THE ELOQUENCE OF THE VULGAR

Language, Cinema and the Politics of Culture

Colin MacCabe

 Publishing

This collection first published in 1999 by the
British Film Institute
21 Stephen Street, London W1P 2LN

The British Film Institute is the UK national agency with responsibility for encouraging
the arts of film and television and conserving them in the national interest.

Cover design: Lewis Revell
Cover image: (front) Dexter Fletcher in *Caravaggio* (1986); (back) Kenneth Williams in
Carry On Cleo (1964).

Set in Minion by Fakenham Photosetting Limited, Fakenham, Norfolk
Printed in Great Britain by St Edmundsbury Press, Bury St Edmunds

British Library Cataloguing-in-Publication Data
A catalogue record for this book is available from the British Library
ISBN 0–85170–677–0 hbk
ISBN 0–85170–678–9 pbk

Contents

With thanks to Margaret Phillips, Davina Nicholson, Esther Johnson, Kate Stables, Kate Mellor and, *prima inter pares*, Sandy Russo.

Preface

The efforts of my enemies in the English Faculty at Cambridge and my friends at King's College meant that I reached the age of thirty-one almost without administrative experience. Save for a couple of years on the Governing Body of Emmanuel College when I was a Research Fellow and one year of directing Studies in English at King's, my entire working life in my twenties was devoted to research and teaching.

That work was profoundly influenced by the momentary confluence of ideas which could later be described as the union of post-structuralism and leftism but which at the time was experienced more simply as a belief that the development of crucial categories in the humanities could be understood as a fundamental political task. This belief had its roots in the flowering of the 20s Soviet avant-garde, when art seemed indispensable to the revolutionary project. And in a smaller but similar way art and politics were interwoven in the student movements of the late 60s. Many sectors of the international research community which I addressed in the 70s had regained an optimistic view of the relations between art, the academy and political change. This optimism manifested itself most noticeably in the attempt to construe accounts of signification which would link the individual and the social in a general theory of revolutionary transformation. Such a theory was the Holy Grail for many intellectuals in those years. Saussure, Freud and Marx formed the Trinity that would provide everything that the revolution had lacked. It was not simply that scarcity would be abolished but sex would be multiplied; it was not simply that the relations of production would be transformed but we would all become poets; it was not simply that commodity production would come to an end but it would be replaced by perpetual carnival.

These dreams still have their merit but they became less and less vivid as the 70s moved on. By the end of the decade, my work both on Joyce and on the cinema had convinced me that the conception of the audience underpinning most accounts of vanguard politics and radical art was inadequate. It also became clear to me that none of Freud, Marx and Saussure allowed one to understand either institutions or audiences. And it was this neglected problem – how institutions and audiences create meaning – that became my obsession as I devoted much of my time to the history of the English language. The historical lessons I was learning were reinforced as I became more and more conscious of both of my role as a teacher and of the claims of my reading in contemporary literature as Rushdie, McEwan and Fenton were added to Lessing, Burroughs and Ballard. All these elements combined to leave the revolutionary conceptions of both art and politics looking increasingly threadbare and unfounded, their truth ever more partial. Any revolutionary politics was going to have to take institutions more seriously than an insurrectionary ideology would allow and any revolutionary art was going to have to be prepared to listen to its audiences much more than any conventional conception of the artist would permit. If much of this was articulated in theory by the end of my time in Cambridge it was in a context in which I participated only minimally even in my own institution and had no audience to listen to save my peers in the research community.

Since 1981 over half my working life has been taken up with administration and often considerably more. In the film world administration is usually called production – which sounds more glamorous, though one of the purposes of my introduction is to show quite how productive, how creative even, administration can be. What is certain is that I have had to address many more audiences both local and national as I have tried to administer effectively within very different institutions. Everything that I have published in this period has been written in direct relation to my administrative work and almost always for a specific audience. To gather these pieces into a book which would address a more general audience, it seemed necessary to provide an account of that work and those audiences and such an account forms the introduction to this volume.

In stressing the situation of these essays, I am also stressing how much they owe to those I have worked with in the past two decades. I have been very lucky. The pleasures of collective intellectual and creative endeavour are little recorded or valued but they are pleasures that I have cherished. To list all those with whom I have worked would be as tedious for the reader as it would be pleasurable for me but I must record the following.

At Strathclyde Alan Durant, Sylvia Adamson, the late Gillian Skirrow and John Caughie.

At BFI Production Jill Pack and Ben Gibson.

At BFI Research Philip Dodd, Laura Mulvey and Tana Wollen.

At BFI TV Bob Last and Paula Jalfon

At the University of Pittsburgh: Dave Bartholomae, Patrizia Lombardo, Peter Machamer, Cecily Paterson and Elayne Tobin.

Finally, I am very grateful to both Ed Buscombe and Paul Willemen for encouraging me to collect these essays. Dave Bartholomae, Alan Durant Stephen Heath and Duncan Petrie read the entire text and made suggestions for detailed alterations. Above all I should thank Rob White who both made the final selection and suggested the order and organisation of the essays.

* * *

The first section 'Theories and Practices' deals with the fundamental categories of author, language and audience. The essays provide accounts of each of these terms in which their perceived autonomy and independence is both recognised and, at another level, disputed. The aim is, particularly using television and film as models, to produce accounts of aesthetic production which both recognise the intense singularity of the creative process and stress its fundamentally communal nature.

The second 'Readings – Cultural Forms and Social Change' provides analyses of the relation between national identity and forms of performance from the Elizabethan theatre to broadcast television and independent film. The aim in all these analyses is to sketch the inscriptions of inclusion and exclusion which constitute a national culture and which are to be found in the very institutions of entertainment – the Elizabethan theatre or public service broadcasting – as well as in individual works

The third section 'Readings – Intellectuals in Transit' gathers together three of the introductions that I have written in the last decade. For me, theory was only important as part of a political project. Its development over the last two decades within the academy signals not only a retreat from politics but more damagingly for the discipline of English, a retreat from the close formal and historical analysis of written texts. But if the development of 'Theory' in contemporary English degrees seems regrettable, it is still the case that theortical questions are inevitably raised by any serious literary and cultural analysis. Both Jameson and Spivak – who are, for me, the most important academic intellectuals of the 80s – distinguish themselves from other theoretical epigones by the subtlety and rigour of their cultural analyses and because of the central role played in their thought by Marx's analysis of exploitation. All three introductions also assume the centrality of film and television to the development of theoretical understanding.

The final essays in this book cover the effort to found a new graduate school which would produce emancipatory knowledge of film and television. The hope was for an education in which theory would be informed by practice and in which academic thinking would automatically take place in the context of non-academic audiences. It was further hoped that this education would feed back both into the formal education system and into the industry. It is an irony so biting that I still do not know whether it should be considered comic or tragic that, at the moment at which this experiment had proved itself an unqualified success, the Governors of the British Film Institute, without any internal or external debate, and under the aegis of a new Labour Government committed to education, decided that the experiment should have no future. A further irony is that the new graduate school's success was so evident that it now looks secure in its future outside the Institute. At the centre of that future is the dream that animated the BFI throughout its long and illustrious history. It is the democratic dream of bringing the highest standards of scholarship and the most demanding vocabulary of critical evaluation to the greatest art-forms of the twentieth century to produce a knowledge available to all.

I remain as convinced today as I did as a teenager over thirty years ago that our cultural present is as valuable as our cultural past and that our educational system should promote both. It is certain that our western educational system has still not yet taken account of the technological and cultural revolution which has followed the introduction of quasi-universal literacy. These final essays suggest some of the terms of a new educational settlement which would place the new forms of mass communication at the centre of a revived and revised traditional curriculum.

Exeter University, November 1998.

Original Sources

(Chronological Order)

CHAPTER 3
'*Righting English*' or Does Spelling Matter?, Inaugural Collins English Dictionary Annual Lecture (Glasgow: Collins, 1984).

CHAPTER 4
'Defining Popular Culture', *High Theory/Low Culture*, ed. Colin MacCabe (New York: St Martin's Press, 1986), pp. 1–11.

CHAPTER 10
Foreword to Gayatri Spivak, *In Other Worlds* (New York: Methuen, 1987), pp. ix–xix.

CHAPTER 2
'Opening Statement' in *The Lingusitics of Writing*, ed. Nigel Fabb et al. (New York: Methuen, 1988), pp. 286–306.

CHAPTER 6
'Death of a Nation: British Television in the Sixties', in *Critical Quarterly*, vol. 30 no. 2, 1988, pp. 34–46.

CHAPTER 5
'Abusing Self and Others: Puritan accounts of the Shakespearean stage', in *Critical Quarterly*, vol. 30 no. 3, 1988, pp. 3–17.

CHAPTER 1
'The Revenge of the Author' in *Critical Quarterly*, vol. 31 no. 2, 1989, pp. 3–15.

CHAPTER 7
'A Post-National European Cinema: A Consideration of Derek Jarman's *The Tempest* and *Edward II*' in *Screening Europe: Image & Identity in Contemporary European Cinema*, ed. Duncan Petrie (London: BFI, 1992), pp. 9–18.

CHAPTER 8
Preface to Fredric Jameson, *The Geopolitical Perspective* (London: BFI, 1992), pp. ix–xvi.

CHAPTER 12
'Cultural Studies and English' in *Critical Quarterly*, vol. 34 no. 3, 1992, pp. 25–35.

CHAPTER 11
On the Eloquence of the Vulgar: a Justification of the Study of Film and Television (London: BFI, 1993).

CHAPTER 9
Foreword to James Snead, *White Screens, Black Images: Hollywood From the Dark Side*, eds. Colin MacCabe and Cornel West (New York and London: Routledge 1994).

CHAPTER 13
'The Case for the Consortium', *Critical Quarterly*, vol. 38 no. 1, 1996, pp. 3–12.

Introduction

Strathclyde 1981–85

In the autumn of 1981 I arrived in Glasgow to take up one of the Chairs of English at Strathclyde University. After my bruising experience at Cambridge, I had few illusions about the possibilities of initiating institutional reform. The media storm which had greeted the refusal of the English Faculty to upgrade me to a full lecturer had concentrated on structuralism and the complexities of French theory. In fact my work at Cambridge had been in the history of English language since the sixteenth century. When I had been appointed, I expected that this work would feed into a thoroughgoing reform of the English undergraduate degree which was going to include the introduction of film and television into the curriculum. I hoped to play a part in sketching a new trivium in which students would be introduced to logic, grammar and rhetoric across both literary and visual media. These expectations had been dashed within a year of my appointment and my personal troubles were only a long delayed after-effect of an argument which had been lost several years before.

While most of the heat and outrage at Cambridge had been generated by petty and specific jealousies, these had been authorised by the unusual level of identification with the curriculum which is one of the features of English departments. While I did not yet know my colleagues at Strathclyde, I assumed that the structure and content of their degree would be jealously defended. If the reforms that I wished for had been impossible at Cambridge where there was a clear majority for such change amongst those holding university posts then it would be impossible where any desire for change would have a very different history.

While I was certainly open to suggestions, I felt no proselytising zeal to convert any reluctant colleagues. I had no doubt that a certain amount of useful education was still possible within traditional English courses. And, if I was also convinced that much better and more effective education was possible, I was also aware that it was not simply a question of altering syllabuses but of teaching new skills and introducing new methods. If I would have welcomed the chance to construct a new kind of English course, I was happy to develop my own research and to throw my new-found professorial weight behind the active group of teachers in television and film working in both Strathclyde and Glasgow.

My expectations were to be completely overthrown by events and the world outside the university was to determine that my major time and effort during my stay at Strathclyde was to be spent developing totally new courses. The first shock came from Mrs Thatcher. Within a month of my appointment in the spring of 1981, her government announced the first of what were to become a series of cuts to the universities. I paid little attention to this announcement. The peculiar nature of Cambridge University with its constituent colleges and its decentred

1

faculties made it possible to ignore the state funding which made one's existence possible. In fact, however, I had been unconsciously briefed some five years before when, in my first term as a Fellow of King's, I had been treated to a masterly disquisition on the relations between University and State by no less an authority than Lord Annan. As a former Provost of King's he was a regular attender at the Annual Congregation of Fellows. On this occasion he stood up to deliver a dire warning. For a decade the government had been asking the universities various questions – questions about the rationalisation of resources and the direction of future development. If the universities did not reply then the government would act and the universities would rue their dilatory and irresponsible attitude. It says a lot about the accuracy of Annan's warning that I, who had already spent ten years in a university, hardly followed what he was saying. What on earth was the old fool going on about, I foolishly thought. Throughout the early 80s I was to hear his grim prognostications echo in my memory, their uncanny accuracy mocking my first reaction.

One result of having heard Annan's analysis was that it was clear to me from the start that the cuts were not, at least in their most important determination, Thatcherite. If the attempts in the later 80s to move towards making student demand effective may be seen to flow from Thatcherite ideology, the early cuts were an alliance between a political desire to cut public spending and a bureaucratic desire to make a nationally funded university system function like a national university system. The cuts were a weapon to impose rationalisation on a system which refused to rationalise itself. What was Thatcherite was that the only political weapon was money. If the universities failed to put their own house in order then money would be used to focus their attention. It was not the government's job to tell the universities what to do; cuts in funding would prompt the necessary thought. It was these cuts that would form the major institutional context of my work at Strathclyde.

Far from prompting thought, which the universities' post-war history and internal organisation ill prepared them for, the immediate reaction was panic. The first result of the cuts was a desperate attempt by the universities to transfer as many of their staff from the current payroll to the pension funds and a whole variety of early retirement schemes were quickly elaborated. Many of those with the most initiative and drive were the first candidates for these schemes. And so, within weeks of my arrival I had to confront the fact that I would have to chair my department for a considerable period.

Furthermore I was taking on this responsibility at exactly the point at which the entire ground rules of university administration were changing radically. From the Robbins Report onwards, the job of a chair had been slowly but surely to seek new posts. Expansion was a simple given of the system. Now not only were there no new posts but there was very little prospect that posts freed by retirement would be filled. The Department of Education was also, at this point, determined to prevent universities solving their problems by recruiting more domestic students. Rationalisation was what the bureaucrats wanted and rationalisation they were determined to get – the home students' fees were reduced in order to make the government block grant the absolutely determining factor in any university's plans. The one area that was left uncontrolled was that of foreign students. An earlier Conservative measure had determined that foreign students would be charged the full cost of their tuition and Britain entered the 80s (and would continue into the next decade) in the extraordinary situation that the only method to undertake any real development in the universities was to provide courses for foreign students.

Insofar as I had adequately formulated to myself the bleak choices for the future I had totally discounted any consideration of foreign students. If my concern was English, my understanding of that term was entirely in terms of the British Isles. But that understanding was about to be transformed by an event as transforming but much more pleasant than the Conservative attack on the universities. At very short notice, in January 1982, I was invited to undertake a British Council tour of Brazil. If the terms of this introduction were not so strictly limited and if I could write like a Chatwin or a Rushdie, I would talk of Brazil in terms of beauty and terror, of limitless hope and unlimited despair. But from the limited perspective of this introduction, the importance of Brazil was that it made me think of English in international terms.

There is one sense in which everyone is aware of the importance of English as a world language. One has only to watch a television news programme in which non-English language speakers hold up political banners in English to be made aware of its astonishing global reach. But it is doubtful how many people are fully aware of how crucial English is to current economic development and it is certain that no one has fully calculated what the cultural and political significance of a world acquiring a second language might be.

The dominance of English is not primarily in terms of the numbers that use it as a first language. Some 6 per cent of the world's population have English as a mother tongue but this is dwarfed by the 20 per cent who speak Chinese and is not significantly larger than the world's population of Spanish and Hindi speakers. The dominance of English is to be measured by the fact that it is the official or joint official language of over 70 states. In addition to those that use it as a mother tongue, there are almost the same number again who use it as a second language in their own countries. Particularly significant is that many of these second language Englishes have taken on systematic prosodic and lexical differences from British English and consider themselves to be genuine examples of a local language. And then a further practically equivalent number of people speak English as a foreign language. In every major area of the world English is either a compulsory subject at school or the most favoured option as a foreign language. In the early 80s Eastern Europe, where Russian was dominant, was the only significant exception to this rule but now there are no major areas where English is not taught widely. Although the figures for second and foreign language speakers are not precise, it is probably the case that if you add them to mother tongue speakers one is justified in talking of English as a language spoken by a billion people.

The importance of English is not, however, in any way exhausted by these already extraordinary facts. One of the reasons that English has achieved such dominance is that it has, to a very large extent, become the language of science. It was also in the 40s and 50s selected in liberation struggles as the language of anticolonialism. What may prove as significant is that it is the language of the new information technology. The fact that the vast majority of databases are in English means that the dominance of English is likely to increase in the decades to come.

Another factor which seems to become ever more important is that English is the language of rock music. While films and television can be dubbed, it is extraordinary the way that rock music has by and large resisted attempts to translate it so that English is now the language of youth culture all over the globe. And that culture informs video, advertising and the Internet.

If you begin to perceive English from this perspective, and it was this perspective that Brazil granted to me, then it becomes increasingly clear that the relations between the current linguistic reality of English and that body of writing that we call English literature is not transparent or obvious. This was a lesson that I had already learned at Cambridge but I had learnt it from a purely national perspective.

In some ways, from the deep interior history of English as a university subject, the row at Cambridge was simply another stage in an old debate which opposed the study of literature and the study of language. In this debate Cambridge had always stood for English as a critical rather than a philological study. The emblem of this was that the study of Anglo-Saxon was not compulsory at Cambridge. But Raymond Williams, for whom literature was as much linguistic as it was social, for whom, indeed, at one level the linguistic was the social, was deeply convinced that the study of modern and early modern English literature needed to be informed by the history of the language. It was Williams who had fought for a post in the history of English post-1500. His arguments were made all the more convincing by the fact that changes in education and developments in modern cultural forms, particularly radio, television and cinema, meant that the traditional assumption of most undergraduate English degrees that English literature since the sixteenth century is unproblematically available to any educated person who reads and writes the language was no longer true. I now saw, for the first time, that the teaching that I conceived in purely national terms was particularly suited also to students for whom English was a second or foreign language.

At Cambridge my job had been to revivify and redefine the teaching of the history of early modern and modern English in relation to literature. This job had taught me two things. The first was that one could only begin to situate the canon of English literature in relation to its complicated social and historical origins when one began to understand properly the history of the language. This history was not most importantly a procession of minor changes in the periphrastic forms of the verb or the development of more regular systems in the comparative and superlative form of adjectives, it was the history of the development of a national standard. This history was of necessity a history of how classes were formed educationally and that narrative could not be told independently of the history of the literature which did so much to define the national standard. So it was not simply a question of teaching the history of the language and then applying it to the literature; the history of the English language and the history of English literature are intimately linked.

Second, and this made the first task potentially easier, contemporary English was now so far removed from early modern English (the English of the great literature of the English Renaissance) that the majority, even of able students at

Cambridge, could not provide decent prose paraphrases of the seventeenth century poetry and drama about which they were writing critical essays. That the poetry and drama resisted paraphrase was, of course, true; that the students were obviously unable to understand the most literal levels of meaning was more than unfortunate.

In other words a teaching of the history of the language which would complicate the canon in a way suggested by a variety of critiques, be they Marxism, feminism or multi-culturalism, was now required given that the canon was now unavailable to the vast majority of students of English at university. Unavailable because they no longer shared the knowledge of Christianity or the classical tradition that the canon assumed but even more crucially because they no longer shared its language. The abandonment of the Authorised Version can be seen here as both effect and cause. Those who urged its replacement by more comprehensible translations were of course merely bowing to the linguistically inevitable but in abandoning it they were also abandoning the three centuries of literature that relied on its rhythms and connotations. From this perspective it should also be said that the rush to introduce theory into literary criticism was simply a way of preserving the traditional curriculum more or less unaltered. As the proliferation of meanings was celebrated, it was easy to ignore the fact that students were unable to read the most literal ones, especially as all such notions of basic meaning were theoretically suspect.

But perhaps even more fundamental was a linguistic change which challenged the very status of the written itself. The advent of television confirmed the transformation of the relation between speech and writing which film, radio and recorded sound had begun. Walter Ong has used the phrase 'secondary orality' to describe the hybrid form used in the new media. This 'secondary orality' challenges and shifts the 500-year dominance (since Gutenberg) of writing in our culture. Any canon inevitably implies an atemporal audience which all texts address across the vagaries of particular historical audiences and the physical facts of the printed word encourage such an implication. The spoken word, with its emphasis on a specific address to a specific audience, lends itself less easily to the task of cultural homogenisation which the canon accomplishes. It is this feature of the spoken word which is one of the crucial elements in our contemporary culture's creation of an enormous variety of audiences and thus of sub-cultures, an ever greater proliferation of differences.

At Cambridge, although many of my colleagues had recognised the reality of the current cultural situation, it had been impossible to persuade the majority of the faculty that a major recasting of the undergraduate degree was necessary or possible. What Brazil made clear to me was that the funding crisis in the universities made possible the construction of a postgraduate degree which would appeal both to English students starting out on a research degree and to the enormous number of foreign students engaged in teaching English language and literature. The linguistics revolution of the 60s and the ever increasing professionalisation of the teaching of English as a foreign language had left foreign teachers of literature ever more marginalised. Those I had talked to in Brazil were obviously fascinated by the thought of a language course which concentrated on literary language. I returned from Brazil determined to construct such a course.

In setting out to teach this history of the language it might be thought that there was little that would be of help. If the great philologists of the nineteenth century, summarised by the great Jespersen, provided some basic descriptions, their concerns were not with the role of literature in the development of the language. Modern linguistics, although again providing very powerful descriptive tools, constituted itself as a science by rejecting any historical perspective and even though some historical linguistics had continued into the twentieth century there was little of relevance to literature.

But it was not a question of starting from scratch. There was a very powerful tradition which, for shorthand, I would call the Cambridge School. At first sight the name itself is a provocation. It was Oxford that had placed philology at the centre of the new discipline of English, it was Cambridge whose English degree was instituted much later that had dispensed with the history of the language as a requirement. But in fact these paradoxes are only apparent. In refusing philology Cambridge had not refused language and indeed it was the work of Richards, Empson and Williams which had provided my constant reference points as I had elaborated my courses at Cambridge in the late 70s.

Although much, of much worth, has been written on the cultural mission that Richards and Leavis set for themselves, much less attention has been paid to the linguistic theories that Richards elaborated and Empson developed. It is curious that they have received very little attention although I would argue that they still constitute the indispensable base for any theory of literary language. Richards's *Practical Criticism*, which he described as 'a piece of field work in ideology', produced in its account of how literature functioned as communication four aspects of language: *sense, feeling, intention* and *tone*.

The force and originality of Richards's position can be indicated by his definition of tone which he defines as 'the attitudes held by the speaker towards the listener'. The dominant meaning of 'tone' would focus on some intrinsic sound properties of a piece of language, and Richards insists on an analysis which defines those properties in terms of the social use of language. Richards avoided both the aesthetic theories which would locate the beauties of poetry in some essential sound properties and the then developing philosophical theses which would reduce language to its logical form.

Richards, however, linked this analysis of language to conceptions of the individual and society which worked against the linguistic analysis, pulling it back into a non-social order. The crucial term in this move was that of 'literature'. For Richards the basic relation between the individual and language is unproblematic: language is merely available as a vehicle for the communication of experience. There is no consideration of language as always social, that the words and meanings available for expression are not produced for the individual. Nor is there any consideration of the difficulty of the category of experience – an attention to the functioning of language should force the realisation that experience is never given as an homogeneous space but is a complicated interplay of pre-existent grids of interpretation in situations where those grids are necessarily never adequate.

For Richards, however, language is only fully social at the moment where there are questions of mis-readings. These mis-readings are analysed in terms of forms of education and expression which are artificial and which abstract language from experience. These forms are, above all, the forms of mass education – compulsory education had been introduced in England some fifty years before Richards was writing – and of mass circulation newspapers which take on a recognisably contemporary form in the 1890s. There seems to be an assumption in Richards, the explicitness of which varies in his writings that it is only these new relations which disturb an ideal homology between word and experience in which the individual has to use one to express the other. Literature then becomes the modern cure which uses all four features of language to re-introduce us to a healthy use of language.

While the original analysis of language stressed its social situation then the further analysis of literature tended towards an ideal situation in which the individual used language independently of social constraints. The concept of 'tone' shows how potentially more productive Richards's analysis was. If we want to understand how an attitude to a listener/reader inflects specific uses of language, it is not enough to talk about individuals. We need to understand the institutions and practices which form the context for particular uses of language. When Sir Philip Sidney produces poems in manuscript to be circulated amongst friends, this is a very different activity from Spenser publishing *The Shepheardes Calender* as a printed book complete with commentary and glosses.

A proper attention to these institutional sites of particular uses of language makes clear that we cannot regard language as unified and homogeneous but need to consider both contradiction and heterogeneity in our analysis. For Richards all contradiction in language is a product of confusion. If the original linguistic analysis allows and indeed encourages an emphasis on contradiction, the psychological and social theories deny its very possibility.

It was Richards's pupil William Empson who developed an analysis of language which stressed rather than minimised contradiction. Empson's three books *Seven Types of Ambiguity* (1930), *Some Versions of Pastoral* (1935) and *The Structure of Complex Words* (1951) are still probably the single most important body of texts for the analysis of literary language. Elliptical and difficult, these texts build on Richards's work. Empson, famously, is not concerned with resolving language into the clarity of a univocal communication. His interests are in the qualities of literary English which render it, particularly in the seventeenth century, such a productive material base for the articulation of contradiction. The virtual absence of inflections in Modern English and the consequent importance and ambiguity of word order are the features which allow for the production of multiple and contradictory meanings. It was these contradictions at the level of the sentence that Empson analysed in *Seven Types of Ambiguity*. Perhaps even more fertile is the attempt in *The Structure of Complex Words* to understand how certain crucial ideological debates are enacted in the complex meanings of words and how struggles over those meanings are part of the production of new structures of subjectivity. In between these two works *Some Versions of Pastoral* sketched the outlines of a theory of the symbolic ordering of social differences across a specific set of examples. Much of this work is susceptible of further elaborations and, indeed, the very terms in which I have described it would not be Empson's. But Empson's theoretical work has been virtually ignored, with the lonely exception of Christopher Norris. This is largely because Empson's own writing, particularly in the theoretical sections of *The Structure of Complex Words* is written in an idiosyncratic private notation which renders it almost unintelligible. This is less a matter of personal idiosyncrasy than the result of the fact that there were no institutionally localisable problems in linguistics or literary criticism to which Empson could address himself. It is the originality of the thought which leaves the text without interlocutors and thus so difficult.

It is also the case that a superficial reading of Empson would appear to limit itself to a narrow literary conception of linguistic history in which language develops only through canonical literary texts. In fact Empson constantly indicates that he is aware of the wider historical and institutional contexts of linguistic development but very often this is implicit rather than explicit. The thinker who places both linguistic and literary development within the broadest social context is a third Cambridge critic, Raymond Williams. In *Culture and Society*, *The Long Revolution* and *Keywords*, Williams makes clear how development of meanings and discourses can only be understood in the broadest historical context. If Empson allowed one to develop Richards's emphases while stressing contradiction, Williams indicated how those contradictions found many of the most fundamental echoes in the wider contradictions of a class society.

My five years' teaching the history of the language at Cambridge meant that I had very definite ideas about the kinds of linguistic knowledge that I felt was essential to any serious engagement with English literature. It was clear to me that any vigorous investigation of the literary tradition needed both to place that tradition within a much more complex institutional history of the language and to consider literature's contemporary position within the whole array of modern cultural forms. If the Cambridge tradition that I have just outlined offered some of the key emphases in developing such thoughts, this historical conception of language was at odds both with modern linguistics and the then ever more fashionable literary theory.

From the mid-60s linguistics had been largely concerned with the theses and theories of transformational generative grammar. If in the very early period there had been the hope that the basic operations of a grammar would provide models for the analysis of literary language, it had soon become clear that the very restricted set of examples with which transformationalists worked could not illuminate language in its broad social and historical sense. In particular, linguists' conceptions of meaning were so limited as to be of very little use for literary or cultural analysis.

If, however, there was no use turning to linguistics as the master science which it had seemed to some in the 60s and 70s, there was every reason to use its techniques for two purposes. The first was simply to provide a clear and agreed vocabulary for the analysis of language. One result of the abandonment of the teaching of traditional grammar was that most students of English either had no such vocabulary or an ill-understood mix of traditional and modern categories. Second, linguistics provided very different models of argument for students reared either on the woolly humanism of traditional literary criticism or the very insulated languages of contemporary literary theory.

It is both shocking and amusing to me in retrospect that my own judgements about the irrelevance and datedness of literary theory were flying in the face of a fashion that was to sweep the universities for the next decade. Theory, for me, had been a specific political experience of the late 60s and early 70s. As those Utopian political hopes receded, so, for me, did theory. Once one had abandoned a messianic view of the contemporary as ushering in a new age, Derrida's scepticism and Barthes's modernism seemed totally inadequate to the historical and institutional realities of language. If Marxism remained a reference it was a Marxism powerfully interrogated by Williams's early work. By a curious irony Williams's later more orthodox work on Marxism seemed several steps back from this early work which was now relatively unread. If Lacan's re-reading of Freud remained a powerful influence it did not offer the kind of historical perspective that seemed crucial if one was to understand the relations between literature and language.

If the ambition of the Master's course that I began to envisage in Brazil was to provide a necessary set of skills and knowledges for anyone wishing to undertake serious research in literary and cultural studies, there were two more specific markets that the course envisaged. The mention of markets in relation to learning may even now seem shocking or scandalous to some. It was, however, in the early 80s that such discourse became part and parcel of the university. Indeed it was exactly my ability to specify these markets which persuaded Strathclyde to allow me the luxury of no fewer than three new posts to build the degree I wanted (two of whom, Alan Durant and Sylvia Adamson, I had appointed by the end of 1982). There was, I felt, a growing demand among teachers for a more adequate understanding of the relations between language and literature. If the attacks on traditional grammar in the schools and traditional philology at university enjoyed a certain justification, there was no doubt that students at every level of English were now woefully ignorant about the history and structure of the language.

There were at that time no courses on language and linguistics which tailored their syllabuses to the interests of literature students and teachers. What Brazil had taught me was that there was also a demand for such courses from overseas. In the 60s traditional literature departments in countries like Brazil had spawned huge language sections which concentrated on applied linguistics and the teaching of basic language skills. Now, however, the younger literature teachers wanted to integrate more linguistic elements into their own work without abandoning their interest in literature.

These multiple determinations were what fed into the Masters course in Literary Linguistics which I designed with Sylvia Adamson and Alan Durant in 1982–83 and for which we took our first students in September 1983. The course is still perhaps original enough to give the brief course descriptions.

TERM 1

Unit 1. Grammatical Description and Analysis
The primary aim of this course is to equip students with practical skills in the grammatical analysis of English; it also provides an introduction to the major concepts, procedures and theoretical assumptions of twentieth-century descriptive linguistics.

Unit 2a. The Sounds of English: Part 1 – Spoken English
A course in the phonetics and intonation of English. In addition to the sessions of

formal instruction, facilities will be available for supervised self-tuition at both elementary and advanced levels. A companion course in the sound-structure of Literary English follows in Term 2.

Unit 3. Appeals to Language: Case studies in literature, education and the history of linguistic thought

This course considers a series of historical debates about language. The aim is to place these debates in their literary, educational and linguistic context, and to reflect on the relations between the conceptions of language delineated in particular theoretical and ideological debates and the conceptions of language embodied in the educational and literary practices of the time. Topics covered will include: the poetry and poetic theory of Spenser; Johnson's *Dictionary*; the Preface to the *Lyrical Ballads*; Matthew Arnold and education since 1870; I. A. Richards and English as a university subject; the Bernstein/Labov controversy and the teaching of English in schools.

Unit 4. The Description and Analysis of Literature: Literary stylistics and practical criticism

This course examines the ways in which the theories, methods and findings of linguistics can be brought to bear upon the practice of literary criticism. The emphasis will be on practical work, with frequent workshop sessions in which students can apply the techniques of textual analysis discussed in the lectures.

Unit 5. Curriculum Developments

This course will consider questions of methodology, evaluation and the concrete relation between language and literature as embodied in curricula. Students will be encouraged to produce work closely related to their own experience as teachers or students. The course will, if possible, be structured around one or more short conferences to give students the opportunity to meet national and international experts in this field.

TERM 2

Unit 6. Grammatical Theory

This course will build on the first term's work in grammatical description and analysis by considering specific theories of grammar. Attention will be focused on systemic grammar and transformational generative grammar, and the course will examine some of the ways in which these theories have handled syntactic and semantic structure. Reference will thus be made to language functions and lexico-grammatical exponents, and to deep structure relations and semantic interpretation.

Unit 2b. The Sounds of English: Part 2 – Literary English

Following on from the work of Unit 2a in Term 1, this course examines the history and structure of sounds in English poetry and prose. Topics covered will include sound symbolism, phonological cohesion, punctuation and rhetoric, intonation, and the history of metrical forms in English.

Unit 7a. The History of English as a Literary Language 1550–1900

Developments in syntax and lexis will be studied through intensive analysis of short sections of the set texts. Wider questions of discourse and audience will be addressed in relation to texts in their entirety. The set texts are: Shakespeare, *Henry V*; Milton, *Lycidas*; Johnson, *Preface to Shakespeare*; Jane Austen, *Emma*; Wordsworth and Coleridge, *The Lyrical Ballads* (including the Preface); Dickens, *Bleak House*.

Unit 7b. Theory of Language Change

This course investigates the question 'How and why do languages change?' Various types of change – phonological, syntactic, semantic and stylistic – are examined in the light of the different explanations of change that have been offered in structural linguistics, sociolinguistics and the psychology of language. The linguistic data will be drawn mainly from English and, wherever possible, from the texts set for detailed study in Unit 7a.

Unit 8a. Broken English: Varieties of English in twentieth-century literature
The subject is approached through the detailed analysis of set works. The diversity of modernism will be illustrated by: T. S. Eliot, *The Waste Land*; James Joyce, *Ulysses*; Hugh MacDiarmid, *Poems*. The contemporary works discussed will vary from year to year, but will normally include a rock film (such as *The Harder They Come*), a contemporary novel (such as *Midnight's Children* or *The Golden Notebook*), and examples of television comedy and thriller genres (such as *Monty Python's Flying Circus*, *The Sweeney*).

Unit 8b. Varieties of Contemporary English
This course provides the linguistic background to Unit 8a by examining some of the major varieties – dialects, registers, styles – of English and their communicative functions in a range of social contexts.

Unit 9. Methods in Literature Teaching
The methodology of literature teaching is still under-represented in most educational curricula. This course introduces students to current research in the area. Subjects covered include: developing readers' responses to fiction; linguistic approaches to poetry; the uses of film adaptation of literary texts; teaching media studies; stylistic analysis and prose composition.

Fifteen years on, the course that we constructed has worn extraordinarily well and Strathclyde still offers a Masters degree in literary linguistics not radically different from the syllabus just outlined. But the current course is much more adapted for the needs of foreign students for whom English is a second language. The hopes that this course would attract the best and the brightest graduate students in English proved groundless. In some ways this is not surprsing. At the most banal level Stathclyde was a new technological university and an unlikely home for arts graduate students. More importantly the waves of politicised graduate students that rolled out from the universities in the late 60s and 70s were now spent. Many of the brightest literature students went off to the metropolitan jobs in publishing or broadcasting which had claimed them in earlier decades. But, most importantly, the argument for the centrality of language to the study of literature was never won at either a national or international level.

At one level this is most surprising. The 1987 Kingman Report on language teaching and the 1989 Cox Report on the English National Curriculum both stressed the importance of the teaching of language. If either had been taken seriously then every undergraduate who was going on to teach English would have had to learn at least some of the material contained in our new degree. But despite the revolutionary nature of these reports which recommended the teaching of the standard without endorsing that standard as 'correct', there does not seem to have been the corresponding and necessary change in English degrees. The reasons for this are undoubtedly many and complex. Simplistically, however, one could suggest that the Right were so disappointed that the teaching of 'correct grammar' had not been recommended that they lost interest. Whereas on the Left any teach-

11

ing about language remained tarred with the historic brush of the imposition of a class-based norm.

University departments of English did not even rise to these two responses; they simply ignored the recommended changes for schools completely. To my incredible surprise the theory revolution which had long outlived its useful life by the mid-70s had by the mid-90s become a new and paralysing orthodoxy. It is impossible to predict with any certainty what the future will bring. In the early 80s I was convinced that if universities still wished to teach the canonical texts of English literature, they would have to provide their students with the linguistic skills to read them. Furthermore those skills would need to be taught in a way that also illuminated the new cultural forms for and linguistic varieties of the English language. I remain convinced that such teaching is imperative but if the Strathclyde degree in literary linguistics continues to provide a relevant model, it is a model which has been comprehensively ignored.

BFI Production 1985–89

In 1985 I left Strathclyde to take a one-semester appointment at the University of Pittsburgh. Pittsburgh does not loom large in this partial history because I have not occupied the kind of administrative positions there that I have held at both Strathclyde and the British Film Institute. Perhaps more importantly the lessons that I am learning at Pittsburgh are still in process. If the history of the literary language and the relation of that history to both the global and local development of English were crucial elements of a renewed study of English, the department at Pittsburgh, which includes important elements in both composition and creative writing, made me think much harder of the place of writing within that renewal. Strathclyde had introduced me to Scottish literature and, in particular, to the astonishing contemporary writing of Alasdair Gray and Jim Kelman. What Pittsburgh further suggested is that the force of contemporary writing must be actively at work in an English department. That thinking is still in process. But Pittsburgh provided an academic base from which I could in the remaining eight months of the year pursue my ever growing interest in film production. By great good fortune the post of Head of Production at the British Film Institute was then free and as I had to spend a year in Britain before returning to the States I took the job on a very short term contract which was then extended to allow me leaves of absence to fulfil my teaching duties at Pittsburgh.

The extraordinarily fortunate combination of Pittsburgh with my position at the BFI allowed me to continue my academic work while pursuing a much more practical understanding of film. I had in the mid-70s written a great deal about film in the magazine *Screen* and this work had culminated in a book on Jean-Luc Godard. As part of my preparation for that book I had spent a couple of days attending the shoot of *Sauve qui peut (la vie)*, the film that announced Godard's return to the commercial cinema. I was astonished, as I watched Godard set up shots, at how little I understood of the process of film-making. This feeling of ignorance was intensified as I sat in on lectures to the crew or uncomfortably observed an explosion of anger directed at an actor. I determined then and there that I would write nothing more about the cinema, once the Godard book was finished, until I understood much better the whole dynamic of the production process.

I had no desire to abandon the pleasures of abstract thought and historical research. Still less did I wish to give up the study of literature but I did have a great desire to throw myself into the world of cinema, to discover how the meanings I had analysed on the screen were related to the collective activity of film-making. And it should be added this was not the world of cinema in general. The 1980s were arguably the most interesting decade of British cinema. On the one hand the Puttnam generation were making their mark in Hollywood, none more memorably than Ridley Scott with *Blade Runner*, while Channel 4 had allowed the enormous talent within British television to find a way on to the cinema screen. I had even had the chance to observe some of this from the sidelines. Verity Lambert had asked me in 1982 to become a member of the British Film Institute's Production Board which she then chaired. So I had seen Peter Greenaway's *The Draughtsman's Contract* become an international hit, had watched Palace Pictures make their mark in distribution with *A Nightmare on Elm Street* and *Diva* and in production with *The Company of Wolves*. Stephen Frears had made his first film in over a decade with *The Hit* produced by Jeremy Thomas and financed by Zenith. The extraordinary excitement that Channel 4's first years bought to both film and television production was palpable. It was an excitement that I wanted to share. As an undergraduate in the late 60s, the universities had seemed the most exciting places in the culture. By the late 70s that moment seemed like an aberrant blip. Universities had returned to the intellectual torpor and administrative rancour with which they had traditionally been associated. The world of film-making seemed full of original ideas and creative excitement.

The Production Division that I became head of was almost entirely the creation of one individual: Peter Sainsbury. In 1951 Michael Balcon, the founder of Ealing Studios, had set up the Experimental Film Fund designed to allow directors to make short films and get a start in the industry. The British Film Institute administered this fund which allowed, amongst others, Lindsay Anderson to make his first film *O Dreamland*. But it was not until the mid-60s with Jennie Lee as Minister of Arts in Wilson's new Labour government that this was incorporated, together with more money from the Eady Levy (see below), into the Institute proper and provided with a Board which represented the great and the good from various sections of the film industry. The brief was still to produce short films for first time directors and amongst the many who took their opportunity in this period one might mention Stephen Frears, who made *The Burning* in 1969. In the early 70s, however, there was an attempt to launch into features with Kevin Brownlow's *Winstanley*. This was a commercial failure and the Board retreated from its experiment. Peter Sainsbury became Head of Production in 1975 and took Production in new directions both aesthetically and organisationally. An editor of the avant-garde magazine *Afterimage*, Sainsbury was fully open to the anti-narrative and anti-representational arguments that were so much part of the counter-culture of the late 60s. Amongst many films funded in this period one might point to Laura Mulvey's and Peter Wollen's *Riddles of the Sphinx* as exemplary. But at the same time he oversaw the final film of the Bill Douglas trilogy and was encouraging a host of new directors from an art school background of whom the most notable was Peter Greenaway.

This wave of aesthetic experimentation posed serious questions about what kind of support the Production Board should be offering. The classic model of state art funding – whereby applicants were given a certain sum of money and left to get on with it – was understood as increasingly inappropriate to film, which required production expertise through the process of production, national distribution expertise to access UK cinemas and world sales expertise to sell abroad and, perhaps most importantly, to be showcased at foreign festivals. The sums of money involved in these low-budget productions as well as the cultural background of the film-makers meant that the existing industry was less than interested in providing this expertise. Sainsbury slowly and carefully built up his division so that knowledge and support could be provided in-house.

At the same time the wilder excesses of 60s aesthetic theory were foundering on the continued demand of audiences for spectacle and narrative, and in 1979 the BFI once again committed to feature production with Chris Petit's *Radio On*. The relative success of this venture ensured that the experiment was continued while the opening up of Channel 4 meant a television market for both the back catalogue and for future productions. Sainsbury's whole amibitious enterprise was finally given its seal of success when, in 1982, Peter Greenaway's first feature *The Draughtman's Contract* was critically acclaimed at Venice and then went on to be a real hit both in Britain and worldwide.

In 1985 I was thus taking over an extremely successful operation with only two drawbacks – there was no money and almost no staff. A major part of Production's funding had come from the Eady Levy, a distribution tax which dated from Harold Wilson's time as President of the Board of Trade in the late 40s. As part of their general dislike of subsidies the Thatcher government had abolished the Eady Levy and, while a final increased tranche had allowed Jarman's *Caravaggio*, Davies's *Distant Voices/Still Lives* and Greenaway's *A Zed and Two Noughts* to be funded, the financial future looked bleak. Partly because of this uncertain future but more because of their recent success many of the staff had moved on to new jobs. All this had led the Institute to reconsider the future of Production, and the argument that it should revert to being a funder and give up providing its range of expertises to film-makers was being actively considered.

At my more cynical moments I thought that Anthony Smith's enthusiasm to appoint me was double-edged. If he thought me the best person to get Production going again, I might also be an ideal person under whom to close it down. But I did not have much time for cynical moments that summer while I received a crash course in film law and finance as I attempted to come to an agreement with the owner of the copyright on Derek Jarman's script.

Nicholas Ward-Jackson was an art dealer who had had the original idea for *Caravaggio* and had signed Derek up to write the script. The contract that Derek signed placed no limit on the length of time that Ward-Jackson owned the script, so that, although Ward-Jackson had failed to find the money for the script himself, anyone who wished to finance the film had to come to terms with him, and with his extremely able lawyers. By the time that the extremely lengthy contract was signed not only was I aware of the crucial role of copyright both culturally and commercially (and also astonished that 15 years' academic study of culture had not prepared me for its centrality) but I had mastered the essential if not very complicated vocabulary of net and gross, advances and allowable expenses. I had also developed a negotiating position, which seemed fair for a public sector body, that although commercial risk might be recognised in terms of speed of return, public sector money could not be regarded as bounty from heaven but must participate in any long-term success.

If contracts and copyright were one element of the summer, the other was the intense pleasure of working with Jarman and Davies. Their working methods could hardly have been more different. Davies's scripts detailed every camera movement and angle: the film existed in every detail before any cast or crew were engaged. At the same time every suggestion or alteration was listened to with great care and, occasionally, some minor detail would be altered or changed, but it was clear that this was only after the most intense reflection by Terence: the calculation of how altering one tiny element of one short scene was going to affect the whole film. Derek was completely different: the script was nowhere near as detailed and in any case was simply a pretext to get cast and crew together. Once assembled, every view was encouraged and listened to with attention and delight, every suggestion was greeted enthusiastically by Derek. Over time, however, it became clear that this enjoyable anarchy was not at all as random as it seemed. Some suggestions were adopted but many were not and it was as though Derek was intuitively riding the wave of the collective talents gathered together but always heading for the shore that was his ultimate destination.

Amid all this creative and legal turmoil, the future of Production was assured. Anthony Smith and Jeremy Isaacs had agreed in principle on an arrangement whereby Channel 4 would provide £500,000 if that was matched by £500,000 by the Institute. Like many Channel 4 deals it was generous and shrewd. Generous because it was money advanced without any creative strings attached, it was the BFI's to spend; shrewd because, in return, they obtained all the output of the BFI in a given year. My job was not simply to spend a million pounds but to use that as a basis on which to raise more money. Indeed as I was expected to produce at least three feature films a year and as their average cost was very nearly one million pounds each, I was going to have to raise a lot of money.

By January 1986 the scale of the problem facing me was clear. If I had enjoyed a flying start with films funded and developed, I must now develop and fund new features and also revivify the production of innovative shorts which had been neglected as the production of features had dominated in the early 80s. To aid me in this task I had a dedicated and resourceful staff, for I had persuaded the Institute of the logic of Sainsbury's mini-studio and filled all the vacant posts. Film production is extraordinarily organised from a financial point of view. Once a film has been 'greenlit', an enormous sum of money becomes available together with a hectic timetable which leaves no room for either thought or error. The result is that any problem is immediately solved, or dissolved, by throwing money at it. Having permanent staff was an enormous advantage since much work on pre-production could be accomplished before the money was in place. If the money never materialised then this was time wasted but, if it did, every such week was, in my opinion, worth about £50,000. In addition to the support of my staff, and most importantly my very experienced and ultra-competent deputy Jill Pack, I also enjoyed the benefit of an enormously talented Board, chaired by Margaret Matheson.

It would be tedious to rehearse the history of each film in this context but I cannot resist telling the story of Terence Davies's *Distant Voices/Still Lives*. Early in 1986 I settled down to watch *Distant Voices*. Although I had thought the script brilliant, nothing prepared me for the force and violence of Terence's memoir of his working-class family. The trilogy of short films he had already made had shown Terence a talented director but with real resources at his disposal he proved himself a genius. There was only one problem. The film was only 45 minutes long and, although it could be assured of a very successful life on the festival circuit, it would never reach any wider audiences. I knew, however, that Terence had always wanted to make a companion piece on the family (set some ten years later) and if one put two 45-minute pieces together one would have a film that could be shown in cinemas round the world. The risk, however, was enormous: we would sit on a great film and let no-one see it while Terence wrote a new film from scratch which we would then have to finance, shoot and edit. If I had any doubts, they were soon dispelled. The Board was adamant we should go for a feature. Channel 4 were equally clear that they would provide additional money to pay for most of the second half. Over the next two years as other films came and went, I was conscious that we had a work of genius up our sleeve – although there were bad 3-o'clock-in-the-mornings when I feared that the actors might die or Terence would lose his touch. Such moments were rare and were more than compensated for when in May 1988 we screened *Distant Voices/Still Lives* in the Director's Fortnight at Cannes to tumultuous acclaim. With the International Critics Prize under its belt, the film went on to be one of the art-house hits of the year around the world.

If my time at BFI Production was valuable and enjoyable in itself, my ulterior purpose was to gain a better theoretical understanding of the process of film-making. While there was no moment on the road to Damascus, there was a clearer vision of the complicated dialectic between author and audience which is fundamental to all art but the very currency of film-making. If it was crystal clear that film was a collective art-form which embodied numerous contributions, it was also clear that there had to be an organising vision to articulate those contributions. On the majority of films that we produced this vision was the director's, but I became more and more convinced that the auteur theory had fundamentally undervalued the role of the writer. Most of the directors who worked for Production were writer-directors, but when these roles were split it seemed clear to me that it was the writer that had the determining role as the initial articulator of the world that the film was to inhabit. The *Cahiers* critics who had historically denigrated the role of the writer had, for the very large part, been writer-directors themselves. If they stressed those elements of film – *mise-en-scène*, performance, articulation of shots – which were not determined by the script, it was also the case that when they came to make their own films, the scripts were theirs.

Much of the detailed historical work that has been accomplished on Hollywood in the last twenty years also casts doubt on the supremacy of the director's role as originally envisaged by *Cahiers*. It is true that their two most favoured directors – Hitchcock and Hawks – never wrote a script but Hitchcock's collaboration with writers often sounds like dictation and much of Hawks's scripts were the result of improvisation with actors.

The other major problem with *Cahiers*'s auteur theory is that it placed all the emphasis on the side of the director: the audience only figures in their theory as the select few who are able to discern the hand of a master. Indeed the function of the audience is no more than the recognition of an auteur, and many European art-house films, in the 70s and 80s, were marketed and sold in this way. This dominance of the director was not a feature of the flowering of British cinema in the 80s and 90s. If Neil Jordan and Stephen Frears were recognised and celebrated, so were Palace Pictures and Working Title – the production companies which were responsible for so many of the most exciting films of the time. This importance of the producer in British cinema undoubtedly owes something to the influence of David Puttnam, whose own conception of his role can itself be traced back to Balcon. As important, however, is the legacy of television where historically the relation between producer and writer has been the key (one thinks, for example, of Potter and Trodd) and the director has been explicitly engaged to realise the writer's vision.

At the Production Board our task was simple: it was to enable a director to realise the best film possible. There were no commercial constraints involved. Indeed, one could define a Production Board film in negative terms – as a film that could not find commercial funding. The non-commercial element, however, was largely confined to the choice of project and director. Once we were committed, our mini-studio was set up to ensure that the film reached the largest possible audience. The producer's role, I realised, was to be the first representative of the audience. The problem with most film-making committed to realising a director's vision is that the dominance of the director is equivalent to the complete disregard of the audience. The time and effort that Hollywood puts into the redrafting of scripts and the editing of films are the visible signs of how the audience is always in play during the process of making a film, in a way which they are not in our dominant models of artistic and literary production. The mini-studio model that Sainsbury had set up and the emphasis on the role of the producer in British film in the 1980s meant that we made every effort to cut out those elements of self-indulgence which frequently handicap director-led films. The director always had the final say but our job was to ensure that this came at the end of a long and animated conversation.

BFI Research and Education 1989–96

In May 1988 Wilf Stevenson was appointed Director of the British Film Institute, following Anthony Smith's decision to accept the Presidency of Magdalen College, Oxford. Very shortly after his appointment he asked me to take on a new job in the Institute. He wished to form a new division, which would include Production, but which would bring together Education, Publishing, *Sight and Sound* magazine and the Library. More importantly it would co-ordinate and develop our existing research activities and, most importantly, it would develop a graduate school and become directly involved in graduate education directly linked to the Institute's activities and audiences.

What made me take up Wilf's offer was the key educational opportunity that was being offered. It had simply never occurred to me that the Institute should teach graduate students directly. But in fact, as I reflected on the possibilities, it became clearer and clearer that there was an overwhelming argument that the BFI's own activities should be used as an educational resource. The film theory that developed in the early 70s around the magazine *Screen* had been resolutely anti-practical in part as a reaction against an identification of film education with the ability to set up a projector and in part as a consequence of the general theoreticism of the times. My own move to Production had been prompted by a desire to let the realities of production inform my theoretical reflections. I had learnt a lot but perhaps the single most important thing I'd learnt was that the film's meaning was not finished with the fine cut. How it was distributed and exhibited, how it was reviewed and archived – the negotiation of meaning and the image ran through all of these activities. The BFI was one of the few institutions in the world and the only one in Britain which housed all these activities under one roof. It was an unparalleled educational opportunity. I was also aware that much of what I had learnt at Production was the collective 'common sense' of the Institute, a 'common sense' that had been developed over the preceding decades by men and women who for the most part did not have many formal educational qualifications but whose commitment to film as the international art was matched only by their insistence on scholarly accuracy. There was a great risk as these pioneers retired and died that their knowledge would not be handed on to the next generation. As I ran the arguments over in my head they pointed to one ineluctable conclusion: I would accept Wilf's offer. It must be said, however, that there was none of the sense of joy that had accompanied my move to Production. This was duty not pleasure.

The first part of the duty was fairly simple. Both book and periodical publishing had developed over forty years of institutional history and like many public sector organisations the only way of understanding the structure was to know the personal histories involved. While there was a more than honourable record it was obvious that the level of subsidy employed in relation to readers reached was ludicrously high. It was also the case that such considerations were simply not part of the culture. In the case of books it was clear that the number of books published per year (about eight) needed to be quadrupled to justify the number of staff employed. Periodicals underwent a more radical rethink with the decision to merge the *Monthly Film Bulletin* and the quarterly *Sight and Sound* into a single monthly magazine.

Neither of these tasks took up much of my time. It was a question of facilitating the efforts of others. Setting up the MA, however, was the central task I had been asked to accomplish and this was harder than I had anticipated. The first steps were easy. Birkbeck College were an obvious partner as not only were they our next door neighbour and had already developed evening classes with us over more than quarter of a century but they shared the same adult education ethos which had inspired the founding of both institutions. Birkbeck welcomed the proposal warmly but this was not a universal reaction. If I had convinced myself fairly rapidly that the idea that the BFI needed graduate students was sound, I was soon to find that it was going to be much harder to convince others. At a meeting called with the leading universities I was left in no doubt that the majority opposed the

18

idea and the best I could hope for was a lukewarm neutrality. I was profoundly shocked by the meeting. Whereas I had hoped for an exchange of ideas and, particularly, a discussion of how the activities of the BFI could be most usefully incorporated into an academic degree, they wanted to tell me that the BFI had no business entering directly into the field of education. I still find it difficult to explain fully the extent of the negative reaction. The main stated argument was that the BFI initiative would compete with other MAs but, in fact, it was clearly different from existing MAs which were, in any case, oversubscribed. The easiest explanation for the hostility to this initiative is that my meeting had coincided with the lowest moment of the universities in the post-war years. The 80s had been a bruising decade for British universities and this had induced a defensive and suspicious attitude. While there is some truth in this explanation, there was also a deeper-seated objection. There are some who argue that the Institute should only be a grant-giving body, like the Arts Council. But this argument ignores the material reality of film and television. If the holdings of the Archive and the full range of world cinema are to be seen, then it is inevitable that the Institute is going to be engaged in distribution and exhibition. The history of the Institute is the history of the development of both exhibition and distribution under a unifying rubric of education. That over time it had also collected various grant-giving functions should not obscure this central history. The Institute's proposal was that it was now time to use its own activities as educational tools. If I was disappointed by the lack of enthusiasm for the proposed MA, it did not deter me from developing the idea. The crucial question was whether we could make the 'research placements' which would occupy the students for a third of their academic year work. The criteria for such a placement were twofold: first, it was essential that the host department – distribution, production, *Sight and Sound*, whatever – really had some use for the student who would work for them. There was no point in having a student stuffing envelopes for four months. Second, however, the student must have a genuine theoretical question which the placement was designed to answer. The account that the students would write up of the placement would combine a description of what they did with an analysis of the ways in which their original question would be answered. If these research placements really worked as practice informed theory then the degree would justify itself not only in terms of its academic innovation but also because the work would feed back into the BFI's central mission, if not, then it would wither on the vine.

What was obvious, however, was that the entire field of the study of film and television was woefully short of resources at the postgraduate level. It was clear in its initial stages, until it had proved itself, that I would have to make sure that the MA was funded outside any existing resources. For the next year I badgered every friend I had in the industry to raid their corporate budgets to get this new MA on the road. At the same time, however, together with Simon Frith who has succeeded me at Strathclyde, I began the long process of bidding to the ESRC (Economic and Social Research Council) for a research programme which would release serious sums of money to develop our understanding of the media. The focus of that bid became the relationship between creativity and money which is central to the whole of film and television but is ill captured by academic disciplines, for which creativity belongs with the humanities and money with economics.

Indeed it was the mismatch between the disciplines and the object of film and television that made me realise that more than the MA was necessary if the Institute was to continue its mission to emphasise the centrality of film and television. There had been a moment in the 70s when film had come to occupy a key position in a rethinking of the humanities but, by a curious paradox, the setting-up of departments of film and media studies, while enabling a great deal of fundamentally important historical work to be done, had separated study of the moving image from both the humanities and the social sciences. This development had impoverished both and, most crucially, media studies itself. The piloting of the MA proposals through the University of London had begun discussions about further collaboration with Birkbeck College and soon we were talking with both the Architectural Association and the Tate Gallery about setting up a new kind of PhD. The aims were ambitious because they involved three innovations. First, we wanted to place the twentieth-century image in all its forms at the centre of intellectual reflection. Second, we wanted to ground the students in taught courses which would emphasise how the analysis of culture inevitably leads one into a variety of disciplines. The call to inter-disciplinarity is an old one but we felt it crucial to emphasise the strength of the traditional disciplines as well as the need to combine them. Finally, and perhaps most ambitiously of all, we wanted the students to think of their doctoral projects not simply in terms of an audience of academic peers but also in terms of the huge audiences that both the BFI and the Tate Gallery addressed.

The planning of the PhD did not really begin until the MA was launched in September 1992 and by then I had cut my links with Production. Ben Gibson, my successor, felt that the Sainsbury mini-studio had fulfilled its historic mission. It had sought to bring the highest level of production, distribution and sales skills to low-budget productions. But those skills were beginning to exist elsewhere as the impact of Channel 4 worked through the whole industry. The BFI needed to develop a different model to work in partnership with the new young producers of the 90s. I agreed with Ben's analysis but, despite this, he felt it important that he was clearly seen to be developing his own policy. I therefore relinquished formal responsibility for Production. I was happy to do this because I had accomplished the major task I had set myself in 1985. It had seemed to me that the only justification for BFI Production was that it enabled images to reach the screen that otherwise would not be seen. If it needed always to be alert to individuals like Jarman and Davies who could not work within the normal industry structures, it also should seek out new areas of experience which even in this too-much recorded age were not deemed worthy of record. For me, the most striking feature of British life that escaped all the dominant representations was the effects of the post-war immigration which had bought millions from the Caribbean and South Asia. If these new Britons appeared on screens, it was in television news and documentaries looking at the problems of racism. If the problems of racism were real, they did not begin to touch on the transformations of the national culture that the new immigrants and their children embodied. The BFI had already made Horace Ove's *Pressure* and Mennelik Shabazz's *Burning an Illusion* but I felt that there was much more still to be done.

There was no question of simply deciding to 'make black films'. The decision to allocate money to a production was made on the basis of the best script available. There was, however, a great deal of latitude in the amount of time, energy and money that were spent in development and black scripts were our development priority from 1985. It says something about how long it takes to move from idea to screen that when I ceased to be Head of Production in June 1989 the two most promising scripts, *Young Soul Rebels* and *Hallelujah Anyhow,* had only just reached their nearly final form. The Production Board was keen to back *Young Soul Rebels,* and although they passed on *Hallelujah Anyhow,* Mark Shivas at the BBC had no hesitation in choosing it for his Screen Two season. With *Hallelujah Anyhow*'s premiere at the London Film Festival in November 1990 and *Young Soul Rebels*'s winning of the Critic's Prize in Cannes in May 1991, I felt that I had accomplished what I had set out to do six years previously.

My self-congratulation was, however, more than a little premature. If someone had told me on the night we celebrated *Young Soul Rebels*'s victory in Cannes that *Bhaji on the Beach* would be the only 'black' film to open in British cinema for the rest of the decade, I would have declared them insanely pessimistic. But such is the case. Films as brilliant as *Trainspotting* or *Four Weddings and a Funeral* continue to offer images of Britain which are, amongst other things, startling in their whiteness. When *Young Soul Rebels* opened in Britain it was greeted with a volley of critical abuse which continues to astonish me. If there were problems at the level of script and performance that I would be the last to deny, there was an energy within the film and clear evidence of a superbly talented director, both of which deserved more generosity from the critics. In retrospect I feel that the critical response to *Young Soul Rebels* was similar to the abuse that was heaped on both Hanif Kureishi's *London Kills Me* and Salman Rushdie's *The Satanic Verses* by English metropolitan critics. In all three cases critics were confronted with representations of their own city which they simply could not recognise and they reacted accordingly.

But if I was to cease producing films for the cinema, I had already started producing television documentaries on the history of film and television. Although it had not been part of the original conversation, Wilf Stevenson soon suggested to me that it was ridiculous that the BFI published magazines and books but didn't use television to reach wider audiences. After some thought I agreed to see whether we couldn't set up a small production arm devoted to documentaries. It must be said that I envisaged a small step-by-step development of this initiative but I had counted without Channel 4 and John Willis who commissioned us to make a series to celebrate the centenary of cinema. The series was to reveal to me not only the extraordinarily rich diversity of the first hundred years of cinema but also a unique insight into the geo-economics and politics of culture as we approach the millennium. In one of the most ambitious tributes ever paid by the small screen to the big screen, I found myself travelling to five continents with films being shot in sixteen countries and a final overall budget which probably exceeded US$5,000,000, none of which came from the BFI.

The first problem was to find the angle. How on earth could one reduce the history of certainly the most popular and arguably the most powerful art of all time to a television series? The problem was redoubled when one added in the fact that the series also needed to recount the history of one of the most important of modern industries. For the first nine months only one principle emerged. There was no point in a history which focused only on the ever more dominant cinema of Hollywood. One of the most striking features of cinema's past is the speed with which the Lumière brothers' invention spread. One year after the first public show on 28 December 1895, cinema had been seen from one end of the world to the other. And it has also been produced across the world in startlingly different forms: from the Latin-American melodramas of the 30s and 40s to the English comedies of the 40s and 50s, from the samurai films of the Japanese to the Third Cinema of contemporary Africa. It was this range that was crucial, for it is the range both geographical and historical which is largely invisible, buried beneath Hollywood's vast marketing budgets. The solution came with the decision to abandon the impossible quest for a total history, to opt instead for individual essays by great directors on their own cinemas and trust that from an incredible variety of approaches something of the complexity of the century of cinema would emerge. If the concept was now in place, we needed stars. In this field there's probably only one global star: Martin Scorsese, not only one of America's greatest directors but also a great film historian, a man who has been described as the Pope of cinema.

The first director I approached was Stephen Frears, then shooting at Columbia with Dustin Hoffman. Could I persuade him to take on the history of British cinema? As importantly, perhaps more importantly, could he recommend the project to Scorsese? Frears's affable not to say scruffy exterior fronts one of the sharpest minds in the business. The answer was as precise as one might expect from someone trained as a lawyer. I could use his name and he would recommend the project to Scorsese but I must understand that he would not make a final commitment until he was sure that there really was a history of British cinema that he wished to recount.

The first problem was Scorsese's schedule. The problem wasn't him finding the time to make a major documentary while he pursued his energetic career as director and producer. The problem was him finding the time to discuss the project. I was finally ushered into the great man's presence in between pre-production meetings for *The Age of Innocence*. Scorsese gave me a masterclass on British movies of the 30s. Not Hitchcock or Korda but the quota quickies and a string of directors whose names, to my shame, I barely recognised. Reluctantly I had to tell him that Frears was inked for the British programme, but it was clear that, however busy he was, Scorsese was going to make a history of American movies; indeed, nothing was going to stop him. About the series he confessed some scepticism. He was not against it but the history of such international multi-partnered projects was grim.

How grim, I was about to find out. With Scorsese confirmed we had the basis for a 'club production': each territory covered the cost of its own production and then exchanged the foreign rights of its film against the domestic rights of all the other films in the series. Everybody who signed up now was guaranteed both Scorsese's name and a feast of Hollywood clips. I had promised Scorsese that we, in conjunction with the Museum of Modern Art, would clear any clips he wanted. Vaguely aware that even with all these cultural brownie points clearing clips was going to be more than difficult, I recruited Bob Last to produce the series with me.

Bob Last is best described as an anarcho-capitalist: a graduate of punk management, he combined a high level of critical awareness with the legal skills of somebody who'd been through the record industry the hard way. Together we were to confront the realities of capital and copyright at the end of the millennium. Many of the Hollywood studios simply have no concept whatsoever of either public record or cultural history. For them, they own material which is theirs to exploit; any other exploitation is potentially in competition with them. No licensing of rights to anybody for any purpose. The full story of how we cleared every clip is long, complicated and beyond the scope of this introduction but I doubt whether without an internationally agreed change in copyright law any future production will assemble together so many clips from so many copyright holders. To give some idea of how difficult our task was, Universal, for whom Scorsese was making *Casino* as he finished our documentary, refused to license clips from such crucial classics as *Scarface* and *Double Indemnity*. Even interventions from the studio head were to no avail and it was only at the last moment that the highest echelons of the company relented. It may seem as though copyright is an arcane aspect of commercial law but in fact it is fundamentally linked to freedom of speech and to the very possibility of criticism. When Milton penned his famous defence of freedom of expression *Areopagitica*, he censured every aspect of the bill licensing publication which the Commons had just passed except for the clauses which recognised an author's copyright. But copyright and freedom of expression are in fundamental contradiction and if there are no practical problems in admitting that an author is entitled to make a living, it becomes more complicated when it is corporations who own the copyright and films that they own the copyright on. Although there are fair dealing provisions in British law, Hollywood studios are so keen to defend their property that they would probably take anybody to court who tried to exercise this right and would almost certainly refuse any further cooperation. In any case we weren't making the series for Britain but for the world and therefore it was American law that we had to confront. American law too recognises fair dealing, but the courts have also recognised very extensive rights which cut across fair dealing. One would require literally unlimited access to money (and also decades of time) to fight the cases that would determine how competing rights stack up. To give some idea how important this question can be, one can take the case of John Wayne. The studios have conceded to the Wayne family that no clips featuring John Wayne can be licensed without their approval. They dislike clips which feature Wayne in scenes of violence and particularly scenes which portray Wayne killing Indians. But one could argue that it is impossible to make a proper documentary history of America which does not contain such scenes. The full implications of copyright run very deep indeed but, by hook or by crook, Scorsese's choices were cleared.

If the Scorsese gave us something to sell, we still had to raise the money around the world. An early boost came from Hong Kong based Star TV who offered to fund India and China. This not only covered two of the most important cinemas in the world but two Third World countries where the fair exchange of a club production turned into imperialist exploitation. In Europe the value of the series was equivalent to the cost of producing one of the films, that is to say US$300,000 an hour. In many Third World countries the value of the series was close to nil. But before the contracts from Star arrived, it was taken over by Rupert Murdoch. I rang a friend in the upper echelons of News International. It was possible that the contracts would arrive but I should know that the company's policy was clear – no money for anything on which they did not take global rights. The very kind of production I was trying to mount would become impossible in a world dominated by global distributors. At this point and as Star pulled out, the series became a mission. The national economies of the first half of the century had allowed many peoples to record their visions on celluloid. I was determined that the series would bear witness to this plurality of vision, to insist that a global culture must recognise local variety.

The director who I felt most shared this sense of the particularity of cinema was Krzysztof Kieślowski. His own perspective was most unusual, he was not interested in director auteurs or in studio histories. He wished to make a film about the audience – to follow the history of cinema in Poland through the memories of the people and, if the technology allowed, to place those individuals in their favourite films. Studio Tor, who had nourished him through the 70s and 80s were not willing to let him direct a project which did not see the studio and Poland receive large sums of money. The notion of an indigent British arts institution was just another rip-off from the West. In the end we agreed that his assistant, Pawel Lozinski, would realise the project. This fascinating documentary gave me some comfort when I saw it months after Kieślowski's death. It provides a fascinating epilogue to the career of this most Polish of film-makers.

Many people have asked me about the various omissions in the series, assuming that we started off with an unlimited budget. In fact the BFI could put no resources at all, except for office space and telephones, into the series. Channel 4, although they generously allowed us to use the money from the few unsold territories to subsidise countries where the money could not be raised, had little interest in the series as such. All the decisions were ours but many were dictated by circumstances. We decided early on that it was an absolute priority to have films from Latin America, Africa and India, and later China was added to that list. Spain was a casualty of this decision because it was clear that we would have to retain one European territory in order to subsidise these choices. Italy was a much later casualty as it became clear, after several years, that RAI were never going to provide the labour to get the necessary clearances. If I had known at the beginning of this mammoth enterprise that the cinema of Rossellini and Pasolini would not be represented then I doubt I would have had the heart to undertake it. We also tried very hard to make first an Arab and then an Egyptian programme but it was impossible to find sufficient funds. None the less, sixteen films were produced, were much shown at festivals, and were received with considerable critical acclaim. If their television audiences round the world were small, they stand as a record of the range of cinema which is unlikely to be duplicated in my lifetime, if ever.

As my time had been engaged in the massive and often hair-raising task of producing the *Century of Cinema*, I had become ever more uncomfortably aware that there was a major crisis in the most vital work of my division: the development of the study of film and television in primary and secondary education. When I had taken over the new division in 1989, both the outgoing and incoming director had assured me that Education was the one department in the BFI that was an unqual-ified success story. Media education had been written into the national curricu-lum and Britain was seen as a world leader in the field. As the 90s progressed it became clear that this picture was partial. While it was true that more and more children were opting to take media studies at every level of the curriculum, it was also true that many of those teaching it were under-prepared and, in general, that the area was massively under-resourced. These developments fed doubts that I had ignored initially. I had always been opposed to the study of media as a single honours degree and unhappy about its development as a separate subject at GCSE and 'A' level. While it seemed to me essential that film and television be studied, I had always believed that this would be most effectively done in combination with other subjects. In 1989 I had kept these doubts to myself not least because it was made clear to me that I was to focus on the other areas of the division. But my own doubts were increasingly reinforced not only by the development of the curricu-lum which offered less and less room for marginal subjects but also by our own research. Perhaps most important of all it was clear that media studies did not by and large serve the aims of the Institute at all. In many cases it did not encourage the study of film and even television was often marginal to what was effectively a study of the print media.

It became clearer and clearer to me that what was needed was an entirely new settlement between the new audiovisual media and the traditional subjects. Other research we had commissioned indicated that almost all classic English drama and fiction was now taught using film or television adaptations but that little of this teaching was equipped to investigate fully the relations between text and image. Quite aside from other areas of secondary education, particularly history, I was convinced that this new settlement needed to run right through secondary and into primary education. For all my work on the history of the language suggested that audiovisual technologies needed to be integrated with the teaching of basic reading and writing.

There can be few more charged educational debates than those surrounding lit-eracy. On the one hand stand an army of conservatives positive that traditional skills of reading and writing are declining. On the other a host of progressives protest that literacy is much more complicated than a simple technical mastery of reading and writing. This second position is supported by the host of academic work devoted to literacy over the past twenty years, particularly in social history and anthropology. These studies argue that literacy can only really be understood in relation to its social, technical and educational context. Our simple notion which makes literacy a pure technical acquisition of the skills of reading and writing is itself a historical product.

In Renaissance England, for example, many more people could read than could write and within reading there was a further distinction in which many more could read print than could manage a manuscript. An understanding of these earlier periods is a useful preparation for a comprehension of the current 'crisis in literacy'. Indeed, the huge volume of academic study is itself a complicated response to the contemporary situation. On the one hand there seems clear evi-dence that there has been an overall decline in some aspects of reading and writing (a comparison between the tabloids of today and those of fifty years ago reveals a clear decrease in vocabulary and simplification of syntax), but the picture is not uniform and doesn't readily admit of the simple distinction 'literate/illiterate' which had been considered adequate since its appearance in the middle of the nineteenth century.

Although little in this area is evident, one might speculate that it is use and interest rather than teaching methods or moral turpitude which produces the confused situation today. While reading and a certain amount of writing is as crucial as it has ever been in industrial societies, it is doubtful whether a fully extended grasp of either is as necessary as it was thirty or forty years ago. While print retains much of its authority as a source of topical information, television has, since the 50s, increasingly usurped this role. At a domestic level the ability to write long and fluent letters has undoubtedly been very hard hit by the telephone and indeed some recent research suggest that for many people the only use for writing outside the educational system is the compilation of lists. At the same time the number of forms of entertainment which do not require command of the written word never ceases to grow. The decision of some car manufacturers to issue their instructions to mechanics as an enormous video pack rather than as a handbook might be taken to spell the end of any automatic link between industrialisation and literacy. In a contradictory movement, it is also the case that ever increasing numbers of people make their living out of writing which is also probably better rewarded than at any other previous time in history. The tendency of the great media cartels to run from the most popular television through printed journalism to the most upmarket publishing gives some idea of the very complicated ecology in which the printed word both gains and loses power.

Historically, of course, the new and old media are simply seen as opposed. School can be defined as the place where films, television and recorded sound have no place; where the book rules. But it is not at all clear that this historical opposition bears any relation to cultural reality. While you may not need to read and write to watch television, you certainly need to be able to read and write in order to make it. Those who work in the new media are anything but illiterate; the skills of reading and writing are central to all production of the new media.

The technological advances of the last few years make even more apparent that the traditional oppositions between old and new media are totally inadequate for understanding the world which a young child now encounters. The computer has re-established a central place for the written word on the television screen which used to be entirely devoted to the image, there is even now anecdotal evidence that children are mastering reading and writing in order to get on to the Internet. However it should not be thought that this re-emergence of writing is equivalent to the printed word. The newest media mix writing, recorded sound and images (both moving and still) in proportions which demand fresh understanding.

What is now necessary is to explore the ways in which the new and old media can be integrated in the schools to provide the next generation of children with all the skills necessary to produce an economically productive and politically enfranchised nation. It must be quite clear that what is being suggested here is not in any way an attempt to minimise the importance of the written word nor the necessity to improve the standards of basic literacy in this country. There is a crisis in literacy and it would be foolish to ignore it. Because literacy studies are interested in the very complicated set of social relations embodied in reading and writing, there is a tendency for this academic position to simply oppose the conservatives who bemoan the present situation. But to understand that literacy may be declining because it is less central to some aspects of everyday life must not be equated to acquiescing in this state of affairs. Traditional literacy remains just as central to any full participation in contemporary society as it has ever been. Indeed, the conservatives' moans may underestimate the dangers of the current situation. It seems to me that there is a considerable risk that the information revolution may intensify the division between classes. On the one side there will be those who come from homes who have full access to the new media and who, partly for that reason, will be literate, on the other will be those who are simply consumers of an ever more diverse audiovisual industry and who lose more and more of the functional skills of writing and reading. A particularly dangerous term in this context is that of 'media literacy'. At best, and this is already being very generous, the term is meant to draw attention to the skills that children have in decoding complicated audiovisual forms and which should be built on rather than ignored in the classroom. But if the term does not include production as well as reception and, even worse, if there is any suggestion that this is equivalent to verbal literacy, then the term simply functions to obscure and legitimate ignorance.

The now pressing question is how these new technologies should be introduced into the schools. The fact that the question is pressing should not lead us to underestimate the difficulties of finding answers. It may seem simple to call for computers, camcorders and edit suites in every classroom but unless there is a detailed and understood pedagogy to go with them, the tools will largely stand unused. Indeed, a great deal of the available evidence suggests that this is the fate of the great majority of information technology which is in the classroom.

The most urgent challenge is to determine how the new technologies can be introduced into the classroom together with pedagogies which will enable those technologies to help children acquire the older and crucial skills of reading and writing. A great deal of experimentation is now going on in this area; if it were possible to provide both theoretical accounts but also, and more importantly, practical models for how traditional literacy and the new media could reach a benign settlement, it would truly mark a new era of education.

It seems very easy in our *fin de siècle* era to adopt the pessimistic view. That these new medias are destroying old skills and values chimes all too easily with a whole variety of traditional pessimisms from both Left and Right. But one should not over-eulogise the past. It may well be true that past generations were more literate but one should be fully aware that this literacy was always a minimal affair. The word itself is a nineteenth-century coinage to describe the divorce of reading and writing from a full knowledge of literature. For Johnson and Milton it would have been impossible to divorce the two. The educational reforms of the nineteenth century produced reading and writing as skills separable from a full participation within the cultural heritage of the nation. The new media are not simply turned towards our economic future, they are also one of the key elements in making our cultural past available to the whole nation. A John Patten can raise bellows of applause when he tells a Conservative Party conference that he wants children taught Shakespeare and not soap opera. The simple fact of the matter, however, is that most children's access to the treasures of our cultural past is initially through television. Each time a Jane Austen or a George Eliot classic is serialised for television, tens of thousands of copies of the books are sold. The success of *Four Weddings and a Funeral* allowed an ever-canny Faber & Faber to sell over 100,000 copies of a special edition of Auden's love poems. These cross-media developments which are the very currency of the modern media industries are to be despised at our peril. Whatever cant is talked about the value of our literary past, it is doubtful whether that past has been available to more than 5 per cent of the population, certain that it has not been available to more than 10 per cent. If the new media are seriously combined with the old, and the much derided public service tradition of British broadcasting makes that a real possibility in this country, then for the first time it opens out the possibility of making our literary tradition available to the vast majority of the population.

But as our discussions about literacy developed, it became clear that there were fundamental arguments which divided opinion within our division. These arguments are complex but I would simplify them in the following fashion. The studies of literacy within anthropology are much animated by a desire to escape the Eurocentrism which is such a distinguishing feature of most of the early study of 'other' and 'primitive' peoples. In particular there has been an effort, most tellingly articulated in Lévi-Strauss, to hold in question the unquestioned superiority of writing-based cultures over those who had never developed an alphabet or ideograms. In history, too, much of the most recent interest in the past has been animated by a desire to understand the motives and desires of subaltern classes whose existence bypassed forms of writing. The problem comes when these attitudes and assumptions are translated to contemporary educational problems and are transformed into educational policy. All too often they become in practice an acquiescence in underachievement and illiteracy amongst the poorest sections of the population. It is these and similar anti-academic educational attitudes which have, in my opinion, so ruined the comprehensive education which, as a schoolboy, I thought would usher in the New Jerusalem. The educational argument which opposes a traditional conception of a single literacy to a more recent conception of many literacies thus conceals a multitude of intellectual and political arguments. There can be few more pressing questions over the next decade as to how the technologies of information and entertainment enter the classroom and how the relation between new technology and traditional culture is negotiated.

It became clear, as these debates continued, that I would have to direct the research on the relations between traditional literacy and the media myself and that the results would have to inform a whole new educational strategy for the Institute. It also became clear that I could not combine this with teaching and the new and ever more daunting commercial problems of our publishing activities. The internal discussions about the future of education had taken place against a background of a series of ever more serious cuts in the Institute's annual grant from the government, and all our commercial activities were being set increasingly demanding targets. I was thus pleased when the Director and Governors agreed to split the division into two, for a three-year period, and to ask me to concentrate on research and teaching while we elaborated a new vision of the Institute's educational tasks.

When the third year of the PhD is in place there will be more than 70 students working in the interstices of the Institute. Their work will be judged not simply on its academic merit but also on the ways in which it feeds into the operations and address of the Institute. The task is to bring the concerns of the academy into more direct touch with an audience which is not academic. In this desire to be the interface between an elite tradition and a democratic audience, the British Film Institute is simply fulfilling the role assigned to it by the art which its celebrates. Film is, *par excellence*, the democratic art. It has brought to audiences that have to be counted in their billions the pleasures of drama and performance, narrative and spectacle.

It is certain that this huge cultural revolution is still very imperfectly reflected in our fundamental forms of academic understanding. While film, media and television studies have burgeoned over the last quarter of a century and have produced much valuable work particularly in terms of detailed history, these studies have by and large been divorced both from the traditional humanities and classic social science. This divorce has been immensely harmful to both sides. Nowhere is this more evident than in the study of literature. It is impossible to write any history of American or English letters in the twentieth century in which the moving image is not central. It is not simply that writers from Waugh to Faulkner or from Pinter to Edward Bond have spent large periods of time working and writing for the screen. It is also that the development of prose, poetry and drama and the development of cinema and television are a joint history which cannot be understood independently of each other. It was Bazin who pointed out some of this complexity when he remarked that it was not simply that Italian neo-realism had developed its style from the prose of Hemingway and Dos Passo but that very prose style was itself unthinkable except as a reaction to the possibilities revealed by cinema.

Furthermore, the lessons of film and television are not limited to the twentieth century. As they have developed new relations between art and audience, commerce and culture they have offered fresh illumination of earlier periods. For myself there is no better guide to the world of the Shakespearean stage than the early history of Hollywood. The attempts to marry elite cultural traditions to vast popular audiences in the search for huge profits make a comparison between early twentieth-century Los Angeles and late sixteenth-century London a genuinely illuminating one.

Film and television produce audiences on a scale which previous forms of information and entertainment could not envisage. Our academic forms of understanding and explanation have still not fully reckoned the implications of these audiences nor the new light they throw on earlier forms. These essays hope to contribute to such a reckoning.

Pittsburgh, April 1997

29

PART ONE

Theories and Practices

1 The Revenge of the Author

There was one massive contradiction in film theory of the 70s. On the one hand there was the elaboration of theories, linguistic, psychoanalytical and Marxist, which challenged the primacy of the conscious subject. On the other, the auteur theory (which depended on just such a notion of the primacy of the conscious subject) was unavoidable: in its weak form simply as a necessary descriptive grid for the archive; in its strong form still a crucial evaluative term. The following essay tried to use my experience as a producer to elaborate an account of the role of the director which would square these particular theoretical circles. Two conferences in the United States, one organised by Fredric Jameson at Duke University in 1987 and the other by David Simpson at the University of Colorado in 1988, allowed me to organise my thoughts.

This essay is an attempt to bring into alignment two major and contradictory areas of my own experience. I have had few intellectual experiences that so deeply marked me as the introduction to the work of Barthes in the late 1960s. Barthes's emphasis on the sociality of writing and the transindividuality of its codes has been a major and continuing gain in our understanding of literature and its functioning. At the same time, I have always been uneasy about the attempt to abolish notions of authorship entirely, and this uneasiness grew when, in the mid-80s, I became actively involved in the making of films. The most general concern of the cast and crew of a film, not to mention the producer, is that the director know what film he is making, that there be an author on the set.

There is no more elegant statement of Barthes's opposition to the concept of the author than the extraordinarily influential essay titled 'The Death of the Author' which summarised many of the most powerful theses of *S/Z*. Barthes's concern, in both the brief essay and the major study, was to stress the reality of the textual: the contradictory series of relations that a text enters into with the writings that precede it. The project may seem to have something in common with the New Critical attack on the author, but its aims are very different. New Criticism sought to liberate the text's meaning from the unfortunate contingencies of an author's time and place. Barthes's attempt is to liberate the text from meaning altogether. The author becomes for Barthes the privileged social instance of this meaning. The massive investment in the author which we witness in contemporary culture is for Barthes an investment in meaning, an attempt to stabilise the fragmentation of identity. Without the author as the crucial function that grounds and identifies the text, we could begin to emphasise how the text obliterates all grounds, all identities: 'Writing is that neutral composite oblique space where our subject slips away, the negative where all identity is lost, starting with the very identity of the body writing.'[1]

Barthes emphasises the priority of language in writing and derides any aesthetic based on expression. All one is able to analyse in a text is a mixture, more accurately a montage of writings, and the writer's only activity thus becomes that of editor – regulating the mix of the writings. It is at the moment we grasp the nature of the textual that we can also understand that the determination of the multiple writings making up the text are to be focused on the reader and not the writer:

> The reader is the space on which all the quotations that make up a writing are inscribed without any of them being lost; a text's unity lies not in its origin but in its destination.

But Barthes goes farther than any orthodox kind of reception theory:

> This destination cannot any longer be personal: the reader is without history, biography, psychology; he is simply that someone who holds together in single field all the traces by which the written text is constituted.[2]

Where are we to locate this etiolated ghost of a reader liberated from identity? How, historically, are we to place a reader without history, biography, psychology, and how can we socially situate his, her or (as the lack of determination obviously includes gender) its emergence? The answer is to be found in considering modernism as a response to educational and social developments that posed readership as a major problem. It is Derrida who has stressed a constant fear of writing in terms of the inability of an author to control the reader's construction of reading. Derrida's concern has been to indicate how this lack of control is general to all situations of language use. What Derrida does not stress, however, is the historicity of this problem, the particular way in which technological advances pose this problem in specific forms to which there are specific responses. The advent of printing radically altered the relations of writer and reader, and our familiar category of author can be read in relation to that new technology. Whereas before printing all reading involved the prior transmission of an individual text, printing suddenly produced an audience which with the author is not, even in the attenuated relation of an individual copying, directly related.

If we look back to the Renaissance, we find that the etymologically prior meanings of the word 'author' stress the notion of both cause and authority without any special reference to written texts but it is in relation to the new technology of printing and the associated new legal relations that our own concept of author is elaborated.[3] Once tied to the printed text, the national author of the vernacular languages replaced the classical authorities – and replaced them by virtue of his or her individual power. There are few clearer examples of this process than Milton. It is rarely stressed that in beginning his famous attack on Parliament's attempt to regulate printing Milton explicitly excludes 'that part which preserves justly every man's copy to himselfe',[4] for its ordinance of 14 June 1643 was the first properly to recognise copyright. But Milton's interest in copyright and his minute concern with the exact details of his printed text make clear how the new category of author relates to legal and technological changes.[5]

Most important, however, is the new relation to the audience which is thus figured. The dialogue implied in both the popular dramatic forms and the circulated manuscripts is replaced by a literal petrifying of meanings. Milton's first published poem, one of the prefatory poems to Shakespeare's Second Folio, uses the metaphor of readers turned into marble monuments to Shakespeare's 'unvalu'd book'. The audience may not be universal, may be fit though few, but it is certainly not an audience actively engaged in dialogue with the text. The act of composition is the poet's alone. Milton's blindness and the image of his solitary composition is almost an essential part of his literary definition. But the solitary author gains, in complementary definition, the possibility of a national audience.

When this concept is given a Romantic turn, the author ceases to authorise a national vernacular, but the new definition in terms of the solitary imagination and a local speech continues to presuppose, in its very definition, a potential national audience, although an audience now seen as at odds with the dominant social definitions. What brings the categories of both author and national audience under attack is the universal literacy of the nineteenth century, the production for the first time of a literate population. As the capitalist economy responded to this new market with the production of those mass-circulation newspapers that herald the beginning of our recognisably modern culture, we entered a new historical epoch of communication in which any author's claim to address his or her national audience became hopelessly problematic. Mass literacy spelled an end to any such possibility. There is now no conception of the national audience not threatened by a vaster audience that will not listen; the traditional elite strategies that defined the audience by those who were excluded are irredeemably ruined by those who will simply not pay attention. This historical situation is one of the crucial determinations of modernism, when all universal claims for art seem fatally compromised. Barthes's fundamental aesthetic is borrowed from the modernist reaction to this problem – a writing for an ideal and unspecified reader, for that reader who, in Nietzsche's memorable phrase is 'far off', that ideal Joycean reader who devotes an entire life to the perusal of a single text.

There seems to me to be a historical explanation of why we get such a powerful resurgence of the modern aesthetic in France, and it is to be found in the delayed but very powerful impact of the consumer society there in the decade from the mid-50s to the mid-60s. The fascination with and distaste for mass culture which runs through work as diverse as that of Barthes, the Situationists, and Godard indicates the extent to which the dissolution of the relations that supported traditional culture were widely felt and perceived. The paradox of modernism is that it fully lives the crisis of the audience while postulating an ideal audience in the future; it fully explores the slippage of significations which become so pressing as a securely imagined audience disappears while holding out the promise of a future in which this signification will be held together. The form of this future ideal audience has been conceived across a range of possibilities throughout the twentieth century. After 1968 in France, however, the favoured solution was the alliance of avant-garde art and revolutionary politics which had marked post-Revolutionary Russia and pre-Nazi Germany and which theorised the audience in terms of a political mandate authorised by a future revolutionary society.

Barthes's classless, genderless, completely indeterminate reader is yet another version of the solution to the modernist dilemma, but it preserves the crucial relation of author and reader bequeathed by the national literary tradition. Indeed, that preservation can be seen in the way that Derrida's project (closely related to Barthes's) was so eagerly seized in the United States as a way of preserving the traditional literary canon against radical curricular reform. Foucault in a famous and almost contemporary article signals this danger. Speaking of the concept of *écriture* and its emphasis on the codes of writing, he warns that the concept 'has merely transposed the empirical characteristics of an author to a transcendental anonymity' and that it thus 'sustains the privileges of the author'.[6]

It is the case, however, that Foucault shares Barthes's commitment to those aspects of literary modernism which concentrate on the difficulty of the author's position. Beckett's 'What matter who's speaking, someone said, what matter who's speaking' acts as a kind of epigraph for the essay.[7] Despite Foucault's emphasis on the need to look beyond literature if we are to understand the functioning of the author and despite his concern to trace the history of authorship, the entire article is still written with an emphasis on the untenability of the traditional Romantic valuation of the author as the originator of discourse. In Foucault there is no consideration of the new forms of education and entertainment which have rendered that position untenable but, in the same moment, have opened up new possibilities.

It is significant that when Foucault does mention he has limited his discussion to the author of the written word that he catalogues his omission in terms of painting and music – arts whose development is contemporary with and indeed dependent on the evolution I have sketched within national cultures. Foucault offers no discussion at all of the cinema, which not only displaced the dominance of the written word but also introduced radical new relations between texts and audiences. This omission is in some way all the more surprising since a mere decade earlier *Cahiers du cinéma* had half elaborated a new concept of the author in relation to cinema. I say 'half elaborated' because the *Cahiers* critics, (François Truffaut, Eric Rohmer, Jean-Luc Godard and Jacques Rivette) never saw their task in theoretical terms. Their concerns were polemical and specific. Above all they were concerned with the importance of the script for the construction of a film. They saw the weakness of the French cinema in terms of its overvaluation of the written element in film, which failed to take account of the *mise-en-scène* which was accomplished by emphasising the role of the *metteur-en-scène*, the director. This emphasis went hand in hand with the second task: the redescription of the huge archive of Hollywood cinema by selecting from its thousands of films a series of corpuses that could be identified through the consistent use of *mise-en-scène*, the consistency being provided by those directors (John Ford, Raoul Walsh, Howard Hawks – the names are now familiar) who could be called 'authors'.

The project is thus curiously at variance with the literary use of the term 'author'. For Barthes, the author is the figure used to obscure the specificity of the textual. For *Cahiers*, the author, while sharing the Romantic features of creativity, inferiority, etc., was the figure used to emphasise the specificity of the codes that went to make up the cinema. It is exactly that mix which makes for the interest and pleasure of those articles and no one was more elegant than Truffaut in his juxtapositions:

> You can refute Hawks in the name of Ray (or vice versa) or admit them both, but to anyone who would reject them both I make so bold as to say this: *Stop going to the cinema, don't watch any more films, you will never know the meaning of inspiration, of a viewfinder, of poetic intuition, a frame, a shot, an idea, a good film, the cinema.*

36

The emphasis of this sentence, which I re-emphasise, is the necessity of under-standing film in terms of the relation between the fundamental articulations of the cinema (viewfinder, frame, shot) and the fundamental themes of great art (inspiration, poetic intuition, idea). The scandal of *Cahiers*, however, is that it insisted on the relevance of themes of great art to a form whose address to the audience neglected all the qualifications of education, class and nationality which the various national cultures of Europe had been so concerned to stress. This pos-ition is interesting because it is a theory of the author produced both in relation to the materiality of the form and also, and this is crucial, from the point of view of the audience.[8]

The attempts, in the late 60s and 70s, to develop this concern with the materi-ality of the form and to analyse further the cinematic codes that *Cahiers* had been the first to bring into discursive focus ran into inevitable epistemological and pol-itical impasses because they attempted to undertake the development without any recourse to the category of the author. The difficulties are clear in the pages of *Screen*, which most consistently attempted to carry out this theoretical project. The logic of the codes revealed in analysis was not located in any originating con-sciousness but was immanent to the text itself. The emphasis on the textuality of meaning, independent of the conditions of either production or reception, brought great gains but, like Barthes's project of the late 60s (to which it was very closely allied), it rested on very precarious epistemological ground, constantly veering between freezing the text outside any but the most general pragmatic con-straints (provided by psychoanalysis) and collapsing it into a total relativism and subjectivism where the reading inhered in the reader.

Parenthetically one might remark that it is not clear even from close reading of the *Screen* of this period that the category of author was ever abandoned accord-ing to the theoretical programme. Perhaps the most powerful single piece from that period, Stephen Heath's exemplary analysis of Orson Welles's *Touch of Evil*, unites formal and narrative determination in the attempt by the detective Quin-lan (Welles) to keep control of his cane.[9] When we consider the significance of the signifier cane in Welles's own biography, then it is obvious that Heath's text as we have it is radically incomplete, needing elaboration in terms of Welles's own life and his relation to the institutions of cinema. *Screen*'s aim of producing readings independent of their grounding within specific determinates of meaning was always suspect. If there was great importance in emphasising the potential poly-semy of any text, its potential for infinitisation, and if there was fundamental sig-nificance in analysing the transindividual codes from which any text was composed, it is still the case that texts are continuously determined in their mean-ings. The question is how we are to understand those determinations without pro-ducing, on the one hand, an author autonomously producing meanings in a sphere anterior to their specific articulation and, on the other, an audience impos-ing whatever meaning it chooses on a text.

It may be helpful in answering this problem to consider from a theoretical per-spective the process of film-making. However one is to understand the collectivi-ties at work in the production of a written text, it is obvious at a very simple level in the production of films that it is directly counterintuitive to talk of one respon-sible author. Even a very cheap feature film involves thirty to forty people working together over a period of some six months, and the mass of copyright law and trade union practice which has grown up around film has largely as its goal the ever more precise specification of 'creativity', the delineation of areas (design, lighting, make-up, costume) where an individual or individuals can be named in relation to a particular element of the final artifact. The experience of production relations within a film makes clear how one can award an authorial primacy to the director without adopting any of the idealist presuppositions about origin or homogeneity which seem to arise unbidden in one's path. If we are to talk of an audience for a film, then, at least in the first instance, that audience cannot be theorised in relation to the empirical audience or to the readings that audience produces. So varied are the possibilities of such readings and so infinite the determinations that enter into such a calculation that it is an impossible task. Indeed, were it possible to calculate the readings produced by any specific film, then the Department of Reader Response would be the most important section of any film studio, and Hollywood would be a less anxious place with much greater security of tenure.

Any future audience can be approached only through the first audience for the film – the cast and crew who produced it. It is the director's skill in making others work together to produce a film, which is of necessity invisible at the outset, which determines the extent to which the film will be successfully realised. It is the collective determination to make visible something that has not been seen before which marks the successful production of a film, and it is insofar as the producers of the film are also its first audience that we can indicate the dialectic that places the author not outside the text but within the process of its production. It might be said further that such an analysis provides an ethic that is certainly important and may be crucial in differentiating among the numerous productions of the new popular forms of capitalist culture. I venture to suggest that those elements in popular culture which genuinely mark important areas of desire and reflection are those where the producers have been concerned in the first place to make something for themselves. Where the determination is simply to produce a work for a predefined audience from which the producers exclude themselves, one will be dealing with that meretricious and toxic repetition that is the downside of the new forms of mechanical and electronic production. A further generalisation would be that genuine creativity in popular culture is constantly to be located in relation to emergent and not yet fully defined audiences.

The process of film-making indicates not only how the moment of creation integrally entails the figuring of the audience but also how that audience is figured in relation to a reality that thus achieves social effectivity. This is a solution to the problem of realism which avoids the trap of representation (which elides the effectivity of the textual) and the snare of endless textuality (which endlessly defers the text's relation to the real). The repositioning of the reader or viewer by the work of art in relation to a social reality is thereby altered by the repositioning that allows the traditional heuristic and oppositional claims of realism without its traditional epistemology.[10]

Considerations of this order enable us to conceptualise the author as a contradictory movement within a collectivity rather than as a homogeneous, autonomous, and totalising subject. If the process of film-making allows us an obvious way of seeing the author in a plurality of positions, it should not be taken as an empirical formula for the studying of authors. If one were to take a specific film and attempt to constitute the author in relation to this first audience, one would be faced by a multiplication of the determinations on that audience to a level that makes any exhaustive analysis not simply technically but theoretically impossible. The usefulness of the film analogy, and the usefulness of the *Cahiers* critics who deliberately adopted a position similar to that of experienced technicians, is that it indicates the multiplicity of positions in which we must locate the author. It should not be thought, however, that the theoretical task is to specify the determinations that would limit the possible meanings of the texts in relation to possible positions in which it could be produced and received. Such a dream of scientific rigour discounts that our own position as reader is always present in any such calculation and that the very fact of a future allows for positions as yet unaccounted for. It should be stressed at this point that infinity once again becomes a real term in the analysis.

The difference between this conception of infinity, however, and Barthes's, is that whereas Barthes's is located in some atemporal and idealist account of meaning, this infinity is rooted in a historical and materialist account of significations. Marx so dominates our thinking about materialism that it may seem at first that any conception of infinite determinations is hostile to materialism. For over two millennia, however, it was the commitment to an infinity of worlds that distinguished materialist thought from the variety of religious views to which it was opposed. Indeed, it may well be that Marx's own unwillingness to produce the philosophy of dialectical materialism derived from his understanding of the centrality of infinity to any materialist philosophy.

If we are to understand the implications of these considerations for any practice of criticism, there is no doubt that the only place to start is with the most important example we have of materialist criticism: Walter Benjamin's fragments, *Charles Baudelaire: A Lyric Poet in the Era of High Capitalism.*[11] In a stunning *tour de force* Benjamin commences with an analysis of Baudelaire's physiognomy and its resemblance to that of a professional conspirator and then weaves in and out of the social and literary text as he moves from the taverns, where the political conspirators gather, to the question of the wine tax and how the tax relates to the poem on the ragpicker. He reintegrates the question of wine into the social spectacle of Paris – as the drunk family weaves its way home – and into its political economy: the *vin de la barrière* produced by the wine tax absorbs several social pressures that might otherwise threaten the government. Benjamin's method is to start with the *doxa* of nineteenth-century life and to work through until connections begin to reveal themselves. Eschewing any theory of mediations, he uses montage to imbricate the literary and social text. There is no question of judging this method in terms of cause and effect within a social totality (all of which categories in this context become idealist): the crucial causal relation is between the analyst and the past and is a truly dialectical one in which the proofs of reading develop in the analysis. Such methods are extremely alien to academic thought, and it is not surprising that the academic Theodor Adorno was so repelled by this text. In that most discouraging of letters which he sends to Benjamin in November 1938 he takes almost personal exception to 'that particular type of concrete-

ness and its behavioristic overtones' and warns Benjamin that 'materialist determination of cultural traits is only possible if it is mediated through the *total social
process*'.[12] But to imagine that the social process can be totalised is to misunderstand the living relation of the present, which determines that the past can be
totalised only for now. It has no totality in itself but rather an infinite number of
possibilities vis-à-vis a future it cannot know but which will bring it to life.

Benjamin saw quite clearly that the notion of 'totality' and its associated concept of mediation were attractive because they were an attempt to fetishise the
past into a controllable finitude and to avoid the risks of scholarly engagement in
the present. His reply to Adorno stresses the personal basis of his own study and
his need to keep the contradictions of his personal concerns in tension with 'the
experiences which all of us shared in the past 15 years'. He distinguished sharply
between this productive contradiction and a 'mere loyalty to dialectical materialism'. Indeed, so deep and productive is the opposition between the personal and
the social that Benjamin refers to it as 'an antagonism of which I would not even
in my dreams wish to be relieved'. And he goes on to state that 'the overcoming of
this antagonism consititutes the problem of my study'.[13] It seems to me that his
disagreement with Adorno was to dominate his thoughts for the short period of
life that remained. The major text of that period is the fulgurant and elliptical
paragraphs which compose the theses on the philosophy of history. I now find it
impossible to read those paragraphs except as a prolonged and mediated reply to
the *bêtise* of Adorno's letter. The constant opposition between the historicist and
the historical materialist is fully comprehensible only if we read the text, in large
measure, as an expression of the opposition between Adorno and himself. Every
line of that remarkable text repays study, but for current purposes I want merely
to quote the first half of the sixteenth thesis:

> An historical materialist cannot do without the notion of a present which is not a tran-
> sition, but in which time stands still and has come to a stop. For this notion defines the
> present in which he himself is writing history. Historicism gives the 'eternal' image of
> the past; historical materialism supplies a unique experience with the past.

Benjamin here makes clear the extent to which the critic enters into a full
relation with the past in which his or her present reveals the past as it is for us. The
crucial problem here is how we are to understand that 'us'. How does the critic's
(and notice that the term must here be considered interchangeable with 'historian') personal constitution relate to any wider social collectivity? Where
Adorno relies on concepts of totality and mediation to constitute a fixed social
past, Benjamin in the theses relentlessly uses the concept of 'class struggle' to
locate us in a mobile social present. The virtue of the concept is that it emphasises
contradiction and division; its weakness is that it is very doubtful that any current
definition of class, either Marxist or sociological, will not limit its contents to a
reductive notion of the economic. The rhetoric function this concept plays in the
theses cannot be sustained when it is given any substantial investigation. Benjamin would find himself limited to another form of the Adorno criticism from
those who would demand 'political correctness' in the present rather than 'the
total social process' in the past.

To elaborate Benjamin it would be necessary to build some notion of a social unconscious into the notion of class struggle. It is interesting that in early drafts of the 'Arcades' project Benjamin had relied on Jung, for it is Jung, of course, who does propose a transindividual unconscious. Unfortunately Jung's concept of the collective unconscious is so historically unspecific that it is completely unequal to the task proposed. But the references to both Jung and Georg Simmel are not to be condemned from the pious position of the orthodox Adorno. They indicate a dimension that must be added to notions of class struggle which would radically transform that notion.

Without presuming on the content of such a transformation, one can indicate some of the effects of introducing the unconscious into the investigation of the past. The historical critic, the critical historian, brings to the past the currency of his or her own epoch; the effort to make the past speak must inevitably draw on resources of which the critic is unaware and which appear only in the construction of the past. The risks are considerable and there can be no question of guarantees. Adorno recalled Benjamin's remarking that each idea of the 'Arcades' project had to be wrested away from a realm in which madness reigns, a realm in which the distinction between the nonsensically individual and the significantly collective disappears.[14] In this respect a critical work shares significant similarities with the creative work it analyses. The author finds him- or herself in their audience.

Notes

1 Roland Barthes, 'The Death of the Author', in *Image-Music-Text: Essays*, selected and translated by Stephen Heath (New York: Hill and Wang, 1977), p. 142.
2 Ibid., p. 148.
3 See Raymond Williams, *Marxism and Literature* (Oxford University Press, 1977), p. 192.
4 *Complete Prose Works of John Milton*, ed. Don Wolfe, 8 vols. (New Haven: Yale University Press, 1953–82), vol. 2, p. 491.
5 See, for example, Mindele Treip, *Milton's Punctuation and Changing English Usage. 1582–1676* (London: Methuen, 1970).
6 Michel Foucault, 'What is an Author?', in *Language, Counter-Memory, Practice: Selected Essays and Interviews*, ed. Donald F. Bouchard, trans. Bouchard and Sherry Simon (Oxford: Basil Blackwell, 1978), p. 120.
7 Ibid., p. 93.
8 François Truffaut, 'A Wonderful Certainty', in *Cahiers du cinéma, the 1950s: New Realism, Hollywood, New Wave*, ed. Jim Hillier (Cambridge: Harvard University Press, 1985), p. 108.
9 Stephen Heath, 'Film and System: Terms of Analysis', *Screen* 16 (1975), no. 1, pp. 7–77; no. 2, pp. 91–113.
10 For details of this argument, see my 'Realism: Balzac and Barthes', in Colin MacCabe, *Theoretical Essays: Film, Linguistics, Literature* (Manchester: Manchester University Press, 1985), pp. 130–50.
11 Walter Benjamin, *Charles Baudelaire: A Lyric Poet in the Era of High Capitalism*, trans. Harry Zohn (London: New Left Books, 1973).
12 Adorno to Benjamin in Ernst Bloch, Georg Lukács, Bertolt Brecht, Walter Benjamin, Theodor Adorno, *Aesthetics and Politics* (London: New Left Books, 1976), p. 129.
13 Benjamin to Adorno, in *Aesthetics and Politics*, p. 136.
14 Adorno to Benjamin, in *Aesthetics and Politics*, p. 127.

2 The Linguistics of Writing

The Programme in Literary Linguistics took its first students in October 1983 and by its second year it was obvious that it had both the intellectual credibility and the student demand to survive. The addition of Derek Attridge and Nigel Fabb to the faculty gave us real international visibility at the intersection of literary and linguistic study and we determined to hold a major conference in the summer of 1986. The conference had two purposes. The first was to promote the particular vision of the relation between language and literature which the course embodied; to anchor the theoretical appeal to language as the key site of the formation of subjectivity in detailed historical and formal analysis. The second was to promote the programme at Strathclyde University.

In many ways the conference was a success. It was not simply that it succeeded in attracting major international scholars to Strathclyde but, more importantly, it attracted scholars from very different disciplines: Williams and Derrida on the one hand, Halle and Halliday on the other. Even the chaotic end of the conference as the audience objected to the form of a conference which had not allowed much space for their participation provided a dramatic climax to the television documentary of the event. If it had the incidental disadvantage of capturing in sound and image the most embarrassing moment of my professional career as the audience voted as to whether I should be allowed to finish delivering the final lecture, there was no doubt that it provided some amusing closing scenes for David Lodge's televisual account of the event.

But in terms of the intellectual ambition of the conference both it and the book that flowed from it were a failure. While much of the anger of the final session of the conference could be written off as conference bile or political fantasy, one charge, that of Eurocentrism, was both justified and, further, seriously undercut the aims of the conference. The initial project of the conference, as of the Programme in Literary Linguistics, was to bring together four very different elements. To a traditional stylistics revivified by discourse analysis and pragmatics was added both a concern with the social and historical development of language and an interest in the workings of language at the level of the signifier. However, all these were informed in the Programme, as it was intended they would be in the conference, by a constant awareness of the status and significance of English; both as a world language, serving as a second language for almost all international interchange, and as a world of languages as the empire strikes back linguistically across the globe. The most important development of English in this century is how a whole variety of peoples subjected to the language of the imperial master have reappropriated it for their own uses. It was this final element, crucial to us as organisers, which we had failed to place centrally in the conference. The arguments of Pratt and Derrida, to which my own paper makes reference, are crucially dependent on these developments in language. However, neither conference nor book contained the material on pidgins and creoles or on Third World debates about national languages which were central to the programme and which would have been essential if the concerns of the programme were to have reached a wider academic audience in the subsequent decade.

Stanley Fish has argued recently that theory can have no effect on practice.[1] This argument depends on defining theory in such a way that it becomes an impossible abstraction and to ignore the very different levels of practice and the relations between them. For me, theory can be sufficiently defined in terms of various kinds of abstraction and idealisation which enable us to discover systems of relationships which can then inform interpretation not simply at the level of individual readings but at the more basic levels of curriculum and pedagogy on which these individual readings depend. How we theoretically place writing in our linguistics will have major consequences for our practice: both educational and social. It is, of course, the case that this century has seen linguistics consolidate itself in terms of conceptions of language which ignored writing as anything but an inadequate record of speech. The reasons for this have been complex. Two important practical reasons can be briefly indicated. On the one hand this denigration of writing accorded with the desire of linguists cataloguing and describing the Amerindian languages to free themselves from Indo-European models.[2] More recently, sociolinguistics has so far almost entirely identified its object as the spoken language.[3] Theoretically, this consolidation of linguistics allowed Saussure to ignore the diachronic in favour of the synchronic, and Chomsky the social in favour of the individual. In fact, in both Saussure's distinction between competence and performance, we find a similar division between the abstract system of the language and the individual speaker.[4] Such theoretical choices mean that any social questions about language are considered to be subsequent to questions of the language's constitution.

These theories are necessarily blind to what one might call either the sociality or the institutionality of language – the different way in which languages reproduce themselves, interact with other languages, grow or decline. Questions of the place of writing within linguistics are a way of focusing this blindness. In thus talking of writing I may seem to suggest, as other references at the conference have suggested, that we talk of a single and unchanging technology. But, of course, writing is not simply a technical matter of reproduction, be it stylus on wax tablet or quill pen on parchment, but a whole system of education and production which produces writers and readers and material texts. Technical and social questions are inseparable when we consider the place of writing in the production and reproduction of a language. To show how inseparable, I want briefly to reflect on the history of English. In talking of English my aim is not to produce an account which could automatically be transferred to any other language, rather it will be, briefly and emblematically, to indicate the kind of concerns we must address if we are to understand a language's social constitution and the place that the dialectic between language and speech can play in that constitution.

English is, in its earliest recognisable manifestations, an Anglo-Latin creole.[5] It was the socially despised language of a conquered underclass. When, however, the French-speaking aristocracy lost their base in France, they gradually adopted the language of their servants and soldiers. The full social history of this development has not yet been written and, given the state of the archive, it is unlikely whether it is possible.[6] It seems probable, however, that it is this complex social history that makes early writers on English from Caxton to Sidney so uncertain of the claims of English. It is not only when compared to the great languages of antiquity but also to rivals in Italy, France and Spain that English seems to be lacking to those who write about it before 1580. Andrew Borde need not be taken as untypical when he writes in the 1540s: 'The speche of England is a base speche to other noble speches, as Italion, Castylion, and Frenche.'[7]

When Caxton writes his famous preface to the *Aeneid* some fifty years earlier he is convinced of English's particular mutability and unsteadiness and he indicates with great clarity the dilemma facing the merchant class, of which he is so notable a representative. It might be hazarded as a guess that Caxton's own super-sensibility to the national and class questions are due on the one hand to his prominent membership of the London bourgeoisie and, on the other, to the fact that he himself originally spoke with a broad Kentish accent, the accent which was already defining the national standard by the fact of its exclusion as sub-standard – a language fit only for workmen and fools.[8] A national language is required for purposes of commerce and identification but these two purposes are not one.[9] Of course, everybody will need to speak the language for the purpose of commerce (and Caxton is not the only writer of the language who includes examples of members of different classes being unable to communicate for purposes of trade as evidence of the failings of the English tongue). But those who will identify the language as theirs, and will identify themselves in the language, must be limited to a ruling class. How that class will be constituted is, famously, one of the crucial political questions fought out until the Glorious Revolution of 1688 put a final seal on the settlement of the Restoration. What is never sufficiently discussed in literature courses is the extent that the literature from the 1580s onwards is a (perhaps the) privileged site where that class question is fought out linguistically. Caxton, and indeed other writers after him, had already indicated that the national language would be identified with a written language which would find its prestige in a privileged relationship to the classics, but what that written language would be, from orthography to vocabulary, and even to syntax, was very definitely an open question. Before 1580 such questions had been discussed in terms of a general pessimism.[10] From thenceforth it is an aggressive optimism which seeks to define what is at stake. What is at stake is as much who is to be excluded as who is to be included.[11] Shakespeare and Spenser make a perfect comparison here. Spenser, working within a traditional pattern of patronage, linked to an aristocratic court, produces a language which is aggressively English but which requires the scholarly gloss of an E.K., the anonymous annotation of *The Shepheardes Calendar*, to make it readable. Whether Spenser and E.K. are one and the same is beside the crucial point that this English text is only to be read by the learned and initiate circle, the language of *The Shepheardes Calendar* fitting neatly with the allegory of *The Faerie Queene* to produce an address which reproduces the allegiance to an imaginary feudal past. It is normal to regard Spenser's linguistic experiments as rather eccentric, but a different history which would have produced an early absolutist court in England might well have determined it as a dominant poetic discourse. However, it is crucial both for Shakespeare's aesthetics and politics that one should be able to move through the various registers and dialects of English. Edgar and Prince Hal are two examples who spring immediately to mind. These alternative politics of literary language relate to the whole variety of complicated social practice but to none more importantly than education.[12] The growth of literacy in this period is very considerable and it is this growing literacy, as much as any other, which fuels the ideological battles up to and through the protectorate. Milton stands in some ways as the climax, within the high literary tradition, of an English absolutely established as a national standard but, theoretically, open to all. For Milton there is no question but that English is superior in its potential to both its contemporary continental rivals and to the languages of antiquity; the opening lines of *Paradise Lost* make this clear. At the same time Milton clearly feels that his poem is open to all those with the correct ethical stance. The paucity of the audience is determined by the lack of religious and ethically fit readers rather than by their social qualifications.

Paradise Lost, however, is written after the Restoration as a ruling class which has constituted itself politically and economically attempts to regulate the ideological sphere. This regulation takes a multitude of forms, most crucially affecting religion, education and literacy (and literacy's concomitant access to freedom of interpretation of the Bible). The language is regulated in all its forms from speech through vocabulary to syntax to text. In this regulation, Milton has a curious role to play. As the writer who has most thoroughly mastered the classical tradition, he becomes a trophy of a narrow class-based definition of English but at the same time his regicide and republican attitudes, as well as his refusal to fix meaning, means that he must be re-written.[13] Bentley sets to work. Later, Johnson, as well as producing the *Dictionary*, will castigate Shakespeare for the varied registers he uses and long for a literary tradition which will observe the linguistic propriety which will render the literature into a language which is not spoken by the majority of the people. Many of these developments are most clearly elaborated in John Walker's *A Critical Pronouncing Dictionary* (1791) which makes absolutely clear that the aim of this regulation is the exclusion of the vast majority that do not share the 'correct pronunciation'.[14] Walker's text deliberately sets out to bring speech into line with writing and thus concludes that identification of the language with the written, and the written with a class-based education which had been at work since the beginning of the sixteenth century.

It is at this point that a fresh difficulty surfaces; the need for a literate population. This is a very different desire from the sixteenth-century wish for a population of Bible readers. The imperative now is provided directly by the developments of capital and the need for a literate workforce to participate fully in the next stage of industrial development. Throughout the nineteenth century, culminating in the provisions of 1870, universal literacy becomes a possibility and a necessity.[15] If we take 1900 as a crucial moment then we can reflect that the language any citizen will speak will bear a complicated relation to this massively reproduced standard. By a deep historical irony, it is at just this moment that linguistics is beginning to free itself from considerations of normativity and undertaking the systematic description of speech forms. It is not belittling that effort, and its necessity, to say now that, in retrospect, we can see that the study should not just have been of the spoken forms but of the relation between those forms and the officially reproduced standard. Before, however, turning to what the consequences of that might be in educational, linguistic or literary terms, I want to complicate the question a little further.

Modernism can be understood, in one of its most important aspects, as an attempt within literature to come to terms with this new educational and linguistic situation in which the vast majority of the population are now literate and the relation between speech and writing, if regulated in the educational sphere, is now deeply problematic. One has only to think of *The Waste Land* and its original Dickensian epigraph – 'he do the police in different voices'[16] – to realise how deep this crisis runs. But Eliot is concerned to find fragments to shore against his ruins, whereas much of the force of modernism – and here Joyce is for me the exemplary figure – deliberately subverts and undoes the identification of the language with the written and the written with a classically defined literary tradition. The introduction into *Ulysses* of an advertising canvasser whose call at the National Library is to search for an advertisement in a provincial paper displays ironically the new organisation of language with which Joyce concerns himself. And Joyce's radicalism is given its cutting edge by his position as colonial subject. The impossibility of merging speech and writing finds its most acute symptom in the need to find definitions of Ireland not wholly dominated by England.[17] Joyce's work, however, suffers from a constitutive contradiction, endemic to much modernism, whereby the attempt to undermine and contest the high literary tradition is enacted within commercial forms and markets which are determined by that tradition. I do not have time in this brief lecture to consider the very complex history of Ireland which condemned Joyce to exclusively written work. Emblematically, however, let us remember that Joyce opened the first cinema in Ireland.[18] And, suggestively, can we imagine a different Irish history which would have seen Yeats and Joyce participating in an Abbey multi-media centre? There the multitude of voices and gestures which crowd the pages of *Finnegans Wake* would have found a more productive cultural and political space in which to operate (it should be obvious that such an imaginary history would necessarily involve a very different national liberation than the one Ireland achieved in 1922).

But leaving aside the particular victories and defeats of Ireland in this century, this imaginary history has the advantage of immediately drawing our attention to the new media of communication: radio and cinema, followed by television and the technologies of recorded sound which have done so much to transform the linguistic space in which we move. The introduction of recorded speech as a massive part of our linguistic environment marks a change in our culture which may come to seem as momentous as printing. It also means that to understand the reproduction of any speech community we must now grasp its relation to the mass media as well as its relationship to the educational system. All this is merely obvious at some political levels (in Britain one immediately thinks of the political struggle for a Welsh language television station) but it is far from obvious at others. Any serious contemporary discussion of language must also consider this phenomenon which Walter Ong has named 'secondary orality'.[19] To continue this kind of social analysis of English into the twentieth century it would be necessary to grasp fully the importance and significance of this secondary orality.

Mary Louise Pratt has argued very convincingly that almost all linguistics is unable to grasp the kind of relations sketched in this brief history because linguistics constitutes itself around the concept of a Utopian speech community in which speakers and hearers communicate with each other in situations of perfect equality and transparency. Pratt argues that typical speech situations actually involve relations of dominance and opacity and calls for a 'linguistics of contact' to replace a 'linguistics of community'.[20] It is in this enlarged linguistic context which I have just sketched that it becomes fully possible to envisage the linguistics called for by Mary Louise Pratt: a linguistics which understands language as constituted across the various institutional struggles and technological transformations that I have just indicated. It is important to realise that this account makes it impossible for us to think first of language, and then only secondarily the speakers that use it or the technologies that transmit it. The language is constituted in relations of power and domination, themselves inseparable from the relations which the technology enacts, which place speakers in a pragmatic situation.[21] There are not speakers and language but speakers of the language in the kind of complex relations I have indicated.

It is doubtful, however, whether 'linguistics of contact' is the best term with which to replace a 'linguistics of community'.[22] It runs the risk of reproducing, in the notion of 'contact', many of the features of a linguistics of communication and the notion of a speech community from which Pratt was seeking to distance herself. 'Contact' does have the advantage of immediately indicating that there is not one single community and it immediately introduces the possibility of language being used to emphasise a lack of communication as well as to facilitate communication. However, the risk is that it would seem to assume two communities meeting and that they meet on equal terms. The risk is, thus, twofold. The notion of community which Pratt so brilliantly unpicked at a primary level is now reintroduced at the secondary level. Moreover, the unevenness and multiplicity of power-relations within a language is likely to be lost because the semantic range of 'contact' would suggest one primary opposition. In searching for a more appropriate lexical item the first alternative that sprang to my mind was a 'linguistics of domination'. This term has the advantage of stressing inequality, and of alluding to the desire which is always at stake in language. However, it still suggests that there are two distinct entities: a dominating and a dominated. In addition it has the further disadvantage of suggesting that domination is always successful, of being unable to account for the play of chance and will which enables subjected sections of the linguistic community to find a voice if only in elaborate forms of mimicry or jokes. The term which I very seriously wish to suggest might perhaps best capture the situation Pratt so well described is a 'linguistics of conflict'. This final term is still misleading if it suggests that what is being described is a conflict between two different entities. There are not two groups of speakers with a different relation to the language; two speech communities instead of one. Rather the language is constituted across a whole variety of relations and struggles. Any given speaker will participate differently in those relations and struggles. It is absolutely essential to recognise that doing away with the idealised speech community also does away with an idealised speaker. There is no more necessary unity to be sought in the speaker than in the community. Just as there are a multiplicity of collectivities striving for definition and identification within a single national language (where it becomes clear that you can replace 'national', but only with some other political social or ideological entity clearly recognised by the speakers), so each speaker is him- or herself a member of a multiplicity of collectivities and is, therefore, constituted as contradictory and divided in relation to the language.

This is not for a moment to deny either that there may be a single dominant conflict between collectivities (classically, in terms of class), nor that it is impossible for a speaker to identify almost completely with the dominant definition of the collectivity (the voice of the dominant and hegemonic sector). But it is important theoretically to recognise the multiplicitly, particularly as within advanced developed countries it is empirically arguable that there are at least four important collectivities in relation to speech (class, race, gender and age) and that no matter how totally there is identification with the voice of the dominant and hegemonic sector, that voice will bear traces and echoes of the conflicts it seeks to conceal.[23]

There is, however, another very important reservation to be made about the linguistics of conflict. It was made clearly at the original conference when Jacques Derrida, while agreeing with the thrust of Pratt's argument, also signalled his agreement with a comment on that paper by someone, speaking in the name of 'hard' linguistics, who insisted that this new linguistics could not supervene or contradict the search for invariants. Derrida went on to emphasise that 'what science has to do, what linguistics has to do, is never give up the necessity, the desire to formalise, to exhaust the analysis of codes, of the invariants'.[24]

The crucial question is how we understand the relations between a 'linguistics of conflict' and a 'linguistics of invariance'. Derrida seems to assume, in the comments he made after the passage I have quoted, that the linguistics of invariance is related to the linguistics of conflict as stability to crisis. This is, I feel, a misleading model and I would now like to outline what I think the relations between them are and the different way in which they would constitute their object and procedures.

In *Knowledge of Language* Noam Chomsky looks back on the thirty-year history of generative grammar. In the first two chapters, he attempts to rework both the methodological suppositions and the vocabulary of generative grammar to make clear how contemporary Government and Binding theory is addressed to the same questions as the older transformational model. For Chomsky the only real difference is that the questions are now better understood. I am in complete sympathy with Chomksy's goals but I feel that he has, in one or two minor but important ways, misunderstood the lessons of the last thirty years' development and has opted for a new vocabulary much more misleading than the one that has become traditional within generative grammar. By following his argument I hope to produce an account which will illuminate the relations between a linguistics of invariance and a linguistics of conflict.

Chomsky's fundamental argument is that the incredibly fruitful conjunction of the study of formal languages and the study of natural languages (of which his own work is the most extraordinary example) led to a fundamental misconception. In any formal language for which one is providing a grammar the sentences of that language are completely explicit; the corpus is easily defined. This completely explicit formal language is the object of study (there couldn't be any other object). When it came to generative grammar and the study of natural languages, the mistake was made to think that once again one was studying the language extensionally, or, as Chomsky says in this text, in terms of its external features.

To define this language, generative grammar used the notion of 'competence', and idealised knowledge of a speaker-hearer in a homogeneous speech community. The important point about this notion, and why Chomsky gets so impatient with those who attack it, is that it provides an absolutely automatic way of constituting the corpus. All the linguist has to do is consult his (or her) intuitions and any sentence will immediately be judged as a well-formed member of the corpus or not. Chomsky is not interested in speakers or hearers or communities, but he is interested in finding a method of constituting his object. At the beginning generative grammar made the mistake of identifying the speaker's knowledge of the language as a method of generating a totally explicit language. There are, as we have seen in Pratt's argument, and as I have indicated here, enormous problems in thus trying to define language, speakers and communities.[25] One solution would be to re-focus on the externalised language, more adequately understood and described. Chomsky, quite rightly from the point of view of the linguistics of invariance, refuses such an option. Rather he redefines what it is that forms the object of generative grammar. So far, so good.

To do this he turns to the great Danish linguist Jespersen in order to define what he calls 'internalized language', a metaphor he quickly swops for a technical term: I-language. I-language is, for Chomsky, what Jespersen referred to when he held that there is some 'notion of structure' in the mind of the speaker 'which is definite enough to guide him in framing sentences of his own', in particular, 'free expressions' that may be new to the speaker and to others'.[26] A grammar is then defined as a theory of the I-language. Chomsky explains the historical mistake of generative grammar by arguing that generative grammar confused I-language with the E-language and often referred to the I-language as the grammar (this is, for example, the case throughout *Aspects of the Theory of Syntax*). But, in fact, it is much easier to say that generative grammar confused its object, 'a grammar', with language. My argument is that, far from making a mistake, Chomsky was correct to call his object of study a grammar and in this technical and specific sense it forms the object of early transformational theory and later Government and Binding theory. This object has little to do with the dominant notions of language, but is constituted by invariant and universal features of language. Crucially we can now define the corpus of the grammar as those set of sentences within English or any other natural language which enable that grammar to be refined and made more powerful. The selection of sentences is now in terms of the questions posed by the theory.

An important problem that remains is the relation between the study of generative grammar and the study of externalised language. Chomsky is convinced that there is nothing to be gained from this externalised language. It is, at best, an 'epiphenomenon'.[27] His attitude to the commonsense attitude which would place externalised language on the agenda is blunt:

> In the first place the commonsense notion of language has a crucial sociopolitical dimension ... A standard remark in introductory linguistics courses is that a language is a dialect with an army and a navy (attributed to Max Weinreich). That any coherent account can be given of language in this sense is doubtful; surely, none has been offered or even seriously attempted. Rather all scientific approaches have simply abandoned these elements of what is called 'language' in common usage.[28]

This is Chomsky at his most painfully polemical for, of course, there is a long history of people who have tried to study language in this sense – Sapir and Firth to name only two of the most influential this century. And I would argue strongly that it is essential to theorise language in ways that relate closely to this dominant conception. However, Chomsky is not alone in feeling that it is impossible to theorise language at any level which corresponds to most commonsense view of languages. Richard Hudson, although extremely interested in the social variation of language, argues very powerfully that it is impossible to give any substantive sense to any unit of language above the linguistic item.[29] All sociolinguistics can accomplish is to study particular speakers or groups of speakers in order to discover what kind of social description can be given for a linguistic item. There is no analysis that will unify these items into the languages, dialects or varieties that both ordinary language and linguists have sought to identify. Hudson comes to similar conclusions about the notion of speech community:

> which seems to exist only to the extent that a given person has identified and can locate himself with reference to it. Since different individuals will identify different communities in this way, we have to give up any attempt to find objective and absolute criteria for defining speech communities. This leaves us on the one hand with the individual speaker and his range of linguistic items and, on the other, with communities defined without reference to language but to which we may find it helpful to relate language.[30]

Hudson moves from the fact that linguistic items cannot be constituted into a language, to the fact that speakers define the language differently, to the conclusion that communities can be defined without relation to language. His problem constitutes our solution, however. One of the most fundamental ways in which we define our communities is in terms of shared language. The fact that linguistic inquiry demonstrates that language is never as shared as we think merely demonstrates the existence of differences within those communities while also giving material reality to notions of the free play of the signifier. The fact that individuals define the community differently merely means that there are important differences of identification. Sociolinguistic research from Labov onwards shows this to be the case, and shows further that the individual is often split him- or herself as a language user, the conscious and unconscious identifications of the language frequently being very different.[31]

What all this indicates, however (and this constitutes a further stage of Pratt's argument), is not that the language or speech community does not exist but that its existence is an imaginary one. One should not confuse imaginary here with inexistent or ineffective. Psychoanalysis has taught us how effective the imaginary is at providing in its unifying images the forms of our most real identifications.[32] Socially, we have only to look at the terrible history of the twentieth century to see the devastating reality of imaginary conceptions of unity. To suppose that these conceptions cannot be studied scientifically is to resign oneself intellectually to Armageddon.

To address this task sociolinguistics will have to develop real modes of social and psychological analysis. At the moment it tends to limit itself to the use of the most banal sociological or psychological categories without any recourse to concepts of class, race or gender which would bring genuine edge and understanding to what so often seems like the barren compiling of evidence (interesting as that evidence often is). It is in the development of such concepts that a 'linguistics of conflict' will have a crucial role to play in a revivifying and recasting of both the social sciences and the humanities. It should not be thought that this is simply a longer version of the tired slogan 'what linguistics needs is Marxism and psychoanalysis'. The problem with that slogan is that it assumes that the necessary concepts are to hand. That is, at best, only partially true. A slogan which would more accurately indicate the real state of affairs would be 'what Marxism and psychoanalysis need is linguistics'. For it is certain that without a real attention to the sociality of language neither Marxism nor psychoanalysis is going to able to solve its currently paralysing dilemmas. For Marxism this is constituted by the impossibility of allowing any real effectivity to political and ideological representations without sacrificing its economic analysis of class. For psychoanalysis it is its inability to provide any account of identification which regards social units larger than the family.[33] Further, it is only in the context of such a linguistics that we could develop the concepts of race crucial to the future development of the planet. The point is perhaps most simply made by saying that sociolinguistics needs to become a lot more dangerous and that it will have to accept that its formulations of problems will need to include not just linguistic description but also the imaginary identifications and real conflicts which are at stake.

What is important to stress is that this imaginary identification of the language has real effects – it is how the language reproduces itself. In this sense the particular way in which national languages reproduce themselves – essentially through education and the media – merely reproduce a tendency within all language.[34] The arbitrary play of the signifier is such that, without such a tendency, language would simply endlessly fragment. From the speech of a mother to a child, through the influence of peer group behaviour to the dictionary and the grammar, we are dealing with different kinds of linguistic regulation, but all such regulation depends on an imaginary identification of the language – it is here that the reality of 'the linguistics of conflict' resides.

From the existence of Chomsky's language-function it does not follow that any languages would exist at all. The crucial question that Chomsky poses runs as follows:

> Surely there is some property of mind P that would enable a person to acquire a language under conditions of pure and uniform experience, and surely P (characterised by Universal Grammar) is put to use under the real conditions of language acquisition. To deny these assumptions would be bizarre indeed: it would be to claim either that language can be learned only under conditions of diversity and conflicting evidence, which is absurd, or that the property P exists – there exists a capacity to learn language in the pure and uniform case – but the actual learning of language does not involve this capacity.[35]

What Chomsky rejects as absurd is to me evident: language is only learned under conditions of diversity and conflicting evidence. There is always present, however (realised at very different levels in different societies) an imaginary unity of the language. It is this imaginary unity which allows property P to function but that unity is not reducible to P. It is the speaker's conviction that there is a unity to the linguistic diversity with which it is presented that enables P to operate. P cannot provide its own definition of its object. It seems to me that this solves Chomsky's problems and also completely vindicates his own continued refusal – most notably when the folly of generative semantics was in full flight – to identify the grammar with the language.[36]

To investigate the constitution of this imaginary unit is a task of pressing educational and social importance. It may provide some of the answers to what Chomsky calls Orwell's question, the problem of how language is misused ideologically and politically.[37] We must be clear, however, that such an investigation will have the characteristics of a critical rather than a positive science. I do not claim for those adjectives any more than heuristic importance as I have no wish to get bogged down in an epistemological discussion which will, inevitably, show that it is impossible to produce any explicit criteria with which to differentiate discourses in terms of their scientificity.[38] However, there are important distinctions between sciences in which the standpoint of the observer is immediately relevant and in which the results of the research programme immediately feed back into the object, and sciences where the standpoint of the observer is not immediately relevant and in which the results of the inquiry do not immediately affect the object. This is an important difference between a linguistics of conflict and a linguistics of invariance. For a linguistics of conflict the linguistic information to be analysed will be initially specified in relation to questions of class, race and gender, which are posed within contemporary political and ideological struggle. This is not, in any way, a prescription for relativism but it does acknowledge that the topics to be studied will not be determined internally by the science. In addition, the findings are likely to alter the object as they feed into dictionaries, grammars and, most importantly, the educational system and the media. A concrete example will make this clear. Let us propose an important research topic: the study of intonation in newsreaders – the study's rationale is in terms of the importance within contemporary advanced societies of the forms of direct address on television. It is very largely within this discourse that a society is given an image of itself, its imaginary identity. It is because of this importance that so much emotion is generated around the topic of bias in the media but, to date, all investigation of this bias has operated at the level of the content of declarative statements. There is no doubt in my mind that a thorough study of intonation would indicate systematic ways in which the viewer is asked to approve or disapprove of developments within society. The results of such a study would be very likely, eventually, to alter the uses of intonation that it describes. Even such a brief example can indicate the kind of controversy with which a linguistics of conflict would have to live. People would dispute the necessity of the research, its results and its consequences.

Before considering how it might be possible to encourage such research, what practical questions we must address for linguistics, literary criticism and education, I want to pose a final and inevitable theoretical question: Are there any relations between the invariants and the conflicts? It may be obvious that there will be relations between the invariants and the conflicts – but I want to suggest that they are two very different kinds. First, and most obviously, the invariants will place certain constraints on the conflicts – the imaginary unity will have very definite limits placed on it by the structures of invariance. It seems to me that the study of linguistic change and of the developments of pidgins and creoles would be the obviously privileged area for investigating this. Second, and here we reach the most speculative of regions: will the conflicts ever affect the variants? Will our deepest syntactic and semantic categories ever be altered by the way we understand our language?

My answer is a definite but purely speculative 'yes'.[39] It is, at this point, that I would appeal to the extraordinarily rich and suggestive article of Michael Halliday's which attempts to grapple with this almost unthinkable problem, unthinkable because it considers how our forms of thought alter and change. Halliday considers language as a dynamic open system: that is to say a system which persists only through change. Crucial to this system is that it constantly represents (better, construes) more than one point of view about reality, while the more determinate meta-languages can only construe reality from a specific viewpoint.[40] Halliday argues that writing encodes language as determinate but that what is needed is to introduce the fundamentally rheomodal (complementary and multideterminate) grammar of spoken language into our written forms. Much of this is persuasive and exciting but I would want to argue that Halliday underestimates the extent to which the ordinary speaker of the language has made certain fundamental identifications, sexual and social, which necessarily deny the complementarity from which they are constructed. Lurking behind this is a question even more fundamental: Is it the case that to speak a language we must ignore its fundamental modes of construction? Or, to put it in psychological, rather than semiotic, terms: How far can we recognise our own identities as provisional? Although Halliday recognises the paradoxes of representation, that it is always by a process of differentiation that we produce a world of identities, he does not consider the extent to which the process of differentiation must be repressed for the identities to exist. Crucially, he does not consider the, for me, vital question: Is it not the case that repressions necessary to produce a world are always anchored in a central repression, sexual or social, whereby we gain a stable identity? Halliday simply assumes (what I feel needs to be proved in both theory and practice) that language can be multiply anchored and not tied to a central semiotic division: male/female, member/outsider. Such questions would temper Halliday's optimism while still allowing us to share it. It would be in this perspective that we might consider limit cases where changes within the linguistics of conflict fed back into the invariant structures of the language. To talk in Halliday's evolutionary terms this would be one clear way to understand the inheritance of acquired characteristics.

The importance and excitement of such questions are obvious but it would be foolish to presume that we are anywhere close to articulating them in a satisfactory manner. Address them, however, we must and the current organisation of departments of linguistics and literary criticism do not, by and large, suggest that we are going to find this easy. It would be wrong to think, however, that this is a local problem limited to two disciplines. It seems to be that the whole organisation of knowledge in the universities often now functions to prevent rather than to facilitate the asking of questions. How far this is due to the micro-politics of institutions, how far to honourable fears about the loss of specific skills, and how far to the deliberate foreclosing of the crucial questions of our society is not a matter I can decide in this paper. All I can voice is an almost consuming despair that the crucial issues for our society, such as ecology or race, are only marginal at best for a western university system which harnesses potential and resources on a hitherto unimaginable scale. Despair is, however, the one unforgivable emotion – as the Catholic Church has long recognised by naming it as the sin against the Holy Ghost. In a spirit, then, of desperate optimism I want to suggest some broad lines of development within tertiary education. It would obviously be a criminal folly for linguistics to abandon the study of invariance, and such a study would be at the centre of a new organisation of the humanities and social sciences. This reorganisation would stress the need to develop the social and psychological concepts to understand the full implications of a 'linguistics of conflict' as the imaginary unity of communities and speakers gives way to a scientific understanding of their divisions and conflicts, as well as the politics, micro- and macro-, which forge those divisions into unities. The elaboration of these concepts will require drawing on the whole range of discipline within the humanities and social sciences in a way which is common at the highest levels of research but scandalously absent at most levels of the university system. It might be said that the great texts of modern and post-modern literature, the works of Burroughs or Joyce, would function within such a reconstituted academy as major and important experiments – the full consequences of which we have not begun to reckon in our more rational calculuses.

But if literature might function as experiment, what of literary criticism? Is it adequate to think in terms of it incorporating a greater historical awareness of the development of language as we study the literary text? Such a local reform is, of course, necessary. I would argue, however, that the kind of considerations advanced in the first half of this paper do not simply appeal to some missing technical skill that must be provided – they indicate the extent to which literary criticism constantly represses the conditions of its own existence. If we fully comprehend the extent to which literature has always been as much an act of social exclusion as shared illumination, if we seriously accept Benjamin's terrible insight that a work of civilisation is also, always, a work of barbarism[41] then we must recognise the extent that one of the major functions of literary criticism as an institution is to preserve a cultural form, with a very specific class history, by ignoring those cultural forms based on mechanical and electronic reproduction which threaten to enlarge the audience in unacceptable ways. If the particular skills of textual criticism and the developed attention to the complexity of textual production must be preserved and reproduced, literary criticism can only develop within a genuine humanities by recognising that its object of study is the whole range of cultural productions. It is only then that we will be able to seriously investigate the cultural movements of the twentieth century and the place of writing within them in ways which seriously engage with the gains and losses of these hugely enlarged audiences, audiences which now cross class and national boundaries in fundamentally new ways. It seems to me merely obvious that this change also involves a change of name, that the chauvinist connotations of English and the class connotations of literature must be abandoned in favour of a commitment to cultural studies. Such cultural studies would find an inevitable place in the analysis of a 'linguistics of conflict'.

All this is proper material for a programmatic statement which is meant both to open and to close a conference. But this is not all vague promises for the future: promises which will run up against the rocks of inevitable resistance as those who identify their very humanity with the most limited notions of taste and standards will fight to the death any attempt to investigate that taste or those standards. The conference on the Linguistics of Writing is an attempt to start something on an international scale but, more realistically and less hubristically, it marks the achievement of something on the local scale. The Programme in Literary Linguistics at Strathclyde University is now three years old and it is one academic enterprise in which the commitment to a linguistics of conflict and a linguistics of invariance is not a matter of verbal promises but real developments. The Masters dissertations which have been produced there already provide a body of work along the lines I have outlined here, and doctoral dissertation and books of much potential are now in preparation.[42]

The practical consequences of the linguistics of conflict are important in the context of tertiary education and the way in which the study of culture is understood, articulated and organised. However, it is possible that they are even more important in the context of primary and secondary education and the teaching of language. The draconian moulding of every child to an artificial standard is, thankfully, a thing of the past, but I would not like anybody to think that the considerations advanced here suggest that a national standard should no longer be taught. In recent years many teachers, in understandable revolt against a 150-year-old tradition of policing their pupils' language, have eagerly adopted the views of linguists that each language, or each variety of a language, is as good as any other. This position, which is true at the level of the linguistics of invariance, is dangerous nonsense at the level of the linguistics of conflict. It is just not true, for example, that Latin is as good as English as a language for science. This is not a comment about some essential feature of the structure of Latin,[43] but a comment on the fact that English has a large specialised scientific vocabulary and that the vast majority of scientific publications are in English. Similarly, no one alive to the vitality of language could pretend that Glaswegian was in any way inferior to standard English. However, to claim that it is adequate either internationally, or for certain bureaucratic or political purposes, is to condemn speakers to their own linguistic ghetto within the national and international polity.

What, then, are the practical consequences for the teaching of English? Do we simply continue to teach the national standard while deploring its history and assumptions? The answer is more complex than a simple yes or no. It is that we teach the national standard but we teach it as a variety. It seems to me that it is absolutely essential that teachers encourage a bi- and multi-lectalism in their pupils; that we find pedagogic means (nothing suggests this will be easy) which encourage people to learn other varieties of their own language, without devaluing their own. In some ways, the development of television seems to have aided this process for, as listeners, we participate in five or six very different varieties of English a night (a full understanding of this is a necessary prerequisite of any full account of the political impact of television). To help develop such pedagogies is a pressing educational and political necessity. Richard Hudson is right to refer to 'national standards' as almost pathologically limited.[44] One of the most hopeful developments in England since the war has transformed us from a monoglot into a polyglot political entity. If we are to build on the diversity of language now spoken in Britain, it will be by developing ways of teaching a standard which does not automatically devalue and disregard other languages or other varieties. It is not too far-fetched to think that if we were to lessen the pathology of our national tongue we might lessen other associated pathological limitations as well.

Notes

1 Stanley Fish, 'Consequences', *Critical Inquiry*, vol. 11 no. 3, March 1985, pp. 433–58.
2 It is difficult to overestimate the importance of the experience of describing and analysing the Amerindian languages for twentieth-century linguistics.
3 Suzanne Romaine argues in *Socio-Historical Linguistics* (Cambridge: Cambridge University Press, 1982), pp. 14–21, that the written language should be a necessary part of sociolinguistic study but this is still a relatively unusual position.
4 In passing it should be said that neo-Firthian linguistics has no such necessary commitment to the primacy of speech.
5 See Romaine, *Socio-Historical Linguistics* (pp. 56–69) for how recent research on pidgins and creoles can explicate the history of Middle English.
6 A brief and useful account can be found in Dick Leith, *A Social History of English* (London: Routledge, 1997), pp. 26–31. For a chauvinist account of this period which nevertheless includes some interesting data, see Basil Cottle, *The Triumph of English 1350–1400* (London: Blandford Press, 1969).
7 Andrew Borde, *The fyrst boke of the introduction of knowledge*, ed. F. J. Furnivall, Early English Text Society, new series vol. X, London, 1870, p. 122.
8 In his preface to Raoul le Fevre's *The Recuyell of the Historyes of Troye*, Caxton tells he 'was born and learned my English in Kent, in the Weald, where I doubte not is spoken as brode and rude Englissh as in any place of England.' W. Crotch (ed.), *The Prologues and Epilogues of William Caxton* (London: OUP, 1928).
9 For a detailed analysis of Caxton's fascinating text see my Collins Dictionary lecture 'Righting English', Chapter 3. For a consideration of the relations between national language and capitalist economies, see R. Balibar, *Le Français national* (Paris: 1973).
10 R. F. Jones in *The Triumph of the English Language* (London: OUP, 1953), locates the change in attitude between 1575 and 1580. Jones's book is a remarkable study but he is resolutely uninterested in the class division that the national standard is both enacting and introducing. None the less many (if not most) of his chosen quotations pick out very clearly what is at stake. Crucial to the discourse of class at this period is the metaphor of dress, a metaphor which is very evident in discussions of language.
11 Leith, *A Social History of English*, p. 42.
12 See Lawrence Stone, 'The educational revolution in England 1560–1640', *Past and Present*, no. 28, July 1964, pp. 41–80.
13 The paradoxes of Milton's position in this general development are explored in work I am currently undertaking: *John Milton: An Epic Poet in the Era of Nascent Capitalism*, London, forthcoming.
14 For example, 'The vulgar pronunciation of London, though not half so erroneous as that of Scotland, Ireland, or any of the provinces, is, to a person of correct taste, a thousand times more disgusting', *Walker's Critical Pronouncing Dictionary*, corrected and enlarged by J. Fraser (London: 1852), p. 17. It is only in the context sketched here that one can begin to evaluate Wordsworth's appeal to 'the real language of men', on the first page of the *Preface to Lyrical Ballads* (1800).
15 D. J. Palmer, *The Rise of English Studies* (London: OUP, 1965).
16 The full quotation from *Our Mutual Friend* in the original manuscript is even more revealing of the link between the growth of mass circulation newspapers and a problematising of the status of writing: Sloppy is a foundling adopted by old Betty Higden, a poor widow. 'I do love a newspaper', she says. 'You mightn't think it but Sloppy is a beautiful reader of a newspaper. He do the Police in different voices.' T. S. Eliot, *The*

Waste Land: A Facsimile and Transcript of the Original Proofs including the annotations of Ezra Pound, ed. Valerie Eliot (London: Faber & Faber, 1971), p. 2.

17 For a more detailed analysis, see Colin MacCabe 'The voice of Esau: Stephen in the Library', in Colin MacCabe (ed.), *James Joyce: New Perspectives* (Brighton: Harvester, 1982), pp. 111–28.

18 For Joyce's involvement with the cinema, see Richard Ellman, *James Joyce* (New York: 1959), pp. 310–14.

19 Walter J. Ong, *Orality and Literacy: The Technologising of the Word* (London: Methuen, 1982).

20 Mary Louise Pratt, 'Linguistic Utopias' in Fabb, Attridge, Durant and MacCabe (eds), *The Linguistics of Writing* (Manchester: Manchester University Press, 1987).

21 It should be said in passing that these considerations most heavily undercut the optimistic account of a general social pragmatics offered by Lyotard in *The Postmodern Condition: A Report on Knowledge* (Manchester: Manchester University Press, 1984). Lyotard ignores throughout his text the importance of those discourses which have totally asymmetrical relations built into the relation between addresser and addressee.

22 At the original conference, Jacques Derrida, while agreeing with the force of Pratt's argument, also voiced doubts about the appropriateness of the term 'contact'. 'Some questions and responses' in Fabb et al., *The Linguistics of Writing*, p. 253.

23 *Finnegans Wake* is the primer for considering the variety of contradictory discourses which constitute the speaking subject.

24 Derrida, op. cit., p. 253.

25 For a more detailed account of Chomsky's concept of competence and its problems, see Colin MacCabe in *James Joyce Broadsheet* 2, May 1980.

26 Noam Chomsky, *Knowledge of Language: Its Nature, Origin and Use* (New York: 1986), pp. 21–2.

27 Ibid., p. 25.

28 Ibid., p. 15.

29 R. A. Hudson, *Sociolinguists* (Cambridge: Cambridge University Press, 1980), Chapter 2.

30 Ibid., p. 72.

31 See, for one example among many, Trudgill, 'Sex, covert prestige and linguistic change', *Language in Society*, vol. 1 no. 2, 1972, pp. 187–8. It should be said that both Labov and LePage have recognised the importance of the imaginary in the constitution of the unity of the language but neither have sufficiently considered its conscious and unconscious characteristics.

32 Jacqueline Rose, 'The Imaginary', in Colin MacCabe (ed.), *The Talking Cure: Essays on Psychoanalysis and Language* (London: Macmillian, 1981), pp. 132–61.

33 My article 'On discourse' in *Theoretical Essays: Film, Linguistics, Literature* (Manchester: Manchester University Press, 1985), deals at much greater length with the relation between linguistics, Marxism and psychoanalysis.

34 Hudson argues very differently. For him the regulating qualities within a natural language are unusual and make them 'the least interesting kind of language for anyone interested in the nature of human language (as most linguists are)', *Sociolinguists*, p. 34. I completely agree with Hudson that standard languages are 'pathological in their lack of diversity' (ibid.), but I feel that by considering other kinds of regulation we might enjoy the benefits of standard languages without some of their consequent pathologies. Standard languages are no more 'unnatural' than other languages, or only in so far as nations are more 'unnatural' than other forms of political and social organisation.

35 Chomsky, op. cit., p. 17.

36 The importance and significance of Chomsky's work and the entire subject that he opened up cannot be stressed enough particularly as his courageous stand on political issues has led the contemptible neo-conservatives of our time to attempt to dismiss it (see Christopher Hitchen's excellent article 'The Chorus and Cassandra: What everyone knows about Noam Chomsky', *Grand Street*, vol. 5 no. 1, Autumn 1985, pp. 106–31). I think that Chomsky's determination to cling to the word 'language', even in the

etiolated and technical term 'I-language', can be explained in part in terms of the micro-politics of the academic institution. To occupy a definite place within the academy is not simply a philosophical question; it involves access to funds, research grants and the whole infrastructure which makes research possible. This is not simply a petty point. Only those who think that institutions are irrelevant or inevitable can ignore the importance of how they reproduce and transform themselves at the micro-level. Particularly someone like Chomsky, who has had the extraordinary experience of discovering (or, as he argues, re-discovering) an important scientific object and a method to investigate it, will be particularly determined to ensure that his scientific research programme can proceed and not be abandoned or neglected. There is nothing objectionable about Chomsky determinedly defending the reality and importance of what I have termed a 'linguistics of invariance' but it is also important to find institutional space for a linguistics of conflict.

37 Chomsky admits himself that he finds little intellectual interest in what he terms 'Orwell's question', op. cit., p. xxix. This is not merely a personal problem. The deep interests of those interested in a language's fundamental structure and those interested in its imaginary functioning are very different and seem rarely to be united in the same person. This seems, in itself, an important problem. The only attempt to theorise this that I am aware of is Jean-Claude Milner's *L'Amour de la langue* (Paris: Éditions du Seuil, 1978). Ann Banfield in her translation of the book *For the Love of Language* (Basingstoke: Macmillan, 1990), has a long introduction which attempts to develop Milner's consideration in the setting of American linguistics.

38 Attempts within both the positivist tradition (i.e. Hempel) and the Marxist one (i.e. Althusser) have all, despite their immense sophistication, ended in failure. To go from this failure to a position of epistemological anarchy (i.e. Feyerabend) is understandable theoretically. It should not, however, lead one to think that there are no useful practical criteria for distinguishing between forms of scientific inquiry.

39 In my opinion it is only on this final point, the possibility of developments in the language actually changing the structure of the invariants, that I am in disagreement with Chomsky.

40 M. A. K. Halliday, 'Language and the order of nature' in Fabb et al., *The Linguistics of Writing*, pp. 135–55.

41 Walter Benjamin, *Illuminations* (Glasgow: 1973), p. 258.

42 See, for example, Alan Durant and Nigel Fabb, *Literary Studies in Action* (London: Routledge, 1990).

43 I would not completely rule out such an argument. Linguists have quite rightly fought shy of comparison between languages, because the historical prestige first granted to classical languages and then European ones was then used to denigrate non-standard or 'primitive' languages. It may be, however, that there are real ways to compare languages. What is certain is that people, particularly writers, constantly do.

44 Hudson, *Sociolinguists*, p. 34 (see also note 33).

3 Righting English, or Does Spelling Matter?

One of the great pleasures of moving to Strathclyde from Cambridge was to move from a campus to a city university. True, Cambridge is located in a city but the university in my day had no contact of any kind with either the local schools or local industry. Strathclyde was a totally different kind of institution. Founded in 1796 specifically to engage with the new forms of industry then emerging along the Clyde, Strathclyde University was very much a part of Glasgow, both educationally and economically. Discussions with local teachers and local businesses were an automatic part of my duties. One such business was Collins the publishers which was still then a Glaswegian enterprise. Part of Collins's core business was dictionaries and when I arrived in Glasgow they were in the middle of an ambitious experiment: to use the power of computers to produce a new generation of dictionaries that would be based on a much more systematic analysis of the language than any previous lexicography. Collins were thus happy to consider funding an annual public lecture which would address questions of language and I was keen to have an audience in the city of Glasgow for the academic work that we were undertaking in the Programme of Literary Linguistics. The lecture explores some of the same themes and arguments as 'the Linguistics of Writing' but for a general rather than a specialist audience.

It is a great honour to have been asked to give the first of these annual Collins English Dictionary Lectures and I am very grateful to Collins for their kind invitation. The establishment of this lecture creates a valuable space in which to confront pressing questions about language. Over the past decade Collins have been consistently innovative in their approach to the production of dictionaries. Most makers of dictionaries have been usually content to reproduce the dictionary that immediately preceded them with only the minimum of variation required to make a claim for novelty (so insistent is this practice that a cynical reader of the history of dictionaries might conclude that the entry for 'lexicographer' in any dictionary should read 'see *plagiarist*'). The production of Collins Dictionary of the English Language in 1979 with its encyclopedic coverage – new to a British audience – signalled very publicly that Collins were determined to experiment and innovate in this most conservative of practices. The most decisive innovation is their Cobuild project at Birmingham University directed by Professor John Sinclair which will, before the decade is out, give us a dictionary composed on entirely new principles, principles I will return to later in this lecture. What is striking about Collins's activity in this field is their commitment to the importance of both theory and practice. Collins's recent output testifies to their belief in the importance of current linguistic theory and their equally firm determination to relate that theory to the practical needs of the language user. It is this dialectic of theory and practice which this lecture will hope to reflect. The annual Collins English Dictionary lecture will find its validity and importance if it can illuminate practical problems and debates about language by considering the theoretical assumptions that underpin them. The task is daunting, the rewards considerable.

Let us start by posing the most general of theoretical questions: What is language? This question has obsessed our culture from the myth of Babel to the present day. There seems to be a persistent belief, which surfaces in very different forms, that in some original state language loses its arbitrary qualities – that in some linguistic Garden of Eden, name and bearer are soldered together by links more durable than the social agreement which determines that, as we cross linguistic boundaries, the same things become different words, or, even more frightening, become different things. We have all probably registered the shock on discovering that the French use one verb *aimer* where we differentiate 'to like' and 'to love' but it is perhaps even more shocking to find the French use two verbs *connaître* and *savoir* while our word 'to know' covers the knowledge of persons as well as concepts. Could it be, and this thought, both frightening and fascinating, is made explicit in the Sapir–Whorf hypothesis, that the world we experience, that apparently given objectivity, is dependent on our language – these weird gurglings that issue from our mouths? The power of language is at once both so immense and so fragile that it is no wonder that it is the locus of endless fantasies in which language and reality would come together – from the cabbalistic search for words that would immediately act on the world (a search we still jokingly acknowledge whenever we use the formula *abracadabra*) to the CIA's funding of linguistic research in the 50s and 60s in the hope of discovering strategies for producing value free languages in which Communist propaganda would suddenly lose its purchase and vanish into the thin linguistic air. Nor is this fantasy to be limited to the world of the Renaissance magus or the Pentagon bureaucrat. Two of the most influential movements in the contemporary study of language – the logical project in which Frege and Russell hoped to ground the truths of mathematics in the operations of a logic purged of the ambiguity of natural languages and Chomsky's belief that the basic operations of language are to be located in innate psychological processes – find much of their emotional power in a dissatisfaction with the arbitrary nature of language.

When I acquire language I acquire the power to summon up entities which are absent – removed into different realms of time, space and imagination. The Athenians, Mrs Thatcher, the unicorn are summoned as I utter them, produced by a mere puff of air. But I also acquire the power to affect those in my presence, to ask, to command, to exhort, to admonish. Any child who has had recourse to the rhyme 'sticks and stones will break my bones but words can never hurt me' knows in the very act of uttering that he or she lies, that words can hurt and maim – in extreme cases they can kill. Even such brief reflections as these make little cause for wonder that in previous times we attributed magical properties to language and that even in this secular age language can provoke deep passions.

But so varied and so heterogeneous are the features of language that it might seem impossible to undertake any systematic study of it. Such at least was the pessimistic thought that haunted the founder of modern linguistics, Ferdinand de Saussure. Although at the early age of twenty-one he had already contributed a brilliant monograph on the history of early Indo-European languages, Saussure was obsessed by the inability of philology, despite its ever increasing understanding of the history of western language, to define its basic object of inquiry. Even a unit as apparently simple as a word with a different pronunciation – you say 'tomahto' and I say 'tomayto' – can scarcely be considered the same word, particularly when a similar change of vowel (m*a*rt and m*a*te) produces a change in meaning in other contexts. Saussure was obsessed by the problem that linguistics' basic units seemed to have no fundamental identity. Like many great geniuses he turned his problem into his solution. Linguistics, he decided, could not study positive identities, it could only study differences. What defined the word 'tomato' was not some absolute sound properties but what distinguished it from 'Tommy's toe' along one axis or potato along another. It was this pattern of differences which constituted the linguist's object of study. The particular properties of specific utterances were defined as '*parole*' – a heterogeneous subject area. When Chomsky came to formulate his understanding of the object of linguistics he followed Saussure in distinguishing between an abstract system, competence, defined as the speaker-hearer's knowledge of the language, and specific uses of the language, covered by the term 'performance'. Although Chomsky defined this competence in psychological terms, his formulations resemble Saussure in opposing, on the one hand, the abstract system of the language and, on the other, its individual realisation.

What gets left out of this account altogether is what one might term the 'sociality' of language. The whole social apparatus for the transmission of language disappears in this account – system and individual speaker exist outside any mechanism of social reproduction. The refusal to consider such features has its reasons in terms of Saussure's wish to separate synchronic from diachronic analysis and in terms of Chomsky's determination to locate the basic structure of language in psychological structures unaffected by social experience. My interest today is not to take issue directly with those decisions but to suggest that both are dependent on understanding speech as the primary material of language and relegating writing to a secondary derivative. Such an understanding means that many of the most important questions about language cannot even be posed within the terms of modern linguistics.

Both Saussure and Chomsky understand the material of language in terms of sequences of sound produced by the vocal apparatus and, secondarily, as writing systems which merely purport to transcribe these sounds. Both definitions ignore as irrelevant the questions about the situation of utterance in the case of the spoken and form of publication in the case of the written. Yet we all know that the relations of power and authority which forms of speech assume are of immense importance. We have Old Testament authority in the story of how Jephthah separated the Ephraimites from the men of Gilead by their inability to pronounce the 'sh' in 'shibboleth' (Judges 12:6) for the social and deadly significance of speech but we hardly need recourse to any authority to prove what we all experience every day – a differential and contradictory sorting of approved forms of speech. And this is as true of the written language as it is of the spoken – only someone insensitive to the imbrication of power and language would confuse, as equivalent, sentences written in popular textbooks and those chalked fleetingly on convenient walls. If we are concerned with how a language reproduces itself then these questions become pressing. For while the interrelation between precept and usage is extremely complicated, it is ludicrous to pretend that the language finds its proper form independently of its forms of transmission. An interesting example is provided by the case of American and British English. In the nineteenth century there were many who foresaw that the languages on opposite sides of the Atlantic would become mutually incomprehensible in much the same way as the Romance languages had developed from their common Latin base in the Dark Ages.

Such a view abstracts from history and ignores the material reality of a language's transmission. In fact American and British English have not grown further apart. The shared technologies of communication from print to the more recent forms of speech reproduction in film, television and gramophone records have made for greater interchange and intercommunicability between the two dialects. But this should not suggest for a moment that these two dialects are merging into a homogeneous speech community. If there is probably a greater uniformity at the level of vocabulary (and certainly a swifter interchange of new coinages), the relationships of power and desire, of identification and counter-identification which run across the basis of shared linguistic material are enormously complicated. Indeed, the last clearly willed shift in usage moved English forms away from American as the punk musicians and ideologues of the New Wave rejected the American intonation which had dominated rock singing since the late 50s and called instead for authentic British lyrics in authentic British tones.

Similarly if we consider the history of radio and television in this country, there were many who foresaw the disappearance of dialect forms as Received Pronunciation ruled the air waves. The results have been very different with the dialect forms fracturing the assured forms of RP so that the BBC standard of thirty years ago sounds, on the one hand, as irredeemably quaint, and, on the other, as socially offensive (which indeed it often was). It is when we consider language in this perspective that we realise that the one-to-one communicational model so beloved of linguistic diagrams is merely one among a whole array of linguistic interactions. Questions of technology, of power, of desire are not additional to a basic communicational situation, they are constitutive of the whole diversity of different communicational forms. We use language for many different purposes and pleasures, it is a considerable mistake to ignore this diversity.

Modern linguistics' insistence on the primacy of speech can be understood historically in terms of a refusal to accept a definition of language purely in terms of a written standard mastered only by a few and which was neither a record of nor a possible form for speech. However, once that unquestioned primacy of writing has been challenged, it should then have been possible, and is now necessary, to refocus on languages as a heterogeneous system of practices. Indeed, if we wish to focus on the reproduction of a national standard, as I wish to do today, then writing may once again occupy a central place but a place which is historicised – the product of a particular series of convergences in human history.

It is a pious wisdom, but none the less true for all that, to trace our culture back to the twin heritage of Hellenism and Judaism. Many have reflected on those astonishing moments when two tiny peoples living on the Mediterranean littoral invented, on the one hand, the astonishing concept of monotheism and, on the other, the categories of rational argument. This heritage has been treated in many different ways but one which is insufficiently emphasised is that both these cultures are inaugurated by writing systems which allowed for the transcription of speech through an alphabet.

The dialectic between speech and writing may well be one of the most important ways of analysing cultural history. We might indeed understand the paradigmatic importance of Socrates and Christ in terms of the transition from the oral to the literate. It may be that these two figures, so uncannily similar in the manner of both their life and their death, are most closely united by the fact that they left to others to transcribe their speech. They stand as figures who epitomise the moment when the word was made text.

Before considering this dialectic between speech and writing in the particular case of English I should stress that what I have to say, indeed much of what I have said, is heavily dependent on the collective effort of planning and teaching of English language and literature. The intellectual excitement of planning the course both at Strathclyde and in other countries and the enthusiastic response from students, who have quickly learned how to teach their teachers, have enormously clarified my understanding of the problems involved in analysing the sociality of language. I would especially like in this context to pay tribute to my colleague Dr Alan Durant whose recent work on the relations between the heterogeneous forms of speech and writing has enormously influenced this lecture.

I have so far talked of writing as though it were a single and unchanging technology but this, of course, is not in fact the case. If we consider technologies in relation to the condition of their social as well as technical reproduction, and my argument is that the two cannot be considered separately, then questions of the differential access to writing produced by changes in the educational system profoundly alter our conception of writing in contrasting historical epochs. But even at the narrowly technical level changes such as that from stylus and wax tablet to pen and paper have considerable effects. It is, however, the invention of printing which registers the single greatest change in the technology of writing. Suddenly it becomes technically feasible to reproduce quickly and mechanically potentially infinite copies of particular text. The history of the language that we know as English is, fundamentally, a history of the printed language.

When William Caxton set up a printing press in Westminster in 1476 he became the first major publisher of a language which is probably best described as an Anglo-Latin creole. The language which is commonly referred to as Anglo-Saxon, and which scholars call Old English, was an inflected Germanic language. When, in 1066, a Norman French ruling class imposed itself on the country by conquest, this language ceased to be the language of law and administration and, indeed, for two centuries virtually ceased to be a written language altogether. When in the mid-fourteenth century it once again became the official language of the courts it was a tongue which relied fundamentally upon word order to indicate grammatical relationships and which had a huge Latinate vocabulary largely derived from Norman French. We can reflect on how intimately this history is still inscribed in our language by focusing, as an example, on the curious fact that we have different words to refer to the beasts in the field and the meat as which they arrive on our table. Beef and cow, mutton and sheep, pork and pig, these couples do not indicate some innate squeamishness in the English but bear testament to the fact that, for at least two centuries, meat was primarily destined for the tables of the Anglo-Normanic aristocracy who referred to it with French words while the animals in the fields were tended by Saxon serfs who referred to them in their own tongue.

It is probably difficult for us to think ourselves back to that moment at the end of the Middle Ages when the vernacular tongues first started to be widely used as written languages. For a millennium education and writing had been controlled by the Church and its language was Latin – there could be no other language for intellectual inquiry. The incredulity with which many regarded the claim that one could write in the vulgar tongue may perhaps be recaptured by using an example of Peter Trudgill's when he translates a passage from an anthropology textbook into a non-standard West of England dialect:

> Social anthropology be a title used in England to designate a department of the larger subject of anthropology. On the continent a different terminology prevails. There when people speaks of anthropology, what to us is the entire study of man, they has in mind only what us calls physical anthropology, the biological study of man.[1]

Our initial reaction is perhaps one of laughter or annoyance. You simply don't write about an academic subject in non-standard English. But this is much closer to the normal language of academic debate than any vernacular tongue was to Latin. Interestingly, however, English at the end of the fifteenth century, and for a long time thereafter, suffered from a particular inferiority complex. A famous and much-quoted passage from Caxton is often used to indicate this:

> For we englysshe men ben borne vnder the domynacyon of the mone, whiche is neuer stedfaste but euer wauerynge wexynge one season and waneth & dycreaseth another season. And that comyn englysshe that is spoken in one shyre varyeth from a nother. In so moche that in my dayes happened that certayn marchauntes were in a shippe in tamsye for to have sayled over the see into zelande and for lacke of wynde thei taryed atte forlond, and wente to lande for to refreshe them. And one of theym named sheffelde a mercer cam in to an hows and axed for mete, and specyally he axyd after eggys and the good wyf answerde, that she coulde speke no frenshe. And the marchaunt was angry, for he also coule speke no frenshe but wold haue hadde egges and she vnderstode hym not. And thenne at laste a nother sayd that he wolde haue eyren then the good wyf sayd that she vnderstode hym wel. Loo what sholde a man in thyse dayes now wryte, egges or eyren certaynly it is harde to playse euery man by cause of dynersite & chaunge of language.[2]

The confusion that Caxton refers to is occasioned in part by the fact that the woman is using the disappearing English plural 'en', retained in the modern language only in exceptions like 'children' and 'oxen', while the merchant is using the already dominant 's' plural familiar to us. Although this must be one of the most cited passage in histories of the English language, I know of no commentators who have dwelt on the articulation of economic and linguistic history in Caxton's little story. Caxton was a member of that London merchant class which was to rise to such dominance in the sixteenth and seventeenth centuries. The establishment of capitalist forms of production in England at this time is crucially dependent on the dissemination of a national language which is the precondition of a national market, and Caxton's little story eloquently demonstrates how crucial language is to the process of buying and selling.

However, the politics of language does not begin and end with the opposition between the necessity of a national language for the functioning of a capitalist state and its irrelevance for a feudal one. Classes do not cease with the transition to capitalism and if it is essential that citizens can speak to each other, they do not speak on an equal footing. Once again, Caxton's preface sets out the terms of this class differentiation in terms of exemplary clarity.

Caxton begins by recalling the immense pleasure that he felt on first reading the French translation of the *Aeneid*. The pleasure leads him into a spontaneous attempt at translation in which he renders a couple of pages into English. On rereading his own translation, however, he is immediately assailed by the fear of linguistic censure. Someone had recently criticised his translations because 'I had ouer curyous termes whiche coulde not be understande of comyn people and [he] desired me to use old and homely termes in my translacyons'.[3] But Caxton is not sure that he wants to write for the common people. When he consults some older English texts he finds that he cannot understand them because, as he says dismissively, 'the englysshe was so rude and brood'. Not only does this language offend Caxton's social sense, it adds national insult to social injury because it reads more like Dutch than English. But if Caxton is determined to write in something which is both recognisably English and is yet not available to the common people, he is determined to avoid the alternative trap of writing in so elevated a style that no-one can understand him. He thus also moves on to reject those critics who want him to coin ever more 'curyous' termes (where 'curyous' carries the implication both of learned and of over-elaborate composition) which will render his text obscure to all. Caxton wishes for a national audience but one composed of educated people who have a ready access to Latin:

> And for as moche as this present booke is not for a rude vplondysshe man to labour therein / ne rede it / but onely for a clerke & a noble gentylman that feleth and vnderstondeth in faytes of armes in loue & in noble chyalrye. Therfor in a meane bytwene bothe I haue reduced & translated this sayd booke in to our englysshe not ouer rude ne curyous but in suche termes as shall be vnderstandenn by goddys grace accordynge to my copye. And yf ony man wyll enter mete in redyng of hit and fyndeth suche termes that he can not vnderstand late hym goo rede and lerne vyrgyll / or the pystles of ouyde / and ther he shall see and vnderstonde lyghtly all / Yf he haue a good redar & enformer. For this booke is not for e[u]ery rude [and] vnconnynge man to see but to clerkys and very gentylmen that vndertstande gentylnes and scyence.[4]

He concludes the justification of his choice of language by saying that he is sending the translation to be overseen by John Skelton:

> But I praye master John Skelton late created poete laureate in the vnyuersite of oxenforde to ouersee and correcte this sayd booke. And taddresse and expowne where as shalle be founde faulte to theym that shall requyre it. For hym I knowe for suffycyent to expowne and englysshe euery dyffyculte that is therin. For he hath late translated the epystlys of Tulle and the boke of dyodorus syculus, and diuerse other werkes oute of latyn in to englysshe not in rude / an olde langage, but in polysshed and ornate termes craftely, as he that hath redde vyrgyle / ouyde, tullye, and all the other noble poetes and oratours / to me vnknowen.[5]

Caxton's preface articulates what becomes the dominating definition of English. The language is identified with a written literary standard, itself guaranteed in terms of an educated audience defined by their access to the classics. I do not have time in this lecture to tease out the linguistic implications of the political and religious conflicts of the next two centuries. Suffice to say that the struggle for power and the struggle for full participation in the language are intimately related. By the time of the Civil War Caxton's doubts about whether 'rude and uplondish men' were a suitable audience for a written text were doubts no longer. When the Earl of Newcastle wrote to the exiled Charles Stuart he dealt in certainties:

> The Bible under every weaver and chambermaid's arm hath done us much hurt ... the universities abound with too many scholars ... But that which hath done most hurt is the abundance of grammar schools and Inns of Court.[6]

With the Restoration of the King, there was an attempt to bring this unsettling spread of literacy, these unauthorised uses of language under control. It took some thirty years to undo finally the educational advances of the Elizabethan and Jacobean eras – to send the English universities back to sleep for over a hundred years and to encourage the great public schools to become barbaric forcing grounds for the country's ruling class. The effects on linguistic practice, however, were much more immediate. From preaching to poetry, every area of linguistic practice was regulated by a conservatism which limited both idiom and audience. It was this political conservatism which informed much of the eighteenth century's desire to control and shape the language.

The eighteenth century is, famously, the great century of linguistic regulation. This covered every aspect of the language from pronunciation (for the first time there is a uniform ruling class pronunciation and both manuals and coaches to instruct you how to acquire it) to literary texts (subjected for the first time to rigorous and thorough editing). It is also the period of prescriptive grammars which try to stretch English syntax to approximate to a Latin standard held more appropriate for a language of Reason. The English authors of the preceding two centuries have become a corpus which consists largely of mistakes. The eighteenth century's confidence that the language's current state is far superior to its unruly past is everywhere evident, every author from Shakespeare down must have his rude and uncouth terms purged and recast, his grammatical errors corrected. It is this confidence in the proper forms of language and appropriate audience for literature which allows Bentley to rewrite Milton and Tate to improve Shakespeare's ending to *King Lear*. There is perhaps no greater monument to this cultural authoritarianism than Johnson's *Dictionary of the English Language*. Johnson's work is one of the great literary and linguistic achievements of all time, but the precision of its definitions, the breadth of its quotations, the sheer pleasure in its knowledge and acuity, should not blind us to the fact that it accomplished that reduction of the language to the written and the written to the literary which Caxton foreshadowed.

Anybody who has ever been troubled by the anarchy of English spelling may be more affected by one of Johnson's more direct debts to Caxton. For Johnson is very conservative in the spellings he adopts. The already extant dictionaries and the sheer volume of printed and published English probably made any spelling reform impossible. But Johnson was undoubtedly the last person who might seriously have affected the spelling of English. Johnson delivers himself of some suitably magnificent periods in setting out his principles:

> In adjusting the orthography, which has been to this time unsettled and fortuitous, I found it necessary to distinguish those irregularities that are inherent in our tongue, and perhaps coeval with it, from others which the ignorance or negligence of later writers has produced. Every language has its anomalies which, though inconvenient and in themselves once unnecessary, must be tolerated among the imperfections of human things, and which require only to be registered that they may not be increased, and ascertained that they may not be confounded, but every language has likewise its improprieties and absurdities, which it is the duty of the lexicographer to correct or proscribe.[7]

The inherent irregularities in the spelling of our tongue are so flagrant that it is a hoary joke that 'fish' in English should be spelt 'ghoti' – 'gh' as in 'laugh', 'o' as in 'women', and 'ti' as in 'potion'. Most of these difficulties stem from the fact that although much of the syntax and lexis of modern English closely resembles that of Caxton, pronunciation has changed dramatically. There are, of course, the evident aberrations like the 'GH' which still had a sound value in most of the dialects of Caxton's time – something like the pronunciation of that stereotyped Scot who announces that it's a 'bricht, moonlicht nicht' – but which quickly disappeared in medial positions and developed into the fricative 'f' in final ones. More crucial, however, is the fact that Caxton established his printing press at the beginning of that period which philologists call the Great Vowel Shift when the whole system of English vowels altered.

However, it is unsurprising that Johnson felt wedded to the agreed spellings that Caxton and his heirs had established by the end of the seventeenth century; Johnson's *Dictionary* testifies in its method and by the very fact of its existence to the identification of the language with the written which printing massively confirms. When in the nineteenth century education becomes compulsory, and with it the study of English, that study is unquestioningly and inevitably the study of the written language. Insofar as speech figures within the curriculum at all it is speech that models itself on writing. To speak well is to be able to recite syntactically complex prose. In his Inspector's reports, which still repay study a hundred years later, Matthew Arnold urges that children should be allowed to recite poetry as well as prose but even poetry offers a limited range of sound possibilities. For generations of schoolchildren the whole mobility of the speaking voice, the different intonation patterns which we play on our breath as a musician plays on the flute, have been limited to the range of those sounds which can represent written language.

Writing is effectively a system for the inscription of meaning which allows a pattern of language to be decoded independently of whoever has made it. It thus must dispose of much that depends on context and utterance. The gestures and intonations with which we annotate out spoken forms are not available when we write. But to stress the importance of speech is not, in a tediously predictable reciprocity, to denigrate the importance of writing. There are many things that speech can do that writing cannot do but just as importantly there are many things which writing can do which are impossible in speech. It is impossible in speech to elaborate thought or narrative over time in the way writing allows. I cannot leave a spoken sentence in the middle and return to it again ten minutes or twenty-four hours later.

What I am trying to stress in this lecture is the variety and importance of both. When I hear the uniform tones and written syntax of speakers like Enoch Powell or Edward Heath, their voices seem an uncomfortable echo of an educational system which told millions of schoolchildren that the only form of the language available to them was a written one. I am sure that there are many who would object at this point that Powell and Heath are formidably articulate and that it is a great pity that all children are not educated to become equally able. My disagreement is not, however, with the articulacy which is admirable but with the fact that it seems to be of only one kind. Of course, control of formal speech patterns is vital in contexts such as the committee meeting or the interview but they are not the only such patterns. When I gave an interview on the radio this morning about the lecture that I'm now reading it would have been totally inappropriate to use the forms of the spoken language with which I described it to a friend in a pub.

But in mentioning the radio we are talking about a completely new form of language and one whose impact has not yet been grasped conceptually or educationally. Film, radio and television have made recorded speech a vital part of our lives but these technological advances have not been considered in their linguistic dimension. To understand the interplay between technology and language in the case of recorded speech may prove almost as difficult as to grasp the full implications of the history of writing. In immediate terms it is certainly more difficult because there is almost no record of scholarship on which one can depend and few obviously appropriate conceptual tools. What seems clear to me, however, is that it has finally displaced that equation between writing and language which has been so central to our culture both in its triumphant achievements and its despicable exclusions. We enter a new epoch in human history when many of the features of speech which cannot be captured in writing can be electronically reproduced. Writing is still crucial, but any serious contemporary discussion of language must also consider this phenomenon of 'secondary orality'. In the domain of secondary orality forms of speech heavily imitative of writing are no longer dominant. It is certainly true that in news and current affairs programmes the spoken forms are still heavily influenced by the written. But if you write out a Monty Python sketch there is often little that transfers to the page. If one takes, for example, the legendary Jean-Paul Sartre sketch in which John Cleese, dressed as a charlady, interrogates the elderly French philosopher over the phone, all the humour resides in the incongruous juxtaposition of register, accent and indeed channel of communication (Plato's dialogues are not telephone conversations) with John Cleese's insistent question: '*Etes-vous libre, M. Sartre?*'

If we pose the question 'Does spelling matter?' then the answer is obviously, immediately and emphatically 'Yes'. But both question and answer are normally understood in the context of a widespread decline in 'standards'. But educational standards, rather like the young, always seem better in retrospect. Both have the quality which they share with the English village, financial probity and sexual restraint, of seeming, since the beginning of time, to have vanished in the last generation. What I have tried to do in this lecture is to make the question and answer seem a little less self-sufficient, to situate them in a historical and linguistic context which makes clear that although spelling matters, writing cannot be considered in isolation from other questions about language.

In the last generation English teachers have made an astonishing advance in freeing themselves from the dominance of that attitude to the language which had the unspeakable arrogance to tell most pupils that they couldn't speak their own language. Very often, however, this liberation has been accomplished by appeals to extremely dubious linguistic and educational assumptions. The refusal of Latinate grammars as the correct model of the language has often been confused with the more dubious notion that you can teach the written language without any vocabulary with which to analyse it. The refusal to impose a form of the spoken language on pupils has been confused with the very dangerous assumption that the pupil's spoken and written forms may be adequate for any linguistic occasion.

Most serious, however – because still very widespread – is the refusal of the use of writing exercises which depend on imitation. Such exercises still seem identified with their use in the early part of the century when the model was to be copied with absolute fidelity and the examples were all in the same register and idiom. It is, of course, ludicrous to impose on children one narrow model of the written form. However, it is equally ludicrous to assume that the pupils will automatically find within themselves the appropriate forms for their experience. It is only by working across a variety of written forms from the sonnet and the essay to the newspaper report or pop song that the pupil will gain the facility with language which is essential to its creative use.

The emphasis in recent syllabus reform on the importance of speaking and listening skills is welcome. But it will be practically useless if teachers were to suppose that forms of speech will develop without the stimulus of models and imitation. There is a deep-rooted and quite justified loathing for those forms of affected speech which are part of the poisonous heritage of our class system and its interventions in the development of our language. However, the ability to move across different registers and idioms is an important skill which can only be learned by imitation whether within or outwith the classroom. Any teacher who looks, however, for textbooks or even research in this area will not find it.

It is usual in lectures of this kind to castigate schoolteachers but the real villains of this piece are university departments of linguistics and, particularly, of English. Teachers looking for aid or advice in the areas I have been discussing will look largely in vain. Much of the recent linguistics research in pragmatics, discourse analysis and sociolinguistics is potentially valuable but it suffers from an overemphasis on speech and speech defined without any serious reference to secondary orality. As for English departments, the identification of the language with a very narrow conception of the written is still dominant. The results both inhibit the analysis of literature and prevent these departments instructing their students in the language.

I want to conclude this first annual Collins English Dictionary Lecture at the University of Strathclyde in an orgy of self-congratulation. For there are at least two areas of important research to which teachers will be able to turn. The first, and more massive, is funded by Collins and the second is located in Strathclyde University. Lexicographers to date have always been caught in the vicious circle that their definitions of the senses of a word always depended on the analysis of a series of examples, examples largely chosen because they were held to demonstrate a sense of the word. The Cobuild project avoids this by the use of computers. The choice comes in the initial selection of the corpus, held to cover the varieties of written and spoken English, but the computer then extracts all the relevant occurrences of a word. This means that when the dictionary is finally published it will properly reflect the diversity of both spoken and written forms, and the relation between them, in a way that no previous dictionary has done. Second, I would like to refer again to the research being generated here in relation to the new Master's degrees which focuses on the diversity of spoken and written forms. The course is unique in paying equal attention to the historical formation and the contemporary importance of our conceptions of language.

Before I finish I would like to deal with a predictable objection to much that I have suggested. It is easy to find in the universities those who, belching with self-importance and simulated outrage, will rise to their feet and oppose the teaching of 'what we all know anyway'. Why should we study the uses of speech in film and television, why concentrate on the ephemeral and the unworthy? Such opposition has been there from the inception of English as a university subject. When, in 1895, Cambridge instituted its first post in English language and literature a sturdy Dr Mayo was recorded in the *Reporter* as objecting

> that the General Board would scarcely be surprised to find that opposition was aroused if it was proposed to make a beginning of the teaching of English in the University. To begin with such teaching would be going back and repudiating the principles of the Renaissance of learning. He and his contemporaries had been brought up to think that learning English should be kept within the first ten years of one's life and that literary attainments should be acquired through erudition in the Greek and Latin languages.

I expect the tones of Dr Mayo will be heard again though the content of the argument may be slightly different. My reply is simple. Both President Regan and Margaret Thatcher pay more attention to the form of their television appearances than they do to their content. It behoves us in the university to bestow at least some of our attention on the play of intonation and gesture which now figure so centrally in our political processes.

Notes

1 Peter Trudgill, *Accent, Dialect and the School* (London: Edward Arnold, 1975), p. 2.
2 W. J. B. Crotch (ed), *The Prologues and Epilogues of William Caxton* (London: OUP, 1928), p. 108.
3 Ibid.
4 Crotch, *The Prologues and Epilogues of William Caxton*, p. 109.
5 Ibid.
6 Quoted in John Laxon and Harold Silver, *A Social History of Education in England* (London: Methuen, 1978), p. 179.
7 Samuel Johnson, *Selected Prose and Poetry*, eds J. Brady and E. Wimsatt (Berkeley and Los Angeles: University of California Press, 1968), p. 217.

4 Defining Popular Culture

The following essay was the opening lecture at a conference on popular culture organised by the John Logie Baird Centre for the Study of Television and Film. The proceedings of the conference were published in a book that I edited entitled *High Theory/Low Culture*. The Centre had been set up as part of the introduction of degree courses in film and television at both Glasgow and Strathclyde Universities.

This book grows out of a widely felt dissatisfaction. The use of psychoanalytic and semiotic concepts in the analysis of film, which proved so fruitful when applied both to classic Hollywood cinema and much European and American avant-garde film, has proved much less successful in its attempt to give an account of either the new Hollywood cinema or, more importantly, television. The forms of analysis which proved so powerful were drawn from Brechtian aesthetic, and particularly those elements of Brecht which stressed art as a practice which could produce knowledge. What was specific to art was the way in which ideological and political knowledge was dependent on the articulations of symbolic acknowledgement of castration. Psychoanalysis was thus added to Brecht to produce an aesthetic of difference.

From within this aesthetic it is possible to account for the failure to deal with so much contemporary art in terms of the failure of that contemporary art. An argument can be produced that such texts as *ET* or *The Sweeney* are so concerned to disavow the reality of sexual difference that it is impossible to do more than dismiss them as stupefying forms designed to retain their audiences in ignorance and inaction.

The problem with such an argument is that it simply reduplicates certain traditional forms of cultural pessimism and denies any effective form of engagement with contemporary culture. From an educational point of view it has the disastrous effect of suggesting that one teach contemporary culture only to denounce it. Educationally, there must be some way of producing procedures for analysing popular forms of television which will interest and inform children, and if these procedures may, at some stage, re-engage with the aesthetic of difference that I sketched above, they cannot possibly start there. This theoretical problem can also be seen from a practical pedagogic angle. Why is it possible to articulate convincingly dilemmas of castration in *Young Mr Lincoln* and *Touch of Evil*, and why does such an attempt become ludicrously or boringly repetitive when applied to other examples? Could the problem be one of register: that within the still confines of the seminar room or weekend school any text can be made to deliver up its sexual meanings, but that in the noisier ambience of the classroom or the first year lecture theatre, the lecturer suddenly appears perverse as he or she gamely struggles to explicate the dilemmas of castration; the dialectic of having and being suddenly reduced to the pathetic ramblings of a sex-obsessed adult?

For the moment I wish to leave both problems of educational theory and pedagogic practice in order to consider popular culture from a political perspective. The insights thus gained and the contradictions revealed may then provide some of the terms with which we can return to the educational problems. 'Popular culture' as a term has a very definite history, but if one part of that history is clear, the other is marked by division and uncertainty. The meaning of 'culture' appealed to in the term is in polemical disagreement with those traditional meanings which attempt to limit culture to a specific corpus of elite practices and a definite canon of works. Instead, to use Williams's famous phrase, culture is understood as 'a whole way of life', embracing a wide variety of practices. Suddenly culture can include much more than the approved genres of opera, painting or literature. But while we can be clear about the polemical meaning of culture, 'popular' remains determinedly evasive. Anybody who has, for example, looked at the very successful Open University course on popular culture might be surprised to find that there is no definition of popular culture as such. The course takes its notions of popular culture from a series of overlapping cultural debates on the Left, and makes no effort to arrive at a precise definition. The reasons for this are outlined in a lucid article by the course chairman, Tony Bennett, in *Screen Education* no. 34 which argues that it is impossible to classify popular culture. The article summarises, in order to reject, four major definitions. The first is straightforwardly descriptive – it defines 'popular' in terms of television ratings, record sales and other quantifiable indicators. Such a descriptive approach suffers not only because it has no positive content but also because it will frequently include forms of 'high culture'. A second strategy simply defines popular culture in terms of what is left over when one subtracts traditional cultural forms from our current types of entertainment. Bennett finds this approach equally unsatisfactory as, once again, there is no positive definition to link the heterogeneous material derived from this procedure. Third, Bennett considers that culturally pessimistic, generally conservative position which defines popular culture in terms of the new mass forms of entertainment generated by capitalist investment. These new forms are opposed to an older popular 'folk' art in which there is no fundamental division between audience and performer and where meanings are democratically produced. By contrast, the 'mass' art of capitalist society addresses a passive audience which simply registers meanings produced elsewhere. The fourth and final position is a culturally optimistic positive definition which perceives this new 'mass' art as enjoying a more active relationship with its audience and aligns this art with the creative impulses of 'the people'. Such impulses are understood as originating within working-class culture and as opposing dominant bourgeois culture. This is a popular culture brimming over with political potential. For Bennett, both pessimistic and optimistic definitions take far too simple notions of 'imposing from above' and 'emerging from below'. Bennett's solution is to adopt a strategy first sketched by Gramsci and elaborated by Stuart Hall and to cease to talk about any definable object at all. Instead, the social is theorised as overlapping terrains of struggle, and then popular culture is simply a way of specifying areas of resistance to dominant ideological forms. No matter how complex the formulations, this approach conceives of the cultural as a unified totality which can always finally, through however many million mediations, be understood in relation to notions of class and class struggle. Strengths this position undoubtedly has, but it reproduces the weakness of the fourth position which, in some sense, it strives to repair. The meanings of texts, whether located as inhering in the texts themselves or in their interpretations, are always finally anchored in a class struggle which is not to be understood in cultural terms. Popular culture simply becomes a way of conducting economic struggle by other means.

The Left's interest in popular culture has always had this element in it: that battles lost economically and politically can be turned into cultural victories. What I now want to consider is how one might pursue a radical interest in popular culture without limiting in advance the politics that will ensue from that interest. A first step will take us to the dictionary. Of course, words do not determine meanings; the flicker of signification can be achieved across the most unpromising material, the fugitive intention can always twist a word into new patterns of meaning. At the same time it is always salutary to recall etymology, not as proof but as a reminder of the semantic fields in which one is operating.

Popular is derived from *populus* – the Latin for 'the people' and 'the people' designated in relation to law. The ruling authority was the Senate and people of Rome and it was from this union that law emanated. Its first recorded meaning in English is also related to law: a popular law was a law that affected all the people. Already we can discern that flicker of meaning which makes popular both so elusive and so central: popular, emanating from the people; popular, applied to the people. The second meaning recorded in the *Oxford English Dictionary* reveals a further element in its centrality as a term for Left politics: 'pertaining to, or consisting of the common people as a whole as distinguished from any particular class; constituted or carried on by the people'. Here we find 'the people' transcending class in a way that avoids objectionable ruling class formulations of the nation or the folk. Here we have the plebeian as Everyman. The appeal of this meaning is inscribed in the history of the European Left since the French Popular Front government of 1936 and is witnessed in the numerous popular fairs held under the auspices of Left parties across Europe each summer. It is Gramsci's concepts of the national-popular and the hegemonic which attempt, within the Marxist tradition, to figure the possibilities of this notion of 'the popular'. Gramsci has the immense merit of refusing the class-against-class positions which debilitated the European Left between 1928 and 1935 and still bequeaths a residual cultural prescriptivism which dooms sections of the Left to a ghetto of 'correct' cultural productions. Indeed, even in the 70s, Gramsci could serve as a useful antidote to those sectarian positions which effectively limited political potential to the archive or the avant-garde. If we are to deprive ourselves of the sounds of the radio and the music centre, of the images of the videocassette recorder or the television, then we risk making difficult struggles unwinnable, of leaving ourselves in an echo chamber of intellectual repetition. But if the appeal to Gramsci has this immense merit, it also has the familiar drawbacks of any Hegelian or Marxist analysis of culture. The Hegelian moment assumes that we can describe our culture as a totality and the Marxist moment then derives this description from a class analysis. The differentiation of cultural artefacts becomes a simple gauging of their political effects. The Gramscian argument describes a cultural terrain in which the dominated's resistance of the dominant is always in terms of meanings already politically defined.

What we must consider is a more radical relationship between popular culture and politics in which it is the culture which may often provide the terms to re-evaluate the politics. At this point the academic category of 'popular culture' would suddenly turn vicious, redefining the political commitments which had first sought to employ it. We can move the argument forward by considering the two key meanings that can be garnered from the *Oxford English Dictionary*. The fourth heading records the meaning 'intended or suited to ordinary people', with a further gloss that this may mean adapted to the tastes or the means of the ordinary people. This notion of adaptation to the taste of the ordinary people has a long history, with the entries running back to Gabriel Harvey's pleas in 1573 'in philosophical disputation to give popular and plausible themes' down to the Longman's catalogue list of 1872 which introduced a series devoted to popular science. The sixth meaning, by contrast, has 'finding favour with or approved by the people, liked, beloved or admired by the people – favourite, acceptable, pleasing'. It occasions little surprise that when we turn to the 1980 supplement it is these two meanings that have produced a host of new examples – on the one hand an emphasis on something produced for the ordinary people, on the other, something approved by the people. It is in the switch between the two emphases that we can locate the problematic of popular culture.

If we stress that popular film and television is produced for the people, then we stress the fact of forms of entertainment which are not generated by the audience either as producers in traditional forms of singing and dancing nor yet in the more active affirmation required by the music hall or the theatre. The audience is figured in forms over which it has no control; in the case of television in a form which invades the home. Immediately a series of criticisms begin to voice themselves around notions of passivity, domination and lack of control. Two options now present themselves. A conservative defence of high culture, a paean of praise for the intellectual effort and social practices required for the appreciation of poetry, painting and classical music. Or a progressive defence of the avant-garde, site of a contestation of the social practices embedded in the high cultural tradition, and a commitment to the intellectual effort of that same tradition. The problem with this progressive alternative is that it inevitably entails attitudes and assumptions which are unacceptable to any kind of committed democratic politics. The millions who daily watch television are discounted in their torpor and their sloth, their tastes held to be of no account, artificial creations of an even more total penetration of capitalist relations of production (the Frankfurt School provides the most elaborate statement of such a position). In fact the only politics which is consistent with such an avant-gardist position would be a traditional Leninist one. A certain form of political organisation, the Party, would guarantee the production of an alternative and more authentically popular view of the society, a fulcrum from which one could move the world, Archimedes as revolutionary. Such ideas now seem to me at best outmoded, depending on a reduction of all practices of the political, and at worst lethal, insisting on such a reduction. What should be stressed, I think, is that many of the avant-garde positions of the late 60s and 70s depend, consciously or not, explicitly or not, on such a conception of politics.

What of the alternative? We are confronted with a whole series of cultural productions which find favour, are approved in numbers which simply beggar historical comparison. Are we thus to go all the way with the democratic argument and claim that in these cultural objects, produced and reproduced throughout the western world, we find the most authentic register of popular desires? The political conclusion of this argument might be that Left political parties should immediately consider a politics that would harness this great machinery of desire and, imitating the Roman emperors, give them circuses as well as bread. If we are to take this option, however, we simply subordinate politics to existing cultural forms as the Leninist position subordinates the existing culture to a future politics.

What I hope to have sketched here are the impasses of the two major Left positions on popular culture in a way that indicates how even a version as sophisticated as Bennett's does not escape the problem of simply anchoring choices in a politics which would appear unaffected by the cultural forms themselves. All that I have argued to date merely sets out clearly the problems confronting the analyst of popular culture. I wish to end the chapter with some positive comments but they are, of necessity, much more tentative and provisional than what has gone before.

What seems positive to me in the commitment to popular culture is that element which is determined to break with any and all of the formulations which depend on a high/low, elite/mass distinction. Those who isolate themselves within the narrow and exclusive traditions of high art, those who glory in the simple popularity of the popular, both effectively ignore the complex way in which traditions and technologies combine to produce audiences. It is in this figuring of different audiences that the political reality of art can be found – the particular way in which an audience is addressed and constituted in relation to the political forms in which it participates. Crucial in this context is the category of the nation, for both the traditional forms of high art and the most closely politically controlled mass forms address an audience, which they thereby constitute, as national. Just as a national literature in the vernacular tongue was an essential component in the constitution of the various ruling classes of the nation states of post-Renaissance Europe, so a national broadcasting system is a crucial element in the current political settlement of the capitalist west. Many of the cultural forms with the greatest political potential, be they works within a high cultural tradition like Joyce's *Ulysses* or Rushdie's *Midnight's Children*, or works within popular forms, like the music of Motown or the Beatles, break this national grid – asserting regional and racial specificities to transnational audiences. What this might suggest is that we should be looking for political groupings along the faultlines opened up by these cultural products.

A traditional Marxist, in the wearied tones of the politically hard-bitten, might well retort that this is all very suggestive but that unless cultural forms are related to the institutions that exercise political power – they are still institutions of nation states – then they will simply obscure political realities. But here, as so often, one may doubt the 'evidence' of the political efficacy of the nation state. If one looks at the most powerful movements in the west over the past twenty-five years – the women's movement, the anti-nuclear movement, the ecological movement, even the movement for black rights in 'western' countries from the United States to South Africa – it is doubtful whether these movements find their deepest reality at the national level. It is also the case that it would be difficult to give an account of the history of women's or black struggles in the past twenty-five years without considering the way in which those struggles have depended on identifications first formulating in cultural terms. It is, of course, the case that the national level cannot be simply ignored. It is in definite demands posed to specific national governments that many concrete political aims have to be realised. However, it is probably wrong to understand the movements that formulate these aims in national terms. It may be added that it is doubtful whether multinational capital is as convinced of the political importance of the nation state as the supposedly hard-bitten Marxist. The crucial necessity for political action is a felt collectivity. It may be that cultural forms indicate to us that politically enabling collectivities are to be located across subcultures, be they national or international. It may be that the opposition between the popular and the national will come to make the radical edge of cultural politics. Much of this may seem speculative. What is less speculative is that the next ten years are going to witness profound mutations in the geopolitics of entertainment. Traditional Left positions, whether couched in the pessimistic tones of the Frankfurt School or the more nuanced accents of Gramsci, are simply unable to provide the terms with which to engage seriously with the coming changes. But engage with them we must.

PART TWO

Readings – Cultural Forms and Social Change

5 Abusing Self and Others: Puritan Accounts of the Shakespearian Stage

Throughout the period covered by these essays the majority of my teaching at the University of Pittsburgh was devoted to Renaissance language and literature. Much of this teaching has been on Milton. Milton is of central interest because his writings and his life focus that century when English literature canonised itself in terms of the written language defined in relation to the classical tradition. One of the many reasons that Milton and the literary tradition that he both inherits and inaugurates is so interesting is its ambiguous relation to the Elizabethan stage. Milton's decision to write *Paradise Lost* in the verse form of that popular theatre, a decision so surprising that he had to defend it in a prefatory note, is merely the most obvious index of this.

In addition, the Elizabethan theatre is a fascinating field of study for anyone interested in cinema. Not only are its business methods and cultural practices closer to early Hollywood than to any subsequent period of English literature but it offers an unparalleled example of an extremely sophisticated popular culture in which print plays an essential but minor part. To put this last point in the terms of the following essay we should imagine Chaplin when he first appears on the screen as having just danced back from Norwich – a worthy successor to the self-banished Will Kempe.

Shakespeare remains a key element within the organisation and authorisation of culture today. He continues to be the major named guarantor of both the dominant form of elite culture and the dominant form of literary education. And yet Shakespeare's work finds its original context far from elite culture or literary texts – in the Elizabethan theatre which flourished in the last two decades of the sixteenth century. Of course, the popularity of that theatre is part of the very function of the texts today – guaranteeing their 'universality' – but if the popularity is acknowledged, much else is not. Despite the enormous efforts of Chambers and his near contemporaries, and the veritable industry of scholarship that has flourished since the Second World War, we still do not clearly understand the social and symbolic functioning of the Elizabethan theatre. Nor is such an understanding merely an antiquarian pleasure. The particular ways in which elite and popular culture were defined in opposition in the seventeenth century continues to have a powerful contemporary legacy, as do the particular ways in which that division related to the organisation of sexuality.

The only writers who have fully emphasised how important sexuality was to the Shakespearean theatre are those Puritan writers who campaigned for their closure. Those eminent, narrow-minded and misogynistic divines have found unresponsive audiences in the twentieth century. Jonas Barish may be taken to be stating a common response when he writes of them:

None of the pamphlets that dropped from the English presses during these years makes

81

an impressive dialectical contribution. Rarely do they pursue an argument closely; more often they disintegrate into free-associative rambles.[1]

Barish's distaste is widely shared and despite a recent edition of Gosson's criticism there has been no attempt to provide any comprehensive account of the Puritan attack on the theatre.[2] In many ways this is unsurprising, for there are few contemporary allegiances to which these Puritan writings appeal. For those whose lives are given over to and whose living is provided by literature, they represent an embarrassing madness which it would be folly to consider. For the historian sympathetic to those forces which brought rebellion and revolt to England in the 1640s, they are equally unsympathetic culminating as they did with an act of political censorship and cultural authoritarianism as the theatres were closed in 1642, not to be reopened till the English people had, in Milton's phrase, 'chosen a captain back for Egypte', and Charles was restored to the throne. It is hardly surprising that the last full-length study was published in 1903 by a convinced Calvinist.[3] The confusion of these texts are, however, a genuine response to the confusions of the Elizabethan theatre and should not be read as evidence of intellectual weakness on the part of their authors.[4] If we are to properly understand and gauge the Renaissance division into high and popular culture, and its relation to a new order of sexuality, then we must come to terms with these confusions. Indeed, paradoxically, I would argue that the Puritan attacks on the theatre are perhaps the best introduction to understanding what Elizabethan theatre was actually like. Far from being incoherent, they indicate clearly what is socially and sexually at stake in the new symbolic spaces created by Burbage and his fellow entrepreneurs.

Between 1500 and 1700 London was transformed from a large medieval town into a modern metropolis. The domination of England's cloth export trade from the early sixteenth century and the Tudor centralisation of power were the two initial conditions of this transformation.[5] But this period saw London move from the periphery of a European system of trade to the centre of one that was worldwide, at the same time as it grew as both a centre of distribution and production.[6] This growth depended on a huge influx of people from the countryside. Even without the plague, urban mortality rates meant that any town needed a constant supply of immigrants. When one added the dreadful and almost regular toll exacted by the plague then the numbers required merely to remain at the same size are extraordinary. Yet the city which in 1500 numbered little over 100,000 had doubled in size by 1600, doubled again by 1650 and by 1700 had become the largest city in Europe.[7] The continual flow of people from the countryside was guaranteed by the ever increasing capitalisation of agrarian production, itself continuously stimulated by the ever growing London market. Recent historians have emphasised the importance of capitalist relations of production in the countryside, but we only need Jonson's plays to recognise how much more striking these relations appeared in towns, particularly in relation to the commodification of pleasure. Crucially important in the economic development of London at this time was the industries set up to benefit from the trend towards conspicuous consumption.[8]

It is difficult to appreciate fully any of the literature of the time unless we read it in relation to these contemporary developments and very few personal histories

82

make much sense outside an appreciation of these fundamental transformations. Stephen Gosson, the first and arguably most famous of the writers against the theatre, is no exception. He was born on 17 April 1554 in Canterbury, the son of a joiner. He was thus one of that artisanal class who were to prove so significant over the next half century in contributing to the establishment of a vernacular literature. Although it would be profitable to compare his career with either Shakespeare or Spenser, the closest parallels are with his near contemporary Christopher Marlowe who left the same school (King's School, Canterbury) some ten years after Gosson had gone to Corpus Christi, Oxford in 1572. Both on leaving university eschewed the feudal options of a career in the Church or service in a noble house in favour of selling their education in the form of commodities – the playscripts that provided the theatres with the raw material that they fashioned into spectacle, a spectacle for which the citizens and apprentices of the City, as well as nobles of the Court and the gentry of the Inns, were willing to pay in very significant coin. Both, also, in fact, worked for the State – not as retainers of a great feudal lord but as spies for Walsingham's secret service, the heart of the modern state. There is a strict limit to how far these parallels can be traced. If Gosson seems to have been more successful as a spy than Marlowe, able to retire from the stress and strain of these new economic and political relations to a conventional and successful career in the Church, there is no indication in any of his writings that he could articulate or reflect on these new relations. Marlowe, by contrast, in the dialogue between Baldock and Spencer in Act II Scene 1 of *Edward II* not only clearly shows his awareness that the new learning is now for sale, but links those commercial possibilities to a programme of perverse sexuality. Gosson's awareness of sexuality in the theatre is acute but it is this awareness which drives him from the theatre and into the pulpit. His writings adopt varied styles and argument procedures, but the fear of sexuality in the theatre is the one constant.

Gosson left Corpus Christi, a bastion of Anglican orthodoxy, under slightly unusual circumstances (possibly lack of funds) in 1576. The date is, of course, a crucial one in theatre history, for it is when Burbage decides to escape from constant harrying of the City by building a playhouse outside the city walls in Shoreditch. In so doing he now seems to have been imitating an earlier venture of his brother-in-law,[9] but it is this building, and the earlier decision by Elizabeth to tightly control the licensing of the companies of players, which mark the 1570s as the clear beginning of the theatre which will become of such cultural significance. It is a curious, and formally unanswerable, question as to whether the great success of the Elizabethan and Jacobean stage was due in large measure to the fact that the theatres play just outside the city boundaries in that wide arc which swings from Shoreditch in the north through Clerkenwell, down Drury Lane and then across the Thames and round to Bankside. Of course all these theatres are not in place in 1576, but the conditions of their existence were coming together and one of the most important was the ever expanding suburbs outside the city walls where all the activities alien to the City's rules and morality were situated – from the brothels to the rapidly increasing manufacturing industry.[10] What is certain is that these large new buildings, themselves the product of very considerable investment, provided an imaginary space in which the permutations of sexuality and power, which the new economic conditions were bringing about, could be played out.

It was for this new imaginary space that Gosson was to write, and to write, as he makes woefully clear, with some success. In reviewing current plays in London, he mentions one on the subject of the Cataline conspiracy which 'bicause it is knowen too be a Pig of myne own Sowe, I will speake the less of it'.[11] Lodge, in a reply to Gosson, claimed that Gosson had also been an actor but Gosson, himself, makes no reference to this although he does make clear how well he knows the abuse he is writing about:

> And they that neuer goe out of their houses, for regard of the their credit, nor steppe from the vniuersity for loue of knowledge, seeing but slender offences & small abuses within their owne walles, wil neuer belleeue that such rockes are abrode, nor such horrible monsters in playing places. But as (I speake the one to my comforte, the other to my shame, and remember both with a sorrowful hart) I was first instructed in the vniuersity, after drawne like a nouice to these abuses: so wil I shew you what I see, & informe you what I reade of such affaires.[12]

What exactly happened to Gosson in the theatre is never made clear. He himself refuses to be too explicit because, he says, of the risk of exciting others but he never ceases to insist that what he found in the theatres was abuse and sin. It is not just prurience stretching across 400 years that makes one wonder as to the exact nature of these abuses which had such a momentous effect on him. However the answer to that question is not likely to be found in any particular sexual act or acts. What Gosson finds so disturbing is a public display of sexuality both on the stage and, as we shall see, in the audience. Gosson stands not only as an unwilling participant within the Renaissance theatre of London, but as a kind of precursor of the bourgeois spectator who will finally fashion a staging of desire which can be controlled and from which the audience will have disappeared.

Crucial to this bourgeois stage is the dominance of the visual and it is not surprising that Gosson finds sound, the sound which sweeps across stage and audience equally, to be the first step on the road to sin. The full title of Gosson's pamphlet is 'The Schoole of Abuse conteining a pleasant invective against Poets, Pipers, Plaiers, Iesters and such like caterpillers of a Commonwealth; Setting up the Flagge of Defiance to their mischieuous exercise, & ouerthrowing their Bulwarkes, by Prophane Writers, Naturall reason, and common experience'. It is Poets and Pipers that are italicised and throughout the text it is the pipes that are the most dangerous. The threat of sound is that, unlike vision, it invades our privacy, penetrating us to the core of our being:

> I iudge Cookes and Painters the better hearing, for the one extendeth his arte no farther thenn to the tongue, palate and nose, the other to the eye; and both are ended in outward sense, which is common to vs with bruite/beasts. But these by the priuie entries of the eare, slip down into the hart, & with gunshotte of affection gaule the minde, where reason and vertue should rule the roste.[13]

Gosson's next great worry is also situated well off centre stage. It is the women in the audience and the behaviour which they affect and cause which bothers him:

In our assemblies at playes in London, you shall see suche heauing and shoouing, suche ytching and shouldring, too sitte by women; Suche care for their garments, that they bee not trode on; Such eyes to their lappes, that no chippes light in them: Such pillowes to ther backes, that they take no hurte: Such masking in their eares, I knowe not what: Such giuing them Pippins to passe the time: Suche playing at foote Saunt without Cardes: Such ticking, such toying, such smiling, such winking, and such maning them home when the sportes are ended, that it is a right Comedie, to marke behauiour.[14]

It is the extent to which Gosson is caught up in the action offstage that he finds the theatre objectionable and offensive.

The Puritan objection to the theatres as sites of public disorder and their objection to the plays as sites of symbolic disorder are never distinguished in Gosson's or other similar texts. The normal critical response to this is to berate the Puritans for failing to make what is, to us, an obvious distinction. But its obviousness to us is a heritage of a very different staging which separates fully stage and audience. It is of course classic that the representational space of Elizabethan stage is less clearly marked. Nevertheless we continue to think of a clear division between representation and audience. For Gosson there is no such division, except, at the limit, that between text and performance.

Gosson tries constantly to articulate the enormity of the theatre but he is as aware as his slightly bored reader that he never quite manages it:

But the abuses of plaies cannot be showen because they passe the degrees of the instrument, reach of the Plummet, sight of the minde, and for trial are neuer brought to the touchstone. Therefore he that will auoyde the open shame of pryuy sinne, the common plague of priuate offences, the greate wracks of little Rocks, the sure disease of vncertaine causes; must set hande to the sterne ... nor goe too Theatres for beeing allured, nor once bee allured for feare of abuse.[15]

If Gosson is unable to produce an argument with premise and conclusion, he can proceed by narrative example:

Bunduica a notable woman and a Queene of Englande, that tyme that Nero was Emperour of Rome, hauing some of the Romans in garrison heere against her, in an Oration which she made to her subjects, seemed vtterly to contemne their force, and laugh at their folly. For shee accounted them vnworthy the name of men, or title of Souldiers, because they were smoothly appareled, soft lodged, daintely feasted, bathed in warme waters, rubbed with sweet oyntments, strewd with fine poulders, wine swillers, singers, Dauncers, and Players.[16]

Once again, continues Gosson, we have a Queen in power but now unfortunately we have become like the despised Romans:

How often hath her Maiestie with the graue aduise of her honorable Councell, sette downe the limits of apparell to euery degree, and how soone againe hath the pride of our harts ouerflowen the chanel ... Ouerlashing in apparel is so common a fault, that the very hyerlings of some of our Players ... iet vnder Gentlemens noses in sutes of silke.[17]

The social confusion of dress, particularly evident in the theatres, calls every category, including that of sexual difference, in doubt. When Mortimer sums up his

85

hatred of Gaveston in Act I Scene 4 of *Edward II*, he claims that it has nothing to do with his sexuality ('his wanton humour grieves not me') but rather his 'over-lashing' in apparel:

> He wears a lord's revenue on his back,
> And Midas-like he jets it in the court

(Edward II, I, iv, 406–7)

And yet what the play persistently makes clear, as does Gosson's pamphlet, is that excessive dress and excessive sexuality are one and the same thing. Social and sexual distinctions are here totally interdependent and nowhere is that interdependence more clearly seen than in the theatre. Commentators who have criticised the incoherence of the Puritan pamphlets have failed to see their coherence, despite the fact that many of the plays, particularly Jonson's, insist on the same symbolic equations. They successfully identify a social space, most evident in the theatre, but spilling over into the streets of London in which social and sexual identity are at risk.

If we concentrate on Gosson's major fears – the music and crowd reaction which threatens to invade and envelop him – then we are inevitably forced to think of the jig that ended the performance of the plays. It is, I believe, the jig, perhaps above all, which renders the Elizabethan theatre so difficult for us to comprehend and it is ignoring the jig that has perhaps misled earlier readers of the attacks on the stage. Baskervill's monumental work of scholarship published in the 1920s is both illuminating and mystifying. Illuminating in that almost all the material that Baskervill quotes emphasises the erotic nature of the jig, mystifying in that Baskervill – who has no contemporary cultural form to use as a comparison – seems genuinely to have little idea of what was at stake. Whenever he quotes references to jigs one can expect to find a reference to sex: 'bawdy', 'misorders', 'ribaldrous', 'amourous'.[18] It probably needs an age which has the stage act of the Beastie Boys to recapture some of that mixture of song, dance and performance that contemporaries deemed erotic enough to send old men scurrying off to brothels.[19] Certainly the collective nature of the emotions it stimulated and the fear it could evoke is well captured in Dekker's horrified description:

> ... as I haue often seene, after the finishing of some worthy Tragedy, or Catastrophe in the Open Theaters, that the Sceane after the Epilogue hath beene more blacke (about a nasty bawdy Iigge) than the most horrid Sceane in the Play was. The stinkards speaking all things, yet no man vnderstanding anything; a mutiny being amonst them, yet none in danger; no tumult, and yet no quietnesse; no mischifs begotten, and yet mischiefe borne: the swiftness of such a torrent, the more it ouerwhelmes, breeding the more pleasure.[20]

But the jig is not simply pornographic and potentially subversive; it is those things in virtue of its links to an older carnivalesque tradition which refused any sharp distinction between player and spectator. Baskervill understands the jig as more or less direct transposition from an older folk tradition. However, Wiles, in a fascinating book *Shakespeare's Clown*, has argued that it must be understood in relation to the development of the theatre in the years after Burbage's first venture. Wiles understands a progressive separation of clown from audience, which begins in dual constraints on the clown's improvisation within the play and in his improvised repartee with the audience. Such improvisation was both politically dangerous, because uncensored, and aesthetically unsettling, because it refused any strict divorce between representation and audience. The compromise was the jig – if the clown was downgraded in the course of the play and limited to the lines written for him by the playwright, after the dramatic finale he issued forth to conduct a jig which established a more direct rapport with the audience.[21] But even this reduced role was anathema to those attempting to produce a neo-classical theatre. By 1600 a liking for jigs already doomed one to share Polonius's outdated tastes and, indeed, it is the submission of the theatre to definite canons of taste from the 1590s on, which marks a very significant break with popular tradition.

It is my own conviction that this break can be dated with some precision. Shortly after February 1599 William Kempe, who had been clown for five years with the Chamberlain's Men, left the company. He had signed the lease for the Globe but he did not move into the new building. I want to argue that Kempe's departure from the Chamberlain's Men was a clear moment of breaking with a popular tradition, a break which Kempe symbolised in his famous dance to Norwich. If we wish to understand this rift in terms of the internal dynamics of Shakespeare's theatre then we can concentrate on the figure of Falstaff. Falstaff, Kempe's most famous role, may well have been the ground of the disagreement. At the end of *Henry IV* Part 2 we are promised sight of the fat knight in France but Falstaff dies before he can appear in *Henry V*. Whatever the details of the historical rift, it is clear that Hal's banishment of Falstaff is a symbolic act of such magnitude that it would be difficult to undo. The enormous polymorphously perverse figure of Falstaff, with his links to the older theatrical figure of the Vice, enacts a carnivalesque role which ignores the linguistic, social and sexual orders of society. The functions, linguistic and sexual, that he carries in the plays he dominates do reappear but they reappear not in a multivalent figure who links audience and representation but as a series of internal conflicts with which the audience now identify on an individual level. To put it in cryptic terms, when we see Hal after the victories over the French he is wearing the mourning clothes of Hamlet and when we next hear Falstaff it is in the language and gestures that Hamlet uses in the mad scenes.

The functions of the clown must now be integrated into action and character and there is no integral place for a concluding jig. Armin, who replaced Kempe as the company's comic actor, had no ability as a dancer and Wiles argues convincingly that he has a very different relation to the action, constituting an alternative world from which to comment on the action of the play, but an alternative world located in his misshapen body rather than in his relation to the audience. For the argument that I am trying to develop, it would be very satisfying if we had definite evidence that the Globe abandoned the jig from the beginning. All, however, that one can say with certainty is that it had no reputation for jigs, unlike the northern theatres. Moreover, there is considerable literary and cultural evidence to suggest that, turning their back on Kempe, the Globe was consciously turning its back on what they saw as an outdated dramatic form and, most importantly, the relation it implied with the audience.

Kempe's response was famous but it has not usually been read as the complicated symbolic challenge that it obviously was. In Lent of 1599 Kempe jigged all the way to Norwich, an event he commemorated in the only book he left, *Kemp's Nine Daies Wonder*. Kempe's action makes a great deal of sense if we read it as a deliberate response to his leaving the Globe. Indeed when he writes that the best way of understanding his journey is that he was dancing 'my selfe out of the world', it is difficult not to read this as a definite reference to the Globe. But it was not just the world of the theatre that Kempe was leaving, but the developing market for entertainment of which the Globe was the most famous and evident example. Kempe only undertook the writing of the book when he was attacked by various anonymous ballads which would seem to have suggested, amongst other things, that the dance had not been a commercial success. Kempe is keen to prove the reverse but he is also keen to locate its economy out of any profit and loss accounting. The journey is successful through gifts and wagers – carnivalesque models of exchange – and Kempe constantly slights any suggestion that you can produce entertainment for exchange. The transformation of language into a commodity is mocked at the beginning of the pamphlet:

> How euer, many a thousand brought me to Bow, where I rested a while from dancing, but had small rest with those whon would have vrg'd me to drinking. But I warrant you Will Kemp was wise enough: to their ful cups, kinde thanks was my returne with Gentlemanlike protestations: as truly sir, I dare not: it stands not with the congruity of my health. Congruitie said I? How came that strange language in my mouth? I thinke scarcely that it is any Christen word, and yet it may be a good worde for ought I know, though I neuer made it, nor doe verye well understand it: yet I am sure I have bought it at the word mongers, at as dear a rate, as I could have had a whole 100 of Bauines at the wood-mongers.[22]

Indeed the whole apparatus of Kempe's dance locates it firmly between carnival and commerce – a transitional form whose status Kempe is keen to defend against those who have opted for commerce, amongst whom in the final address he would seem to identify Shakespeare as the most important. If one attaches this kind of significance to the move to the Globe and Kempe's departure then it may be possible to readdress the hoary but crucial question of Harbage's rival traditions, aptly summarised by Gurr as follows:

> The question of a division between the popular and the privileged, when it came into existence and what playhouses it separated people into, is the most knotty item in this whole history of playgoing.[23]

Much of the recent debate has turned around the exact composition of the audiences and this is obviously a vital question. If, however, we want to read the social significance of the various theatres, it may be as vital to understand how the audience was addressed as much as what its composition was. If one allows the jig the significance that Kempe would attach to it then the crucial division between the theatres may not be between those that address their audience within a neoclassical framework which insists on the division between representation and audience and which plays on mechanisms of individual identification, and those which continue to allow interchange between audience and stage in what is a collective event rather than a private experience.

Any analysis of the politics of the Shakespearian theatre which does not address these questions of form and audience ignores the real political choices that faced Shakespeare in the development of his art. Consideration of such choices is, for example, more or less totally missing from Stephen Greenblatt's long and fascinating essay on the Henriad, 'Invisible Bullets'. Placing itself in the context of the colonial discovery and subjugation of the New World, Greenblatt reads the sequence of plays as a complicated interrogation of political power. By ignoring the significance of the move to the Globe and the importance of the theatrical situation for that play, Greenblatt is able to produce Shakespeare, once again, as the myriad-minded ground of all political possibility rather than as a dramatist whose forms themselves make political commitments.

Greenblatt's strategy is made possible by displacing the very concrete analysis that the plays produce of the relation between sex and politics in Europe into a much more generalised account of power. The political thrust of the plays and the significance of *Henry V* cannot be read independently of the dialectic set up between Wales and France. Wales and the Welsh language represent an archaic, almost bestial, condition which must simply be suppressed and eradicated. France and the French language represent a civilised condition which England and English must rival and appropriate. The opening of *Henry IV* Part 1 indicates clearly the threat posed by the Welsh:

> the noble Mortimer
> Leading the men of Herefordshire to fight
> Against the irregular and wild Glendower,
> Was by the rude hands of that Welshman taken,
> A thousand of his people butchered
> Upon whose dead corpse there was such misuse,
> Such beastly, shameless transformation,
> By those Welshwomen done, as may not be
> Without much shame re-told or spoken of.

This threat of a sexuality which escapes the control of language is carried throughout the plays, not only by the Welsh but by the figure of Falstaff himself, and Hal's assiduous study of language is what enables him to bring both nation and body under control in the concluding play as he moves from his conversation with the ordinary soldiers on the eve of battle to his mastery of the French princess. But in this final play, the resolution has been achieved not simply at the level of plot or dialogue but in the very form of the theatre itself, the theatre from which Kempe and the traditions which he represents has been expelled.[24]

The fear that Gosson and his fellow pamphleteers of the 1580s experience is one of the collapse of identity within a new symbolic space, itself located in the incomprehensible new economic and social conditions of developing London. Twenty years later, with London beginning to divide itself more clearly into rich and poor areas and the theatre developing different addresses for different social classes, the acute threat posed by the theatres may have passed.

If we are to adopt such an analysis then the development of taste in seventeenth-century London is not a minor item of an obscure social and economic history but one of the crucial mechanisms which came to stabilise the new civil and sexual life of the city. The developments in the Globe that I have alluded to did not, however, touch the neuralgic focus in the Puritan fear of sexual confusion, and it is the cross-dressing of the boy actors which becomes the major Puritan complaint against the theatre by the beginning of the seventeenth century; indeed, Gosson makes it the centrepiece of his second attack on the theatre *Playes confuted in five actions*. In this pamphlet Gosson drops the Euphuistic style and humanist position of his earlier offering in favour of a Ramistic logical demonstration that no plays at all are 'to be suffered in a Christian commonweale'. As he proceeds through the Aristotelian causes he finds that under every description the theatre is damned. The formal cause of plays is the act of counterfeiting and the crucial basis of that counterfeiting is an impermissible method of representation:

> Whatsoeuer he be that looketh narrowly into our Stage Playes, or considereth how, and which waye they are represented, shall find more filthiness in them, than players dreame off. The Law of God very straightly forbids men to put on women's garments, garments are set down for signes distinctiue betwene sexe & sexe, to take vnto vs those garments that are manifest signes of another sexe, is to falsifie, forge and adulterate, contrarie to the expresse rule of the worde of God.[25]

Shortly afterwards, in one of those rare passages which illuminate these dull texts we suddenly, in his description of the boy actors, get a sense of how deliberately erotic the Elizabethan stage was:

> ... shall they bee excused, that put on, not the apparell onely, but the gate, the gestures, the voyce, the passions of a woman? All which like the wreathings, and windinge of a snake, are flexible to catch, before they speed; and binde vppe cordes when they haue possession.[26]

Concerned that some may think that the prohibition in Deuteronomy has some other particular application, Gosson reinforces his position with an argument from natural law:

> The profe is evident, the consequent is necessarie, that in Stage Playes for a boy to put one the attyre, the gesture, the passions of a woman; for a meane person to take vpon him the title of a Prince with counterfeit porte, and traine, is by outwarde signes to shewe them selues otherwise then they are, and so with in the compass of a lye.[27]

In Gosson any fear of sexuality is immediately linked to a certain uncertainty about social order. For Prynne, writing in the 1630s, many of the complaints that bothered the earlier pamphleteers of half a century earlier have disappeared. In particular, there is little sense of that social disorder so threatening in Gosson or in Munday. What has replaced it, however, is a pathological hatred of any form of cross-dressing, a hatred which seeps out from almost any page of his *Histriomastix*. Its rampant homophobia can be read clearly in the enormously prolix index, the entries of which are almost little aphorisms. An enormous number of the entries link themselves to some vice associated with sodomy or effeminacy. I take, almost at random, the entry for apparell:

> the end and use of it, overcostly new-fangled Play House apparell censured ... Mens

putting on of womens, and womens of mens apparell (especially to act a Play) unlaw-full, abominable, unnaturall, the occasion of Sodomie, and lewdnesse.[28]

It is very difficult to know how general was Prynne's fear and horror. All we do know is that when Charles II restores the theatre, it is recognised that this Puritan complaint had some foundation, and actresses are summoned to the stage for the first time. Whatever other rationale is provided, it can be seen as a final adjust-ment to the norms of neo-classicism with the removal of a feature which would always puncture notions of verisimilitude. If, however, one was to pursue the argument of this essay, it might also need to be explained as part of a growing specification of sexual desire in terms of individual identity. As the theatre becomes increasingly a site of identification rather than participation then a much clearer demarcation of sexuality and sexual roles is called for. Indeed this clearer demarcation of sexual roles is one of the features of the developing metropolis. The first recognisable homosexual sub-culture is to be found in Restoration Eng-land.[29] It is as though the complicated social transactions of city life can be at least partially held in place by fixed sexual identities. But if this hypothesis were true then Prynne's horror at recognising in himself desire for a man is very different from Gosson's terror at an undifferentiated sexuality which threatened all social categories. Indeed Prynne's texts can be seen as addressing what is already a much more socially conservative cultural form.

The Puritan attack on the English stage tells us much about the cultural devel-opment of England in the period up to the Civil War. It is amongst the most strik-ing evidence that major questions of social order and sexual identity were intimately linked to the drama and its forms of performance. It is not clear, how-ever, that they should be seen as an unbroken series of texts stretching from 1580 to 1642 and the closing of the theatres. Much that was socially threatening in the English theatre had been neutralised long before Parliament finally bowed to the pressure from the City. Indeed much of it had been neutralised on the stage itself as the players and the playhouses developed from 1580 to 1600.

Any attempt at a political reading of Shakespeare must take that development as one of its starting points if it is to gain any real purchase on history.

Notes

1 Jonas Barish, *The Antitheatrical Prejudice* (Berkeley and Los Angeles: University of Cal-ifornia Press, 1981), p. 88.
2 The standard historical accounts are to be found in E. K. Chambers, *The Elizabethan Stage*, vol. 1 (Oxford: Oxford University Press, 1923), pp. 236–307 and J. Dover Wilson, 'The Puritan attack upon the Stage', *Cambridge History of English Literature*, vol. VI (Cam-bridge: Cambridge University Press), pp. 373–409. See also Russell Fraser, *The War against Poetry* (Princeton: Princeton University Press, 1970). The recent edition of Gos-son is Arthur F. Kinney, *Markets of Bawdrie: The Dramatic Criticism of Stephen Gosson* (Salzburg Studies in English Literature, 1974). All quotations are taken from this work. Biographical details are taken either from the introduction to this volume or from William Ringler, *Stephen Gosson* (Princeton: Princeton University Press, 1942). It is now conventional to say that Gosson was not in fact a Puritan. While it is true Gosson never took up Puritan positions on Church government, and while it is true that the

Schools of Abuse is written within a humanist discourse, *Playes confuted in five acts* is impeccably Puritan in both style and content.

3 Elbert N. S. Thompson, *The Controversy Between the Puritans and the Stage* (New York: Russell and Russell, 1966). A reprint of the 1903 edition.

4 Barish can again be said to be expressing more than his personal opinion when he writes 'It is a relief to turn from the heavy-handed Puritan tracts, with their clumsy invective and their lumbering repetitiousness, to the Cartesian lucidity of the French treatises. The debate in France proceeds on an altogether more analytical, more intellectually responsible plane', Barish, *The Antitheatrical Prejudice*, p. 193.

5 A. L. Beier and Roger Finlay, 'The significance of the metropolis' in A. L. Beier and Roger Finlay (eds), *London 1500–1700* (London: Longman 1986), p. 14.

6 For London's position in the international market, see Brian Dietz, 'Overseas trade and metropolitan growth'; for the growth of production, see A. L. Beier, 'Engine of manufacture: The trades of London', both in Beier and Finlay (eds), *London 1500–1700*, pp. 115–67.

7 See Roger Finlay, *Population and Metropolis: The Demography of London 1580–1650* (Cambridge: Cambridge University Press, 1981).

8 F. J. Fisher, 'The development of London as a centre of conspicuous consumption in the 16th and 17th centuries' in *Transactions of the Royal Historical Society*, 4th ser., 30 (1948).

9 See Janet Sloengard, 'An Elizabethan Lawsuit: John Brayne, his Carpenter, and the Building of the Red Lion Theatre', *Shakespeare Quarterly* 35 (1984), pp. 298–310.

10 A. L. Beier describes how trade increased in relation to production within the city in this period while outside the walls trade declined and production increased. There are few more important divisions to be borne in mind when trying to understand the culture of renaissance London, as Beier writes: 'In passing through the City's gates, one entered another world. The sights and smells of the busy, rambling extra-mural parts must have presented a sharp contrast to the well-ordered world of merchants and professional men within' (*London 1500–1700*, p. 153).

11 Kinney, *Markets of Bawdrie*, p. 97.

12 Ibid., p. 86.

13 Ibid., p. 89.

14 Ibid., p. 92.

15 Ibid., p. 95.

16 Ibid.

17 Ibid., p. 96.

18 This list is taken from Charles Read Baskervill, *The Elizabethan Jig and Related Song Drama* (Chicago: University of Chicago Press, 1929), p. 36.

19 As a much-quoted stanza from Guilpin puts it:

> And she with many a salt La volto jest
> Edgeth some blunted teeth, and fires the brest
> O many an old cold gray beard Cittizen
> Medea like making him young againe
> Who coming from the Curtaine sneaketh in,
> To some odde garden house of sinne.

Quoted in Baskervill, *The Elizabethan Jig*, p. 112.

20 Ibid. Similar feelings seemed to have affected Paul Lashmar when he reviewed the Beastie Boys in the *Observer*, 31 May 1987:

> (the audience) are there to indulge in mass psychosis, with the Beasties as a focal point. Within a few minutes of the Beasties arriving on stage, the packed hall was charged with a tension like the Milwall terraces before a riot. For nearly an hour the Beasties baited the audience to near explosion. The grinding beat, the 20-foot inflatable penis and caged go-go girls all contributed to an air of intense sexual violence … what is meant to be black humour actually plumbs the much darker depths of the adolescent condition. Instead of making contact with an amiable spirit of hedonism,

they have provoked the frightening forces of youthful nihilism and repressed sexuality.

21 David Wiles, *Shakespeare's Clown: Actor and Text in the Elizabethan Playhouse* (Cambridge: Cambridge University Press, 1987), Chapters 1–4.
22 William Kempe, *Kemps Nine Daies Wonder*, ed., G. B. Harris (New York: Barnes and Noble, 1966), p. 6.
23 A. J. Gurr, *Playgoing in Shakespeare's London* (Cambridge: Cambridge University Press, 1987), p. 67.
24 Some of the same criticisms might be levelled at Steven Mullaney's reading of the Henriad in *The Place of the Stage: License, Play and Power in Renaissance England* (Chicago: University of Chicago Press, 1988). I was very unfortunate in not having read this fascinating book, which parallels many of my themes, when I wrote the essay. While I agree wholeheartedly with the importance it stresses for the positioning of the London stage and of the significance of the Liberties, I feel that it does not appreciate the significance of the move to the Globe. The final chapter of the book which deals in masterly fashion with the importance of the acquisition of Blackfriars and the constraints of the romance does not, in my opinion, give adequate weight to the earlier history of the company and the growing importance of tragedy in the early 1600s.
25 Kinney, *Markets of Bawdrie*, p. 175.
26 Ibid.
27 Ibid., p. 177.
28 Prynne, *Histerio-Mastix: the players scourge* (London, 1633), p. 207.
29 See Alan Bray, *Homosexuality in Renaissance England* (London: Gay Men's Press, 1982).

6   Death of a Nation: Television in the Early 60s

When Melvyn Bragg asked me whether I would give the annual South Bank Lecture in 1987, I was both honoured by the invitation and delighted at the chance to talk about British television in the 60s. It was this television that had provided me in my early teens with the most excellent of educations. I wanted both to celebrate the medium that had meant so much to me personally and to inscribe it centrally in the modern development of Britain and its self-definitions. The lecture was also intended to contribute to the debate about the new forms of television which technological and economic developments were about to deliver. Those debates are ever more important for an understanding of contemporary definitions of democracy.

Television came into my home in 1957 – I was eight years old, ITV was a baby, albeit one that I couldn't receive on my first set. For the next decade, until I went up to university, television was to offer me education and entertainment on a scale that I still find difficult to credit. It would be silly to discount the value and importance that I found in both traditional schooling and traditional culture. Equally, the new technology of recorded music and the older technology of the cinema offered pleasures and insights unknown to television, but it was television, more than any other institution or medium, which opened up the world for me.

The suburban London of the 50s into which I was born was a very limited world: limited in class, in history, in behaviour, in politics, in information. If I were to pick a television programme which seemed to epitomise the limited pleasures of that world, it would be *Dixon of Dock Green*. Each week George Dixon would stride forward to address us in our comfortable suburban homes and to offer us a cautionary tale from life at Dock Green. The character of Dixon had been stolen from the film *The Blue Lamp* which had attempted to articulate a post-war British consensus and, for George, the values of family, authority and tradition were as evident as they were simple. When *Z Cars* spilled on to our screens in the early 60s, we were suddenly transported from the traditional certainties of Dock Green to the more complex and complicated world of Newtown. Love, work and crime were no longer evident categories which could be allocated to preordained moral pigeonholes. When, in a moment etched in my memory, Jeremy Kemp's wife hurled his supper at him in anger and frustration at the demands of his job, we were not being invited to sit in moral judgement but to witness the conflicts between work and family which the new modern home of consumer society (and the set design was as important an element in that scene as any other) made all the more acute. It was small wonder that the Chief Constable of Lancashire took the next train to London to complain. Television was suddenly discussing the most pressing and disturbing moral and social problems and discussing them in the living room. Ibsen's dramas or Hollywood films still shocked the private sensibilities of the bourgeoisie in public spaces. Television brought the public sphere right into the breeding ground of that private sensibility – the home. In doing so, it immediately became the focal point for all serious questions of censorship.

It is my own personal belief that if one wishes to estimate the importance of any art form one should immediately consult the censors. Censors are unhampered by aesthetic theories or the critical responses of previous eras; they know what they don't like and they don't like it because it's important. When Ben Jonson published his collected plays in the second decade of the seventeenth century, he was mocked by a literary establishment who ignored the theatre as too popularly based to be anything but aesthetically insignificant. Elizabeth I's and James II's Lord Chamberlains, on the other hand, had no doubt that what happened on the stage was so crucial to culture and politics that it had to be rigorously policed and monitored. When Matthew Arnold bemoaned the state of poetry in the mid-nineteenth century without seriously considering the novels of Dickens which he so much enjoyed, he was refusing to accept that the evidence from across the Channel, where Flaubert was being tried for the publication of *Madame Bovary*, showed that the novel had become the central literary form. The intellectuals at the beginning of this century who despised the cinema and its immense popularity understood less about its potential than the asinine Hays who elaborated the moral code which ruled Hollywood for thirty years.

My teachers at school might affect not to watch television and to regard it as insufferably vulgar, but looking at *Z Cars* I knew that those who wished to censor it were absolutely right – this was the most important drama of my time and I was determined not to miss it. I did not, at that stage, make any fundamental distinction between a popular series like *Z Cars* and the more culturally respectable single plays. It was, however, the single plays which produced greater pleasure and genuine awe. David Mercer's extraordinary trilogy which moved through three generations of protest to end with a mad young man dying on the wall in Berlin, Dennis Potter's extraordinary plundering of autobiographical material to bring us Nigel Barton and the move from mining village through Oxford to Hampstead and a prospective parliamentary seat – if I turned on my set all the contradictions of my society came pouring out. The play which stands for all the socially conscious drama of that time, although 'socially conscious' is far too limiting and lame a phrase, is *Cathy Come Home*. Brilliantly acted and directed, it showed how fragile was the affluence of the post-war years and how easily one could fall into a grim urban underclass which did not know that poverty had been abolished. The ending is still powerful and upsetting.

To dwell on the drama of the period is, whatever its riches, misleading. Drama is the oldest of the literary genres, and it is all too easy to regard television simply as a medium of transmission uninvolved with the forms it records. If we turn to situation comedy, then we are dealing with a genre whose very form and structure depends on the rhythms and repetitions of television. And there is another advantage. Although the drama of the time was superb and still repays viewing, as the recent Potter retrospective on the BBC demonstrated, I cannot be certain that its value will endure beyond the period when its contemporary references and allusions are easily understood. I have no such doubts about the great situation comedies; *Hancock's Half Hour, Steptoe and Son* and *Till Death Us Do Part* will still provoke laughter as long as there are television sets and viewers. It would need a whole other lecture to do full justice to these masterpieces and, given time, I would like to consider them in relation to the works of Beckett, particularly in their joint demonstration of the ways in which we shore language against our ruin, desperately utilising forms of communication always inadequate to the experiences which they attempt to capture.

What I do want to emphasise, however, is their coruscating analysis of the dominance of class in Britain. Again and again these comedies mercilessly and hilariously dissect the social subtleties of dominance and subservience that cripple so much of our daily life. While today's sitcoms seem content to reproduce the class stereotypes – which, in one of the bitterest historical ironies of my own life, become ever more dominant – a Hancock or a Steptoe rendered the stereotypes more and more ineffective by exposing the shame and humiliation that underpinned them. In the painful laughter of recognition that they provoked lay some hope of liberation. And that liberation drew on some of the most profound historical changes of the twentieth century. The situation comedies grew out of the sketches and routines of music halls. This development was intimately connected with the Second World War and the fabled entertainment arm of the services: ENSA. As the situation comedy developed its radio form, which television was to borrow, its comedy was heavily dependent, in personnel and tone, on that great social upheaval. The carnivalesque atmosphere which the threat of death and extinction can evoke combined with the intense social mobilisation of the people's war to produce an immense guffaw at the paralysing poison of class. If the drama I have already evoked came largely from the pens of a grammar school generation produced by the Butler Education Act, the situation comedies depended for their deepest energies on the radicalising social mobilisation of the Second World War.

This deep-seated plebeian anarchism was joined on television by a very different strain of subversive humour. From Nash to Oscar Wilde, university wits have descended from Oxford and Cambridge keen to pit their youth and learning against the repressive torpor of an establishment to which they will inevitably submit or succumb. Television, in its range of audiences, offered an unparalleled chance to thumb a nose at authority. There is no doubt that *Monty Python* or the fall-out from *Not the Nine O'Clock News*, both products of later university generations, offered incomparably more entertaining and sophisticated comedy. However, it is difficult to explain to someone even a few years younger the excitement and liberation offered by *That Was the Week That Was*. Saturday night after Saturday night the sacred cows were led to the slaughter, the shibboleths were mocked, and it was easy for a fourteen-year-old glued weekly to the screen to think that a brave new world was at hand.

One of the specific strengths of television is that it is not limited to fictional forms of entertainment; it can also deploy direct forms of education and instruction. Much of what I understand about politics, the arts and even the structure of ideas themselves comes from television. I'm not sure that any subsequent television programmes have conveyed the enthusiasms and excitement of ideas better than A. J. P. Taylor's simple history lectures delivered straight to camera. Or that politics and current affairs have been more effectively illuminated than by the early episodes of *This Week* and *World in Action*. And I am almost certain that Huw Weldon's regime at the BBC produced arts programmes which have still to be surpassed. Most memorable of all for me was Jonathan Miller's moving dramatisation of Plato's *Symposium*.

The list is literally endless and it is a constant source of wonder to me that this incomparable archive is not used more regularly by television. But rather than continue in this elegiac vein, I want to consider some cynical objections that might be raised by somebody who saw this glorification of the past as simply yet another distressing sign of middle age, at one with receding hair and an expanding waist. These objections will lead, I hope, to an understanding of why that period can rightly be considered as a Golden Age.

The most powerful objection would argue that to treat television as a unified cultural form is already to misunderstand the nature of the technology. Television as a medium has so many different relations to so many different aspects of our experience that it is ridiculous to try to understand television as any kind of unity. Take sport, for example. One of the major pleasures which television provided and which I have not mentioned was that it provided me with a ringside seat at Wimbledon, the Cup Final, the Test Matches, the Olympics. What is a routine and expected right for my children was, for me, a valued privilege. But one could argue that it is impossible to compare television coverage of sport in 1957 (the first year I watched a Cup Final) with television coverage in 1987 because sport itself has been transformed by television. If we take cricket, for example, and the recent coverage of the World Cup, we can note that neither the event itself nor the form of cricket played – one-day limited-over cricket – would exist without television. Perhaps more significantly, it is impossible to compare early television coverage of politics where for a few brief years – perhaps in Britain up until 1964 – television functioned pre-eminently as an observer with political coverage, where now most of the rhetoric of politics is organised in terms of television. To sum up: to talk of television as such is to confuse electronic hardware with cultural form – all TV is is a transmission device. All that it is possible to do is to examine the diverse and incomparable ways in which the developing technology interacts with the reality or fiction that it frames.

This important and cautionary argument has much to recommend it but it ignores the fact that television was, and to a certain extent is, unified in two ways. Unified at its point of reception in the home and unified at its point of production in the huge broadcasting institutions. For the teenage viewer I tried to evoke at the beginning of this article, it was crucial to the impact of television that all these diverse programmes, to which I have already referred, were available in the same mode, often on the same night and, for almost all the examples I have taken, on the same channel – the BBC. This does not mean that ITV was not crucial to the developments of the early 60s. Almost all the programmes I have talked about were developed and produced in direct response to the challenge mounted by Independent Television. Some, such as *Z Cars*, are unthinkable without reference to ITV productions such as *Coronation Street* and *No Hiding Place*. Others may lack such immediate influences but were, none the less, the product of the BBC's rethinking of the whole concept of television after ITV had first exploited the real popular appeal of the medium. Indeed, this interdependence of BBC and ITV is a continuing feature of television – the complex interlocking nature of the system is such that the excellences of one channel cannot be understood independently of the other channels with which it is competing.

For the moment, however, all I want to stress is the importance of the unity conferred on television by the very fact that a multitude of diverse forms are juxtaposed in a very concrete way by the set that receives them. The single most important result of this juxtaposition is that television in Britain refused to separate the traditional forms of high culture from the traditional forms of popular entertainment. That division, endemic and crippling to western culture since the Renaissance, was challenged by a technology which could provide both, and the ethos of public service broadcasting, which ensured that both were provided.

The BBC's historical attitude to popular forms of entertainment on radio was deeply paternalistic. If the population had to be provided with circuses, then the circuses would be carefully managed by mandarins. But, to pursue the metaphor a bit further, the carnival atmosphere of the circus is seriously contagious, and even mandarins have been deeply affected. The inevitable result of producing a wide variety of programmes within the same organisation was that there was a great deal of cross-fertilisation, and the major comedies like *Hancock* or *Steptoe* are genuine hybrids, products of a wide variety of cultural traditions. This was the second real unity of television, the unity of production and broadcasting functions in large organisations, particularly the BBC, and the real possibility of creative interaction between very different departments. One has only to think emblematically of the career of someone like Jeremy Isaacs, traversing current affairs with *This Week* and *Panorama*, documentary with the *World at War*, and drama with *A Sense of Freedom*, to see concretely how creative such interaction could be.

So television has a real unity, but perhaps its history is very simple to understand and has nothing to do with television as such. What has happened to television in the thirty years since the opening of ITV is simply what happens to any new institution. When television started it was the province of the young and enjoyed a technology which militated against tight editorial control. As youth has aged and the technology has allowed much more effective editorial intervention, television has simply submitted to the iron laws of Weber – 'Bureaucracy rules'.

In my more pessimistic moments this account seems all too true, but it ignores the place of television within its wider social context, and it is that wider context which enables us to understand fully why we can indeed talk of a Golden Age of television. The official culture of England was, for over 300 years, identified with a printed language which inevitably ignored specific differences of class, region and gender. It would be the wildest of McLuhanite fantasies to confuse medium and message and suggest that somehow print was intrinsically the property of a male ruling class, but it is a medium in which any differences relating to speech, be they of class, gender or region, do not register in the evident way they do when people talk. The notion of unified culture is thus peculiarly plausible in a print-based culture, and when the BBC started broadcasting they attempted to reproduce the terms and assumptions of such cultural unity. The Reithian news announcer, clothed in his dinner jacket and articulating the precise tones of Received Pronunciation, can serve as an image of that unified national culture and the terms of that unification. Many might perhaps be forgiven for thinking that, with the advent of broadcasting, we would finally see regional speech forms disappear and Professor Higgins rule all our tongues. Such unity of speech would, of course, reflect the unity of the national culture. Such a possibility was not completely alien to the technology, and the history of radio in Nazi Germany gives one a glimpse of the horrors of such a culturally unified nation. The reality of the development of broadcasting in Britain was that it has led to an ever greater diversity of accents and speech patterns and an ever more fragmented national culture. The example of Germany would, by itself, rule out uncritical acceptance of the notion that the introduction of a speech-based form of national communication inevitably entails that differences and divisions will suddenly make themselves heard. But the very forms of speech, even in the specialised forms required by broadcasting, admit more readily a multitude of possible positions and perspectives. The potential of radio to introduce differences of class and region into a institutional structure deliberately set up to reproduce a national culture was realised by the medium of television. Historically, the regional structure of ITV was an important factor in this, but more important than the role of speech in the medium or the structure of its institutions was television's place in the radical social transformation produced by the advent of the consumer society. The energies released by the new forms of marketing-led production have still to be evaluated fully. They cannot begin to be understood without analysing television, which both as advertising medium and consumer durable is an integral part of these new patterns of consumption. The paradox of television in this period, and the reason that it generated such excitement, was that it used a cultural form which presupposed (and indeed to some extent guaranteed) the traditional conception of the nation to both reflect and produce a very different kind of national culture: more pluralist, less dominated by the forms of writing and traditional high culture, more open to both international and local variations.

What happened in the late 50s and early 60s was that a nation gathered to witness its own transformation. Television, while by no means the only or most important cause of this transformation, became its focus. There are, in the history of the west, three particularly important moments of dramatic innovation: fifth-century Athens, the Elizabethan stage and Hollywood in its earlier silent heyday. In each of these cases there are some important and striking parallels. All three witnessed an extraordinary combination of both official and popular culture. All three, while intensely concerned with art, found their justification elsewhere – in Athens in terms of religion, in Elizabethan England and Hollywood in terms of commerce. Perhaps most extraordinary of all, all three combined an extraordinary intensity of commitment to particular productions with a complete carelessness about the preservation of the artefacts thus produced. The details of Athenian stage productions are gleaned from a few lines in Aristotle, we lack even one manuscript of a Shakespeare play and many silent films decomposed before latter-day archivists could preserve them.

It is a curious fact that all these comments apply equally to British television of the 60s and none more significantly than the final one. To talk to anyone who worked in television at that time is to become aware that the excitement I have tried to evoke was not simply felt by viewers like myself. People worked and argued with a fierce passion and yet, curiously, much was not preserved – the archive for this period is extraordinarily bare. But one should not be surprised nobody then took television as a serious art form. I do not want to suggest that television of the 60s should be ranked in some all-time artistic hit parade with *The Bacchae, Hamlet* and *Intolerance.* But I do want to suggest that the importance and vitality of these historical moments is directly related to very deep and momentous political changes, and the way in which a new medium for artistic expression can articulate those political changes. Both the Athenian drama and the Elizabethan stage provided the aesthetic and symbolic space in which the emotional and personal possibilities of the new political forms of the Greek *polis* and the European nation state were examined. Hollywood, and the television of which I have been talking, seem to me to relate to political changes as momentous but which, as the processes are by no means completed, are more difficult to grasp. Furthermore, cinema and television seem to be linked as aesthetic forms, with both their possibilities and their failures, to a new political order which may well prove stillborn. If we think back to the beginning of the century and to the Valley of the Angels in Southern California, where mid-European Jews organised actors from every ethnic background into narratives written in English, it is no surprise that many thought that this was the artistic medium which would reflect a new international order. Of course, from the Hays Code through the McCarthyite witch hunts, the history was written differently and the medium and possibilities of film were tied to the last, greatest and most paradoxical of European nations – the United States of America.

The history of television in the early 60s prompts some analogous political reflections. Night after night the set brought forth fresh images, which fresh images begat in a cycle that denied any possibility of simply identifying any one of them, or any combination of them, with Britain. One might have anticipated that the political analogue of this would have been an ever decreasing decentralisation of national power, not simply in relation to regional definitions but in relation to a whole number of differing and competing collectivities. Certainly, developments in television itself have followed that logic. The multiplication of channels, the advent of the video recorder, the general pluralisation of special forms of entertainment, particularly the home computer, mean that the unified set of the 60s is now itself a multitude of different possibilities. At the same time the founding of Channel 4 with an explicit remit to break the link between transmission and production and to foster much smaller groups of producers has seen the television institution subject itself to a process of fragmentation and splitting. The period of the paradoxical Golden Age, when the two channels of BBC and ITV could use their cultural dominance to bring the message that such a dominance was at an end, is over. What, however, can we expect to replace it, and can we anticipate that the age to come will be Silver, Bronze, or some even baser metal?

As we enter the most important era of television reform since the 60s, I hope that my brief account of the past has demonstrated that the choices made now will have the most serious social and cultural consequences. The current government's desire to ease the monopolistic culture of television is, in itself, no bad thing.

Indeed, it could be seen as the development of the cultural logic I have sketched, in which ever more differences find articulation in more pluralised forms of entertainment. But beneath this explicit aim one can possibly discern two far more sinister agendas. The first is a hatred of the power of television and hatred that identifies that power with the existing structures. Why not dismantle the existing structures, break up the big existing organisations, and the host of small independents will never wield that power again. More bluntly, and this thought must have passed through the mind of many a harassed politician, do away with BBC and ITV and no politician will have to fear television again. These thoughts are the merest folly. Television will wield its power over politicians more or less whatever structures are used other than direct state control. It is therefore crucial that this power is wielded with the responsibility of a regulated institution and not with the irresponsibility of an unregulated tabloid press. Concretely that means that while access for independents must be encouraged, the existing institutions must command enough resources to allow them genuine autonomy.

Second, and working at a much deeper level, is a desire to reproduce the nation that has died and the moral and social certainties which have vanished with it. One can see the desire surface in the attempts to arraign television for the tragedy at Hungerford. Even the sparsest details of Michael Ryan's life speak volumes on the fragmentation of any shared national culture. However, our contemporary politicians are unwilling to address seriously the particular mix of economic, social and psychic reality revealed by the sub-culture of the gun club and its associated macho magazines and networks. There must be one simple explanation for Hungerford and television is the visible example of the new semiotic world in which we live. Little matter then that there was no evidence that Michael Ryan watched television and less consideration of the fact that if it was images of sex and violence that fuelled his fantasies, they were almost certainly culled from the magazines and videos provided by his local newsagents and not from national television channels subject to rigorous policies of self-censorship.

The attempt to blame television as a cause rather than analysing it as a part of much wider social and economic processes is most evident in the activities and role of Mrs Whitehouse, for more than any other individual she symbolises the failed potential of television in the 60s and the society which flashed across its screens. What Mrs Whitehouse relentlessly reiterated was the necessity for a society to agree upon a set of shared values. That she assumed definitions of society and values which were hopelessly inadequate is, in this context, less important than the fact that the questions she raised were unanswered except in her own rather limited terms. Beyond her media transformation into a rent-a-quote figure and beyond her peculiarly Anglo-Saxon obsession with sex, she represented and articulated the claim of the ethical. Both makers and viewers in the 60s participated in the pleasures of the wake, a rowdy and raucous farewell to the dead. What was less clear, what is less clear, is what was being born.

The most serious danger facing television is that there will be an attempt, under cover of an appeal to market forces, to fudge and forge a false unity based on faded images of the nation. Let every broadcaster find the widest possible audiences under straightforward commercial pressures and we will once again recapture a nation untroubled by difference and diversity. The reality of this policy would be a television dominated by game shows and banal sitcoms punctuated by the national anthem playing over the portrait of the Queen. This would not involve the elaboration of values for our increasingly differentiated society but the assumption that they exist for a falsely unified one. Independently of the moral and cultural vacuity of such a policy, it will fail in its own terms because the economies and technologies of television are no longer national. The satellite footprints across the globe and the increasing importance of co-productions and foreign sales in the funding of television production would mean that this unified nation of viewers would be watching American sitcoms and game shows made under licence from Hollywood. Television would cease to have any active relation with the society it serves.

If we wish to think of an alternative, it is impossible to do so without some concept of public service. It is, of course, the case that it is currently unfashionable to talk of a public sphere with its assumption that social policy can be formulated in terms of shared goals. The coincidence of private economic interest and public social good is widely held to be a self-evident truth. It is not the purpose of this article to demonstrate that, at every level of society, from the family to large private corporations, the making of decisions is constantly informed by notions of a common good irreducible to notions of profit and loss. What is clear is that, given the existing technology, free-market television would deliver a range of undifferentiated programmes which would leave us, as citizens, considerably impoverished.

If, however, we are appealing to the concept of public service, it is itself a concept much transformed by the history of the past forty years. It is not inaccurate to say that Reithian notions of public service depended on a clear understanding of the existing values of the national culture and a determination to transmit those values. It has been the paradoxical thesis of this article that the television service informed by these values became the focal point for their fragmentation. If we are to take seriously the advances of the 60s, we cannot attempt to turn the clock back and produce a unified culture from on high. Public service must be defined and defended in contemporary terms. Are we to understand it as television entirely devoted to difference, the endless proliferation of fresh images and identities? This would be all television as Channel 4, with all broadcasters constantly seeking out new audiences. Such a strategy is still not technologically feasible, because if it were to cover the entirety of television production and broadcasting, it would inevitably require pay-per-view systems which have not yet been developed. More importantly, this vision of the future ignores the cultural reality of television. Much of television's appeal springs from the fact that viewers know they are watching what others are watching. The tabloids' fascination with the soaps is not an aberrant eccentricity but the reality of a society for which the common currency of much national life is provided by these continuous dramatic narratives and, in particular, the contradictions between the fictional characters and the real life of the actors who portray them. It is across these figures, both real and fictional, that many of the debates about private and public morality are conducted. In our current forms of social organisation, television will inevitably produce mass audiences: the problem is to provide a television system which will allow those mass audiences to divide and reconstitute in ways which allow both unity and difference.

It is this tension between mass and minority audiences, between innovation and repetition, that provides the real basis of the contemporary appeal to public service. It is also, in fact, the conception of television embodied in the differing remits and constitutions of our existing four channels. But if this is the case, why is there any need for reform? Have we not already got the television of the Silver Age? Those who urge reform claim that technological advance will inevitably transform television as we know it and that these changes should be used as an opportunity to allow more independent access to the airwaves. Technology and independence are brave new words and both have genuine meaning, but they carry with them profound and dangerous confusions.

Anybody who thinks that television is going to be transformed by the introduction of satellite broadcasting should consider the disastrous fate of cable in this country and its very partial success elsewhere. It is difficult to draw any very positive conclusions from the global evidence to date but broadcast network television is showing remarkable resilience in the face of competition from both cable and satellite and even from recorded cassettes. If it is important to encourage the new technological developments so that the viewer has greater choice, it is well to remember that choice depends as much on variety of production as on alternative channels of distribution. If we have eighty channels which spread existing resources between them then we will have eighty channels providing a diet of *I Love Lucy* re-runs and the golden hits of the BBC liberally interspersed with soft porn. Any appeals to new technology should not fudge the question of where the funds for production are going to come from and it would be a criminal folly if our resource-rich industry was dismantled in the name of a quite illusory notion of consumer choice.

The arguments in favour of independent access are not more important and potentially more dangerous than the appeals to technology. Legislating for non-existent technological futures is a harmless pastime of twentieth-century governments. The demand that independents be allowed on to the airwaves is both more of a reality and more of a fiction. (The BBC and ITV have, by and large, always functioned as monopoly producers for their own systems of distribution. The current government has been increasingly convinced that this monopoly position has allowed production costs to balloon and all we need to drive them down is genuine competition.) The problem with this argument is that with such a limited number of distribution outlets, it is not clear that you can ever achieve real competition between producers. None the less, the government has decreed that 25 per cent of both BBC's and ITV's output must be opened out to independents. The immediate effect is that, day by day, producers within both BBC and ITV are leaving to set up production companies that qualify as independents. It may be that the net effect of these developments will simply be the loss of huge economies of scale and an enormous increase in reduplicated overheads.

If, however, the economic arguments are double-edged, there can be no question that the cultural argument for independent production is overwhelming. The broadcasting organisations are enormous bastions of power and privilege which find much of their tone from the elite educational establishments of this country. They inevitably confer their style and attitude on those who work for them, and, at their worst, they manifest a complacent arrogance which refuses to see alternative points of view. It is essential that other perspectives, other working practices, other social groupings have the possibility of projecting their sounds and images on the national screens. If one is to develop fruitfully the process of social pluralisation that began in the 60s, then it is essential that ever greater numbers of people should have access to production facilities. The ability to produce and broadcast images should, at a Utopian vanishing point, become as easy and obvious as the ability to write and publish. This, of course, is substantially the philosophy that underlay the campaign for Channel 4. Unfortunately this cultural argument is becoming increasingly confused with the economic one. At its most unpleasant the campaign for independent access risks degenerating into the current union-bashing, a rather distasteful attempt by those outside the big institutions to grab the jobs of those inside. It is crucial that independent access really does broaden the base of those that make television and that it does not mean that exactly the same individuals go on making increasingly commercial programmes while more and more production monies are diverted into profits. The worse scenario would see the power of the broadcasting institutions pass to the City without any change in the programme-making personnel. The best would see the existing broadcasting institutions allowing access to a much wider variety of programme-makers while using the rigours of competition to strengthen their own institutional autonomy. For the reasons I have sketched, we cannot go back to the Golden Age of the 60s with its wealth of entertainment and education. If, however, the next stage of television reform is done properly, we will continue to have a television system which is part and parcel of a pluralistic and democratic society. If it is not done properly then we will enter a dark age of broadcasting in which television will never educate and barely entertain.

7   A Post-national European Cinema: A Consideration of Derek Jarman's *The Tempest* and *Edward II*

As Head of BFI Production, I spent much of my time dealing with Europe, and those deal-ings took place on two very different levels. The first was the network of small art-house dis-tributors and public service television commissioning editors who provided the audiences, and sometimes even a little money, for the films that the BFI was producing. The second was the bureaucrats and administrators in Brussels. The first were a joy to work with and con-vinced me, if as an English-born Irishman who had done graduate studies in France I needed convincing, that Europe was both a reality and a joy. The second convinced me that Brussels was a sink and a sewer in which any popular idea of Europe was likely to perish. In particular I found the whole thrust of European film policy deeply misguided. The econ-omic definitions of film which looked to Europe to provide competition for Hollywood ignored both the cultural traditions of European film from Rossellini on and the economic reality whereby Los Angeles is the only focus for the most important economic asset of the global industry: stars.

As Head of Production I had spent a fair amount of time at conferences debating the future of European film; as Head of Research I was in a position to call a conference which would look at the future of European film in terms of its past. It was at this conference at which I gave the first version of this paper that I made my final attempt to hold together my two experiences of Europe. 'My final attempt' because in my interview with Jean-Luc Godard which formed part of the proceedings, Godard said to me, with visible amazement, 'I'm surprised at you, Colin, showing this interest in Europe, you should know that histori-cally Brussels has never produced any great art.' If the exact terms of this comment were perhaps too literal, its spirit was all too accurate. My efforts to participate in the formation of a European cultural policy had been, in retrospect, the product of bureaucratic delusions.

At the conference I had taken as my text Derek Jarman's version of *The Tempest*, to argue that the Europe of the future only begins when we come to terms with the Europe of the past. Ten days later Derek showed me the fine cut of *Edward II*. It is difficult to describe the effect that this film had on me. It had always been clear that Derek was a film-maker of enormous talent and working with him on *Caravaggio* had been one of the most pleasur-able lessons of my life. But in his adaptation of Marlowe, he had reached a new level of intensity and analysis which he was to sustain throughout the final years of his life. I am very grateful that my preparation for the conference on Europe meant that I was able to write immediately on *Edward II* for *Sight and Sound*. Like so many others I loved Derek and it was a great personal pleasure to produce an article which he enjoyed and appreciated.

The following article combines both conference paper and magazine article.

In some senses it is almost impossible to question the notion of European culture; the two terms seem necessarily to define each other. But this definition of culture is specifically European: it relates to the great national cultures of Europe and to their founding fathers, the Dantes, the Shakespeares and Goethes. But you have only to sit, as I have sat, in conferences on Europe with Europeans whose forebears come from the Caribbean or from the South Asian continent to realise how point-less such a litany can sound, how far removed those national cultures are from the contemporary realities of multinational and multi-ethnic Europe. The real question is: How are we to understand the founding moments of those great national cultures in conjunction with a Europe whose other founding moment has come back to haunt it? If we think back to that period in the sixteenth century when western Europe expanded to asset-strip the globe, what comes back in the twentieth century is the fundamental asset of labour which is now imported to service late capitalism.

The problem is that if we wish to grasp the reality of this moment it becomes difficult to know, or to understand, how we can define it as specifically European. In the movement from the sixteenth to the twentieth century we pass from a European to a global perspective, a perspective which demands that we analyse contemporary culture in terms of an imperialist imposition of authoritative norms which are then contested, negotiated, mimicked in the crucial emphases of our post-modernity. But that post-modernity would seem to have no more time for European than for national cultures as the crucial terms become the global and the local.

It might seem that we can short-circuit these theoretical difficulties by appealing to a practical political level at which European culture makes sense. Independently of the particular political rows about the single currency, or the powers of the European Commission, the European Community is becoming an ever increasing political reality, and it is that political reality which is increasingly part of any European cultural agenda. It is such pragmatic realities which dominate much of the institutional concerns of bodies such as the British Film Institute, and have dominated the multitude of conferences on Europe and the cinema which have taken place in the last few years. These concerns and conferences are not without their successes. The MEDIA 95 programme for European Film Funding proliferates, growing new arms like a monster from a 50s sci-fi movie. But it is when one reflects on an initiative like MEDIA 95 that one realises that there is no real way to short-cut the theoretical problems by appeals to political reality. All the discussions around MEDIA 95 make two massive cultural assumptions: the first is that American cinema is a cultural threat, and the second, as a necessary corollary, is that there is some evident meaning to the notion of European cinema and European culture. Within such forums any attempts to raise genuine questions about European culture are treated both as impertinent and irrelevant. Impertinent because we all know what European culture is, irrelevant because we must eschew such intellectual levity for the realistic rigours of 'policy'. In fact, almost all appeals to 'policy', like its repellent semantic cousin 'management', are appeals away from a reality which is too various and too demanding. But it is the cultural reality of Europe which must be faced, and faced urgently, if we are not to bungle the enormous possibilities offered by the growing movement towards political unification.

To understand our current cultural situation, it is my own deep belief that one must step into the 'dark backward abysm of time'. These are the words that Prospero uses at the beginning of *The Tempest* as he reveals to his daughter the world beyond their island. The world that we need to understand is not the Milanese court and its intrigues, which Prospero addresses, but the cultural space of the Elizabethan and Jacobean theatre which Prospero and Miranda inhabit. The film-maker who has been most preoccupied with this historical reality is Derek Jarman ever since, in *Jubilee* (1978), the magus John Dee escorted Elizabeth I on a tour of her kingdom four hundred years on. For Jarman the investigation of what it is to be English is inseparable from a reworking of the controlling myths of the English Renaissance. Three years after *Jubilee*, Jarman made his own version of *The Tempest*.

Let us start with Shakespeare's version. The play starts eponymously with a tempest and a consequent shipwreck. The ship carrying the King of Naples back from the wedding of his daughter to an African (itself an interesting fact in the light of the play's concerns) is separated from its flotilla and wrecked on an island. The wreck itself divides the passengers and crew: Ferdinand, the heir, finds himself alone; the nobles form one group and the crew, with the exception of Trinculo, are confined to the ship and kept there for the duration of the play. It is at this point that we learn from Prospero, the magician who rules this tiny kingdom, the history of the island, or rather the history of his arrival and conquest of the island. He disposes of the former ruler of the island, the witch Sycorax, frees her captive Ariel, the airy spirit, who is then bound to him for twelve years (a period which will coincide with the end of the play), and enslaves her son Caliban, this 'thing of earth'. The play then pursues two sub-plots in which the nobles plot against the king and Caliban conspires with Trinculo to overthrow Prospero, while the main theme follows the courtship of Ferdinand and Miranda, all these events obsessively supervised by Prospero with the help of his spy Ariel.

While the play may seem entirely European, set in the Mediterranean, its source is not (as for almost all of Shakespeare's other work) a European story but a contemporary event in the Caribbean. In 1609, while sailing off Bermuda, an expedition led by Sir Thomas Gates was caught in a tempest, his ship was separated from the rest, and he was presumed lost. A year later Gates arrived in Virginia, having spent the intervening year on a magical island, which furnished the survivors with all they needed to eat and drink. It is from this contemporary story that Shakespeare actually weaves his tale. In this context it becomes clear that the problematic of *The Tempest* is the problematic of the relationship between Europe and the New World which had only been discovered a century before and was in the process of colonial appropriation. Caliban is not simply 'this thing of earth', the savage man who has a long history in European thought, but also an anagram of his own name: the cannibal, the inhabitant of this new world. Prospero's relationship with him is evidently, among other things, an allegory of Europe's relation with the New World.

It is fashionable at the moment, in the current jargon of post-coloniality, to read *The Tempest* entirely in relation to Caliban, to stress the extent to which one must understand the play as Shakespeare's meditation on the particular way in which the colonial is constituted as what is not civilised but then, in a complicated and reciprocal moment, is considered to be that which defines civilisation.[1] In the contemporary critical climate this is defined as the political reading. From this point of view Jarman's *Tempest* is an embarrassment, for his Caliban is white and the concerns of colonialism are largely absent from his film. But these contemporary readings ignore another, and as important, political reading which concentrates on the formation of the new nation states which will dominate global history for the next four centuries. Explicitly, these concerns are present in *The Tempest* in terms of the politics of the court of Milan. Jarman rigorously excludes all such concerns from his film.

In *The Tempest*, however, he makes clear how Prospero's reign is one of terror. It was, not that long ago, fashionable to imagine the Elizabethan age as one of social harmony. More recently, and in the wake of the new historicism, political divisions have been understood as contained by cultural power.[2] What both ignore are the twin foundations of the Elizabethan terror state, torture and espionage. If one wants to think of London at that time then what I always think of first are the gates, the walls of the city, outside which are the theatres along with the brothels and the new factories, but mounted on which are the bleeding quarters of those who have just been executed – noted by contemporary Protestant tourists to London as signs of England's civilisation.[3] The crucial element in this machinery of terror was Walsingham's secret service, and we can read Ariel in *The Tempest* as an allegory of that secret service, forced under pitiless conditions to spy on every corner of the island, and to bring to his master Prospero that information which underpins his power. It is for this reason that Jarman's *Tempest* concentrates on the relationship between Prospero and Ariel with its barely suppressed sexual undertones. Jarman's homosexuality is what leads him to concentrate on the repression at the heart of the English state from which all the other repressions follow: the complete containment of sexuality within sanctified heterosexual marriage, the rigorous policing of desire and excess, the focusing of male sexuality and the denial of female sexuality. These are the fundamental themes of *The Tempest*, the sexual politics which underpin the birth of capitalism as it appropriates its colonial surplus.

But Jarman clearly understands, even more clearly in his art than in his discourse, how this sexuality is linked to certain traditions of representation. For if the security apparatus is the skeleton of the state, then the new national culture is the flesh. At the heart of this culture is a rigorous divorce between representation and audience. The traditional and much mocked reading of *The Tempest* is that it is autobiographical, that Prospero is Shakespeare and that when Prospero at the end says that 'every third thought shall be my grave', it is Shakespeare's own voice that we should hear as he bids adieu to his audience. In fact, if that traditional autobiographical account is placed within the wider context of theatrical history then it once again becomes very plausible. The theatre in which Shakespeare started to work at the beginning of the 1590s and in which Marlowe was already the transgressive star was a very different theatre from that to which he bid farewell in 1611. Not only was it more directly popular and addressed a much wider social audience but it was also one which posed direct political and cultural threats to the State. By the time he wrote *The Tempest*, Shakespeare was writing for a representational space which was much more contained both aesthetically and socially. That is the crucial point of the masque that Prospero puts on for the lovers in Act IV, the masque that will celebrate their wedding. In his instructions to Ferdinand and Miranda, his attempts to control them as they sit, his order that 'No tongue! all eyes! be silent!', Prospero reproduced the new relationship to the audience, a relationship where without tongues, reduced to vision, the audience is excluded from the representational space. It is this space, directly filiated to an aristocratic culture, which disinherits the popular traditions on which Shakespeare had drawn so contradictorily. The biographical nature of the farewell comes in the recognition of what has been repressed and disinherited.

It is the fracturing of that representational space which makes *The Tempest* such a subversive film, for it sets itself not on an island, but in a ruined aristocratic house, an imperial monument. If the viewer grasps that this is a house, there is no way in which he or she can organise the space that is presented. We cannot connect room to room or inside to outside. And, as if to make the point more explicit, Caliban is played by Jack Birkett, the blind actor. It is this Caliban's blindness which places him categorically outside Prospero's cultural space. But if we can understand Jarman's undoing of the space of *The Tempest*, if we can see him using the cinema to undo the rigid distinctions of culture and sexuality which *The Tempest* so brilliantly performs, we must also admit that, in many ways, and whatever the borrowings from the popular culture of the twentieth century, it remains caught within that exclusive cultural space that it seeks to undermine. Brecht's 'fundamental reproach' to the cinema was that it could never escape that divorce between representation and audience which he termed 'Aristotelian' but which is more properly understood in terms of the Renaissance theatre (Brewster, 1977).

In the aftermath of *The Tempest*, one could be left wondering where this filmic subversion of the relation between representation and audience could ever do more than endlessly interrogate itself. Jarman's disruption of cinematic space (in terms of costumes, sets, and articulation of shots and scenes) seems to invite (like so many Leftist critiques) a nostalgic Utopia in which the ideal is a carnivalesque union of audience and representation, a return to a moment before any of the divisions of labour on which capitalism constructs itself. That carnival is, of course, realised for Jarman in the Super-8 films of the 70s, but they remain irredeemably private, films which can only be truly enjoyed (as in their original screenings) by an audience entirely composed of their actors.

The counterpart of this personal privacy is the absence of any real public political sphere in *The Tempest*. Jarman excises the power politics of the kingdoms of Naples and Milan, but the film is then left in a curious vacuum in which the critique of representation and sexuality remains curiously unanchored. Jarman triumphantly solves this problem in *Edward II* (1991) when the political plot is made to turn (and turn even more emphatically in Jarman's version than Marlowe's) on direct sexual repression. *Edward II* would seem to mark a final settling of accounts with Jarman's chosen historical space: that interface between the Renaissance and the present which was first unveiled by John Dee in *Jubilee* and which had been investigated again and again, in *The Tempest*, in *The Angelic Conversation*, in *Caravaggio*. But all these films fade into apprentice works beside the achievement of *Edward*. Christopher Hobb's sets and Sandy Powell's costumes triumphantly realise what one now sees was only hinted at in *Caravaggio* (and Italy may always have been a diversion): a world which is always both now and then (both twentieth and sixteenth century) but is always England. At its heart is the constitutive relation which founds the modern English state on a repressive security apparatus and a repressed homosexuality. Jarman makes all these arguments with the deftness and lightness of a painter's hand. From the moment that Mortimer appears with the dress and bearing of an SAS officer in Northern Ireland, the equations between past and present, between state and sexuality, are clearly visible on the screen.

Jarman's *Edward* continues a debate about national and sexual identity which goes back four centuries to that moment at the beginning of the 1590s when the Elizabethan stage became the privileged symbolic space for a whole society. The exact date of Marlowe's play might seem of interest only to the most pedantic of scholars but, in fact, it is crucial to the play's significance that it comes right at the end of Marlowe's career, probably in 1592. Crucial both personally and culturally, for by 1592 Marlowe was a man deeply engaged not only with the Elizabethan theatre but also with that other alternative employment for a man of letters who did not want to join the Church or to occupy the position of learned scholar in a great lord's house: he was deeply implicated in the modern foundations of the Elizabethan state – Walsingham's secret service.

Culturally the play can be seen as a direct response to Marlowe's new rival, Shakespeare, whose trilogy *Henry VI* had attempted to produce a version of English history which would find ethical and political meaning in the bloody shambles which had produced the Tudor dynasty. Marlowe's response is that of the arrogant intellectual who has known the pleasures of both political and sexual transgression. There is no meaning to be deduced from these chronicles of blood and treachery, except Mortimer's wheel of fortune (a sixteenth-century version of Ford's dictum that 'History is bunk' but with none of that twentieth-century tycoon's optimism), and to emphasise the nihilism Marlowe places a perverse love at the centre of his story. But for Marlowe this perversity is very closely linked to the new learning from which he draws his own legitimacy. There is absolutely no warrant in the chronicles for turning Gaveston and Spenser into intellectual parvenus. Edward's minions they may have been, but they were as well born as Mortimer and the other barons. For Marlowe they represent the new class, of which he is a prominent member, who will sell their learning to the new state but will, in the end, be crushed by that very same state. It is Gaveston's and not Edward's death which uncannily foreshadows Marlowe's own end, that great reckoning in a small room when Ingram Frisar, almost certainly with the Privy Council's blessing, stabbed Marlowe days before he was to appear before that same Council to answer charges of blasphemy. Four hundred years on, Marlowe's death remains no less of a mystery but it is not unreasonable to speculate (as become wearingly and repetitively obvious in our own century) that political and sexual secrets make the most likely of bedfellows and that in an age when sodomy was a capital offence there may have been more than one member of the Council who was concerned that Marlowe's testimony might end with a lethal outing.

Jarman's film is not, however, Marlowe's play. Marlowe's identification with new knowledge and learning of the Renaissance gets no response from the director ('such an intellectual queen', as Jarman remarks in a marginal note to the script), and Jarman's Gaveston and Spenser are not overlearned smart young men working for MI5 but very rough trade indeed. What Jarman has always insisted on is that he be recognised for what he is, and *Edward II* is, in that sense, unquestionably his most autobiographical work in what has been a consistently autobiographical *oeuvre*. But it is the bovine, middle-class ox Edward that Jarman identifies with, not the street-smart Gaveston whom he loves but who is here presented without redeeming feature except that 'he loves me more than all the world'. The film is also much more ambiguous in its misogyny than ever before. In that gay dialectic where identification with the position of the woman is set against rejection of the woman's body, *Edward II* is entirely, and without any textual foundation, on the side of rejection. For Marlowe, as for his age, the love of boys is merely the ultimate sexual transgression, not in any sense an alternative to heterosexual sex. It is here that Jarman does violence to his source, making Edward's passion for Gaveston a consequence of his inability to be roused by the queen's body, a truly chilling scene at the beginning of the film. This is itself horribly overturned at the end, however, by the murder of Kent when Tilda Swinton's magnificent Isabella literally tears the life out of him with her teeth; every fantasy of the castrating woman, the *vagina dentata*, rendered into all too palpable image.

But there is love in this film, and a love which redeems history. The film is punctuated by scenes from the end of the play as Edward and his murderer-to-be, Lightborn, discourse in the bowels of the castle where the king is imprisoned. We await throughout the film the fabled end, the vicious poker which will leave a king dead and humiliated and without a mark on him. It is this end that the film has prepared us for as we see the homophobia which courses as a vicious lifeblood through our history and our culture. No fault of Gaveston's can possibly excuse or justify the hatred which is spat out at him as he is forced through a gauntlet of hatred on his way to exile and a death unbearable in its explosion of destructive violence. As Mortimer comes to upbraid the king for his moral turpitude, the barons at his back suddenly reveal themselves as a moral majority stretching back and forth across the centuries, an endless, and endlessly unpleasant, Festival of Light.

But after the end that Marlowe and history has prepared us for, Jarman has contrived a happy end from the resources of his own fight against death. As Lightborn approaches the king for a second time with the dreaded poker in his hand, it falls from his hands and in a moment of real tenderness he bends and kisses the king. That Lightborn is played by the great love of Derek's life, Keith Collins, the 'H.B'. of the diaries, gives this most powerful of scenes almost unbearable force. With this kiss a whole history of homophobia and violence is annulled, a whole new history becomes possible.

It is at this point that *Edward II* becomes possible, drawing the audience into the most private of worlds, not merely as spectator but as participant (and in this respect the published screenplay is an integral part of the film). The Outrage slogans which punctuate the text, like the film itself, demand reaction. It is in the multiplication of the forms of address around the text that Jarman provides a solution to Brecht's 'fundamental reproach'. For Brecht, the theatrical setting is still a unity, the alienation devices simply fragment that unity from within. Jarman, here working with the grain of advanced capitalism, breaks the unity of the cinema experience from without. The celebrity interview, that crucial tool of marketing, is here turned into a method of disrupting any separation of public and private, and thus depriving the moment of viewing of any simple aesthetic unity.

It is this multiplication of address, and its refusal of the divorce between public and private, which enables Jarman to solve the problems of *The Tempest* in *Edward II*. The private is made public and, as a result, the public sphere can be incorporated into the film. The state, which disappears from his *Tempest*, is now centre stage but that stage can now contain the most public proponents of the abolition of privacy, the militants of Outrage. It is not, I think, unreasonable to suggest that it is the pressure of death, that unique meeting of the public and private, that has been the catalyst for the extraordinary experiments that marked the last five years of Jarman's work. This is signalled within the film itself when, as the screen dims, the final lines, which are Jarman's rather than Edward's or Marlowe's, are:

Come death, and with thy fingers close my eyes,
Or if I live let me forget myself.

It is striking at this point, and in the context of the politics of any future European film, to compare Jarman's film with Kenneth Branagh's *Henry V*. *Henry V* is a crucial play for Shakespeare – both the final answer to the problems that Marlowe had posed him seven years earlier in *Edward II* and the first play in the new Globe theatre. The power politics with which the bishops open the play is transcended by the national divinity which Henry represents. And the final farewell to an older cultural space is witnessed in the death of Falstaff, standing in for Will Kempe's (the great clown who had embodied Falstaff) refusal to join the new company. It can come as a surprise only to those who refuse to understand the links between sexuality and representation that it is in this play that the formal mastering of the female body is accomplished by the naming of Katherine's body in English and her marriage to the English king. It says a lot about the sheer bad taste of Branagh's film that his idea of taking licence with the text is to have Falstaff appear in flashback and to rehearse the famous Chimes at Midnight speech (which only makes sense as a conversation between two old men) as a dialogue between Hal and Falstaff. But this is all of a piece with the cultural nostalgia of Branagh's project (which is exactly captured in the name of his company). The Renaissance theatre will now use the cinema to reproduce the Elizabethan stage shorn of all its contradictions. What in Olivier's magnificent film is the cultural corollary of the last tragic moment of the English state (extinguishing its own empire in the fight against Fascist Germany) becomes in Branagh's tepid offering the farcical analogue of Thatcher's hideous mimicry of Churchill. Jarman's use of his Renaissance model has absolutely nothing to do with Branagh's. The text of *Edward II* (as in Olivier's *Henry V*) is placed at the service of pressing contemporary concerns. Unlike Olivier, however, Jarman's film responds to both public and private need and calls the very distinction into question.

I think that these reflections should enable us to understand something of the specificity of European film. What is specific to Europe, within a global context which emphasises the local and the international, is the question of the nation state. It is no accident that Jarman never hesitates to stress his cultural conservatism, for what he returns to, again and again, are the founding myths of Englishness. Jarman, it could be argued, is trying to rescue, from underneath the monument of the nation, the last ethnic minority – the English. It is exactly the release of these buried ethnicities which constitutes the reality and risks of European culture and politics today. This is not to say that there is no question of cultural prescriptivism, that all European film-makers should now address the question of the nation. What it does say is that in so far that European film-makers make films that are specifically European, those films will focus on the reality of national identities and the possibilities and risks that are contained in their transgression.

Notes

1 See, for example, Stephen Greenblatt, *Learning to Curse – Essays in Early Modern Culture*, New York and London, Routledge, 1990.
2 See Stephen Greenblatt, 'Invisible Bullets: Renaissance authority and its subversion – Henry IV and Henry V' in J. Dollimore and A. Sinfield, *Political Shakespeare: New Essays in Cultural Materialism*, Manchester, Manchester University Press 1985, pp. 18–47; and Steven Mullany, *The Place of the Stage: Licence, Play and Power in Renaissance England*, Chicago, Chicago University Press, 1988.
3 Auon (n.d.), 'A short admonition or warning upon the detestable treason wherewith Sir William Stanley and Roland York have be trailed and delivered for monie unto the Spaniards, the town of Deventer, and the sconce Zutplier'. Sig A iiii, recto. My attention was drawn to thus pamphlet by my colleague Curtis Breight, *Surveillance, Militaryism and Drama in the Elizabethan Era*, London, MacMillian, 1996.

PART THREE

Readings – Intellectuals in Transit

8 Fredric Jameson

One of the major intellectual tasks that I set myself when I became Head of Research at the British Film Institute was to try to bring leading cultural critics to the Institute in order to get them to speak specifically about film in a general intellectual context. Cornel West, John Berger and Marina Warner were among those who took up this invitation. Fredric Jameson was one of the earliest of such visitors and his lectures on four aspects of world cinema in 1990 were so compelling that the British Film Institute decided to publish them in book form the following year. My publishing colleagues felt, however, that Jameson's difficult style and complex intellectual allusiveness required an introduction which I should provide. I was more than happy to undertake this task. Jameson is one of the few academics writing today who uses the vast array of scholarship at our disposal to address genuinely important questions. Any effort of mine that could bring his work to a wider audience, particularly to an audience of film scholars, was an effort well worth undertaking.

Fredric Jameson is probably the most important cultural critic writing in English today. The range of his analysis, from architecture to science fiction, from the tortuous thought of late Adorno to the *testimonio* novel of the Third World, is extraordinary; it can truly be said that nothing cultural is alien to him. He is one of the very few thinkers who genuinely ignores the conventional distinctions between cultural objects: he will as readily bring the same care and attention to the deliberately complex works of high modernism as to the very different complexities of cyberpunk. As importantly, he will move between media: the analysis of a text will be followed by a social description of a building, the criticism of a mainstream film will be succeeded by an appreciation of an avant-garde video.

At the same time it must be admitted that his work is particularly difficult, the first encounter with these long and complex sentences in which the sub-clauses beat out complicated theoretical rhythms can be almost vertiginous. At one level this difficulty must simply be encountered – Jameson's style is an integral part of the effort to understand the world as both one and multiple, and if there is difficulty and awkwardness there is also pleasure and grace. But Jameson's work is difficult in another way. He is a systematic thinker, like Sartre and Adorno, his two great masters. That is to say that even the most local and specific analysis finds its place within an overarching theoretical framework. The specific analysis is always related, albeit in dialectical fashion, to an extraordinarily sophisticated and detailed theory of culture and society. That theory, however, provides the underlying assumptions and reference – it is not present explicitly in every text. It is thus the paradoxical case that to read Jameson is always to read the entire *œuvre* rather than a single particular text. It is a feature of such systematic thinking that it may very often have a slow start – as the basic premises are worked out – but once these premises have been elaborated, more and more material is illuminated by their perspective. Jameson's own bibliography and career follows this pattern as a patient understanding of French and German theory throughout the 60s and 70s then gives way in the 80s to a riot of cultural analysis, starting with *The Political Unconscious* (Cornell University Press, 1981) at the beginning of the decade and working through a whole variety of media in the aftermath of that book.

Although an intense private interest in film had emerged in the 70s with articles on *Zardoz* (*JumpCut*, no. 3, Sept/Oct 1974) and *Dog Day Afternoon* (*Screen Education*, no. 30, Spring 1979), Jameson's full theoretical engagement with film is a product of the recent past, with the lectures at the British Film Institute in May 1990 – which form the basis for this book – and the publication in the same year of *Signatures of the Visible* (Routledge, 1990). It is thus possible that readers will be unfamiliar with some of the crucial assumptions of Jameson's thought. A full exposition, which also took account of the way in which the engagement with film feeds back into the theoretical assumptions, would be material for yet another book but it is worth very briefly glossing three terms which are crucial to Jameson's endeavours: the political unconscious, post-modernism and cognitive mapping.

The Political Unconscious

Jameson is a Marxist and traditionally that has meant granting a primacy to the forms of economic activity in an understanding of cultural forms. The most traditional form of Marxist analysis presupposes that an analysis of the economic base will then enable one to read off elements of the cultural superstructure from law to literature. There are two classic theoretical difficulties with this position. The first concentrates on the difficulty in defining the mechanism which leads from base to superstructure. How exactly does economic organisation cause effects at levels which cannot be directly related to it? The second, possibly even more serious, questions how one can define the economic base without having recourse to categories which are themselves superstructural – how, for example, can one describe any set of economic relations without notions of ownership which are legally inscribed?

These two theoretical difficulties are perhaps of less importance to cultural analysts than the practical difficulty that if one adopts a classic Marxist position then all cultural forms end up with the same content. One must resign oneself to endlessly analysing the same messages – in the end, there is simply the endless recoding of property relations which are themselves to be analysed in economic rather than cultural terms.

It is to this practical difficulty that Jameson's theory of the political unconscious responds. Jameson is by training a linguist and a literary analyst – trained to respond to the smallest variations of meaning. For him, it is crucial to develop a form of Marxist analysis which will respect and utilise these differences rather than collapsing them into an undifferentiated reflection. To accomplish this, he makes the radical theoretical move of assuming that the relation to the economic is a fundamental element within the cultural object to be analysed – not in terms of the economic processes within which the cultural object takes form but in the psychic processes which engage in its production and reception. For Jameson's every text is at its most fundamental level a political fantasy which in contradictory fashion articulates both the actual and potential social relations which constitute individuals within a specific political economy. In postulating this textual level Jameson is fundamentally influenced by the Christian tradition, and its most important recent literary critic Northrop Frye, rather than any of the theorists or critics who have addressed this problem within the Marxist tradition. The religious perspective allows a non-sociological approach to the connection between the individual and the universal.

The great advantage of this solution is that it allows Jameson to respect levels of textual and cultural differentiation. In fact, these differences become a primary element in the development of analyses of new social and economic relations. This advantage is much more striking in *The Geopolitical Aesthetic* (1991) than it was in the original *Political Unconscious*. The original theory was elaborated in the context of a reading of nineteenth- and early twentieth-century fiction. The political unconscious at work in texts by Balzac or Conrad provides a way of reading a social history and an economic analysis – which are in their outlines very well understood within the Marxist tradition. Balzac and Conrad provide the material to produce a more nuanced account of what is in essence, a well understood story. *The Geopolitical Aesthetic*, on the other hand, addresses contemporary texts and provides readings which suggest radical new ways of formulating both a social history and an economic analysis.

At the same time, Jameson's theoretical originality enables him to maintain an orthodox Marxist position which allows primacy to economic forms or organisation, with the nuance that those forms may well need to be understood in the light of analyses produced within cultural texts. Jameson is thus locating himself on very different ground from the various forms of cultural materialism which are currently the dominant academic inheritors of Marxism. For these last emphasise the impossibility of splitting cultural and economic analyses at any theoretical level and thus refuse the primacy to the economic which Jameson still allows. Jameson's position has the advantage of being able to draw fully on the traditions of both literary and cultural criticism as well as classical Marxism. It also provides an original solution to the need to provide some account of a dialectic between economic and cultural categories. However, it falls prey to the most obvious question that has to be asked of any base/superstructure model: What mechanisms translate social organisation into cultural forms? What is novel for a Marxist theory is that what Jameson's account lacks is a psychology rather than a sociology. What Jameson requires is an account of the mechanisms which articulate individual fantasy and social organisation.

Post-modernism

If the political unconscious provides the key theoretical term for Jameson's endeavour, the key historical category is that of post-modernism. Post-modernism is a term notorious for its extraordinarily fluid meanings and extremely complicated history. For our current purposes let us simply identify three meanings which contribute to Jameson's use of the term. From the 50s onwards, particularly in America, post-modernism was a term used by literary critics to refer to contemporary works ranging from the Beat movement to campus novels which obviously indicated a new sensibility but, equally obviously, could not simply be linked into the concerns of what was becoming an increasingly institutionalised modernism. As modernism came to dominate the university curriculum, a new term was needed for new literary movements. Some twenty years later in France, and particularly in the work of Lyotard, post-modernism gained increasing currency as a term which would cover both contemporary culture and the new post-industrial economy and society which nourished it. By then it had also gained polemical currency in architectural debates in a devastating attack on modernism and the concerns of the modernist movement, a meaning only hinted at in the previous two uses.

For Jameson the term is crucial as a means of designating a completely new social positioning of art. Post-modernism is not fundamentally a question of subject-matter or themes but of the full entry of art into the world of commodity production. Jameson's definition is thus a fully Marxist one crucially linked to Mandel's analysis of the current stage of global multinational capitalism as marking a new stage in capitalist development. Post-modernism is the cultural form of the current movement of late capitalism just as realism was the privileged artistic form of the first stage of capitalist industrialist development and modernism corresponded to the economic moment of imperialism and monopoly capitalism.

Jameson's analysis, which emphasises the full integration of economic and culture, can thus be understood as both congruent and completely opposed to the modernist perspective of Adorno and the Frankfurt School. For Adorno the commodification of art marked the final abolition of any autonomous perspective from which to criticise the dominant forms of economic development. For Jameson the moment at which cultural production is fully integrated into economic production opens out the possibility of a cultural politics which would fundamentally intervene in the economic.

If the first cultural reaction to capitalism is a realism which attempts to provide forms of representation which will comprehend this new stage of economic development, modernism is the appalled recognition that any such representation is itself subject to social and economic forms which relativise its comprehension in relation to changing audiences. Modernism is the attempt, after a loss of innocence about representation, to invent forms which will determine their own audiences, to project an interiority onto a future unmediated by any form of commodity. It is for this reason that the history of modernism is marked by new forms of sponsorship and above all by an avant-garde ethic which, be it of an aesthetic or political form, looks into the future for an ideal Joycean or proletarian reader. Modernism thus constitutes itself, well before the cultural analyses of an Adorno, as an area of art constitutively opposed to commerce. The effort to project the self onto reality is premised on a perfected future man who will become the ideal audience for ideal art.

Nowhere are these assumptions more obvious than in modernist architecture and nowhere have their inadequacies been made more apparent. Architecture, which has always been the traditional art most fully integrated with the economy, is the neuralgic point of modernist breakdown as the pretensions of a Le Corbusier and Frank Lloyd Wright run up against the realities of the post-industrial city. It is for this reason that Jameson's analysis of post-modernism is so firmly anchored in the architectural debates of the late 70s. But if architecture is the traditional art most difficult to disassociate from the economy then film is properly the post-modern art – impossible to understand outside the full development of the first stage of capitalist development. Cinema is a product of the most sophisticated forms of industrial production; it is, in Hollis Frampton's memorable words, the last machine.

One then has to reckon with the historical paradox that this post-modern medium recapitulates the basic realism/modernism/post-modernism aesthetic development, with the classic Hollywood cinema representing realism (and a moment of innocence about the means of representation), the European cinema of the 50s and 60s reliving all the paradoxes of modernism (and Godard is here the exemplary figure) and a fully post-modern cinema having to wait until the early 70s. It is now a cinema in which the distinctions between high and low art (always precarious) have more or less vanished and where culture and economics cross and recross at every level of both fields. It is cinema which still more than any other medium provides – if not the universal form – at least the possibility of combining the most ancient and local artistic traditions with the most modern and global advertising campaigns. It is a cultural form permeated at every level by the practices and paradoxes of marketing – a post-modern practice which oscillates between the passive reproduction and the active remodelling of audiences. If the politics of realism are implicitly reformist (the understanding of society leading directly to its control) and those of modernism vanguardist (in which it is the future tendencies of the system which provide the basis for political action), it is not yet clear what the politics of post-modernism will be, though it is clear that they will articulate the ever increasing levels of micropolitics with those almost paralysed stirrings towards global forms which date back to the League of Nations.

If film is the most post-modern of art forms (the discussion about its relation to rock music and television would be a separate book) then it will also be one in which the current political unconscious may most fruitfully be analysed. This is the wager of Jameson's book as he attempts to analyse the geopolitical realities of post-modernism cinema. His method, however – the selection of four disconnected moments in current world cinema – depends on a further term: cognitive mapping.

Cognitive Mapping

Cognitive mapping is the least articulated but also the most crucial of the Jamesonian categories. Crucial because it is the missing psychology of the political unconscious, the political edge of the historical analysis of post-modernism and the methodological justification of the Jamesonian undertaking. The term is taken from the geographer Kevin Lynch's *The Image of the City* (MIT Press, 1960) and is used by him to describe the phenomenon by which people make sense of their urban surroundings. Effectively, it works as an intersection of the personal and social, which enables people to function in the urban spaces through which they move. For Jameson's cognitive mapping is a way of understanding how the individual's representation of his or her social world can escape the traditional critique of representation because the mapping is intimately related to practice – to the individual's successful negotiation of urban space. Cognitive mapping in this sense is the metaphor for the processes of the political unconscious. It is also, however, the model for how we might begin to articulate the local and the global. It provides a way of linking the most intimately local (our particular path through the world) and the most global (the crucial features of our political planet).

Most importantly, however, it provides a justification for Jameson's own cultural analyses of the past decade and of this book in particular. There has been a considerable amount of criticism of Jameson for attempting to generalise about global situations from limited information. Should Jameson ever choose to respond to such criticisms it would have to be in terms of the fact that such generalisation is an inevitable cultural process. The point is to make sure that the information (which will always be limited) is none the less sufficient to produce a map which will overlap at certain crucial points with other grids of interpretation and which will produce the terms for further political and economic analysis.

Theoretically speaking, cognitive mapping needs more than mere development – it is fundamentally a metaphor which needs to be unpacked into a series of concepts which would link the psychic and the social. At the same time, it proves a very adequate account of Jameson's own personal project. As life in general, and academic life in particular, has become more global there is no figure who has more thoroughly attempted to expand his field of analysis accordingly. There may be more assiduous travellers of the airlines of the world but I know of no-one who more systematically and thoroughly attempts at each new destination to experience both the local cultural forms and their local forms of analysis. In these terms Jameson can be understood as attempting to join the journalistic function of reporting to the intellectual project of cultural analysis. From this perspective, the theoretical underpinnings are beside the point. What those who attended the lectures at the National Film Theatre in May 1990 were privileged to hear and what this book now provides for its readers are a series of cultural reports. What these reports make clear is how crucial it now is to understand film in its global complexity if one is to hope to understand it in its local specificities.

One of the great excitements of this book is the way that the perspective it obtains enables an entirely fresh look at the whole question of film and politics. Ever since the mid-70s questions of politics within film theory have largely been couched in vanguardist terms. The positions elaborated by *Screen* now seem in retrospect to be a terribly belated last gasp of modernism in which a figure like Godard promised to articulate the relation between art and politics prefigured by Mayakovsky and the Formalists in the Soviet 20s or Brecht and Benjamin in the German 30s.

Since the *Screen* of the mid-70s there really has been no new attempt to theorise the relations between politics and film. While there is always the production of local ideological readings, particularly fuelled by identity politics, these rarely engage with film as form and history. What Jameson suggests is that we must now analyse film comparatively – that we can only understand a film's politics when we place it both in its local political context and its global context as film – for any film will inevitably reflect on what one might call its place in the global distribution of cultural power. In this, Jameson's analysis relates very neatly to the massive new importance of festivals as forms of exhibition.

One striking feature of this text is how the analysis advanced in May 1990 has been amply confirmed in the following two years. The fundamental figure of conspiracy and, particularly, the confusion between conspirators, victims and police finds text-book confirmation in films like *Total Recall* (1990) and *JFK* (1991). Even more striking is that the fundamental grids that Jameson offers – the encounter of the former Soviet states with capitalism, the resurgence of local realities in the successful economies of the Pacific, the continuing 'underdevelopment' in the 'Third World', the complicated search for a European culture – seem ever more pertinent in a world where the political dominance of America is now equal to the cultural dominance that Hollywood achieved over half a century ago. Any future attempt to analyse politics and film will have to take issue with arguments advanced in this book.

9   James Snead

One of my saddest tasks of the past decade has been the editing of the posthumous papers of my student and colleague James Snead. The following article served as an introduction to the book on black cinema *White Screens/Black Images* which he had all but completed at the time of his death. With Kara Keeling and Cornel West I have edited a further collection of published and unpublished papers and stories which will be published in the near future.

James Snead died on 26 March 1989 in Pittsburgh. In my last conversation with him, and when I was completely unaware of the terminal nature of his illness, he said, apropos of the fact that he had had to abandon teaching for the term, 'One good thing about this illness is that I am going to get both books finished.' The books he was referring to were the history of black representation in American cinema on which he had been working for the previous three years and a book on African-American culture which he was writing with Cornel West and which the three of us had discussed in a memorable all-night session the previous year in Philadelphia. When James died, both I and his brother George, to whom he had spoken at much greater length and who he had charged with the responsibility to ensure posthumous publication, were overwhelmed by the state of Jamie's papers and computer files.

The volume of work accomplished by someone who was only thirty-five at his death and who had spent (unusually for an English academic) a couple of years working as a banker for Chase Manhattan was simply staggering. Four novels, numerous short stories, papers and lectures without end – and all this in addition to the published work on Faulkner. However, there was not, as we had both been expecting, two books almost ready for the printers. Of the planned collaboration with Cornel West there were only the merest traces. Of the book on American black cinema, there was too much and too little. Too much in the sense that there were three or four versions of each chapter. Too little in the sense that there was no definite outline of the book and no clear sense of James's own priorities in the versions of the chapters he had left. Indeed, the best indication of the book James had planned was a version that he had given me a year earlier. What then began was a long editorial process which, in different geographical circumstances, would have been much shorter. George Snead and the physical material were in Los Angeles, Cornel West on the East Coast and I was split between Pittsburgh and Europe. A first collation, with the three of us, was attempted in February 1990 in Los Angeles. More work was carried out by Cornel West and George Snead that autumn and a final version and a division of responsibility for the introduction arrived at by Cornel West and myself in the extraordinarily unlikely setting of

Reno, Nevada in September 1991. The editorial process was completed by a diligent and talented copy-editor at Routledge.

The text of the book that one can now read is not the text that James would have himself approved. The arguments of the second half of the book would have been worked into a continuous text and there would have been a very full illustration of all the arguments through impeccably researched stills. None the less I feel confident that in this book one can read Jamie's major arguments: the centrality of black representation to a history of Hollywood, a refusal to read that representation as merely a positive or negative, and a linked determination to read it in relation to the deepest of political and sexual fantasies. There are, however, two omissions which must be noted. The first is, apart from one or two sentences, a lack of any material on the blaxploitation genre (*Shaft, Superfly*) of the early 70s. Any attempt to give a general history of black representation in America would have to deal with this first Hollywood reaction to black power, which appeared to code certain blacks positively while establishing that definition within a cripplingly limited and stereotypical view of the ghetto. This absence is not of crucial importance – it was clear how to develop Snead's analysis to deal with what was never more than a relatively minor genre. The second absence is both more important and absolutely inevitable. Spike Lee's *Do the Right Thing* premièred at Cannes a mere two months after James's death and the last three years have seen an explosion of films by black directors, financed by the mainstream. James's death robbed these films of the one intellectual who was really prepared for their arrival, and it seems to me that it is impossible to read his reaction to them from the terms that he develops in this book. Indeed, this book should have been part of the cultural context into which these films first appeared. Instead it will appear in the aftermath of that first wave which culminated in John Singleton's *Boyz N the Hood* (1991). One can only hope that it will contribute to the debate about them, the debate that Snead foresaw when he wrote about black film-makers:

> It will be interesting to see in the coming years whether the oppositional aesthetics and thematics of their earlier 'independent' films can be adapted for mass-market consumption. Some would doubt whether white Americans can ever learn to see blacks and themselves from a black, and not a white, vantage point ... Perhaps the greatest challenge for future black film-makers, independent or not, is to find a way to prevent an imagistic co-optation in which an insincere, ritualized tolerance of recoded images may itself become just another way of keeping blacks out of the picture. (p. 119)

It is certain that the debate will go on without James Snead but it is also certain, and this gives a real idea of Jamie's stature, that the debate will be missing a crucial voice. In this age of ever increasing specialisation it is important to recognise that Snead was not a specialist in film studies. His scholarly interest in film came about because in 1985 Cornel West was invited to give a lecture about black film which he felt unable to attend. As Cornel himself said in his memorial lecture delivered at Pittsburgh in April 1989, the invitation was itself a sign of the crucial scarcity of black intellectuals – so that those that do exist are constantly being asked to comment on areas outside their specialisation. Cornel, however, suggested that Jamie take up the invitation and it took very little time for him to see the scholarly and intellectual challenge offered by the whole question of blacks and cinema. While important empirical pioneers had opened up the field in the 70s, they had opened it up using very simplistic forms of analysis in terms of positive and negative images. They had not used the crucial terms of cultural analysis developed from the insights of French thinkers like Roland Barthes and Jacques Derrida. For Snead the first crucial step was to recognise the structuralist insight that all signs can be defined diacritically – and thus that any analysis of race must recognise that any definition of black always involves definitions of white. The second and complementary step was to adopt the post-structuralist perspective that diacritical definitions were always in process – articulated in a perpetual process of signification where it was impossible to isolate the couplet black/white without further examining its ramifications in relation to other fundamental distinctions, particularly sexual ones.

What Snead saw quickly was that the cinema, the major cultural form of the twentieth century, bore eloquent witness to W. E. B. Dubois's claim that the 'Negro' is the central metaphor of the twentieth century and this book is nothing more nor less than the investigation of how that metaphor was deployed in the cinema to articulate the unconscious bases of the power relationships embodied in master/slave, civilised/primitive, good/evil. In these days of easy academic superlatives, in which every assistant professor is an outstanding scholar making a groundbreaking contribution to our knowledge, it is difficult to find the terms which convey the power of Jamie's intellect, the ferocity of his industry, his absolute commitment to the life of the mind. To many it will be surprising, indeed difficult to believe, that someone could master both the theoretical terms of film theory and the history of Hollywood so quickly but one should not underestimate the speed at which Jamie could work nor the genuine mastery that he could achieve.

As his PhD supervisor at Cambridge I was the last person to so underestimate him. He first burst into my life at Cambridge in an absolute rage. He had arrived in Cambridge, as many American students before him, to discover that he was expected to spend his two years there completing another undergraduate degree (the Part 2 of the English Tripos). To someone as ambitious, in every sense of the term, as Jamie, such marking time was almost criminal. He therefore besieged the administrative instances of the English faculty and they, surprisingly (but Jamie was very black, very big, and very mad at the thought of wasting two years), said that he could indeed register as a PhD student if he could find a member of the faculty willing to supervise him. He arrived in my office having already been turned down by a number of my more cautious colleagues. I immediately asked him if I could look at some of his work and he gave me his Scholar of the House dissertation from Yale on Mann and Joyce. When I read it I was astonished both by his grasp of literary modernism but also by his profound philosophical culture, by his intimate understanding of Hegel and Nietzsche. I had no hesitation in accepting him as a pupil because, by my own reckoning, his undergraduate work was, staggeringly, already of doctoral standard. However, I was more concerned about the topic. He himself wanted to continue his work on Joyce and Mann but I was against that for a number of reasons. I felt not only that he had to a large extent already mastered European modernism and that his doctorate would thus just repeat reading he had already accomplished but also that a great deal of work

129

was currently being published on these topics (including my own book on Joyce). More importantly I felt very strongly that if the power of post-structuralist reading was to indicate more than its own virtuosity, it was important to anchor those readings in real historical contradiction and I therefore suggested to him that he consider Faulkner. Not only was *Absalom! Absalom!* the great modernist text which had received relatively little critical attention but in Faulkner the paradoxes of modernist writing were integrally linked to questions of race. It was at this point that I was made aware of the truly phenomenal nature of Jamie's appetite for work. Within a few months he had not only read through the entire Faulkner corpus with an intensity of attention which made every line yield up its formal strategies as well as its content but he had also worked his way through the secondary Faulkner literature and made a very good start on the contextual history and sociology. In the thesis, in which Faulkner was linked to Joyce, and in the subsequent book which concentrated purely on Faulkner, Jamie read the modernist disruption of representation around the impossibility of and necessity to establish difference in the world. His work showed clearly how Faulkner is intent on engaging his readers in the problem of representation, the very process of differentiation through which we divide the world into identities. The racial segregation of the South is overlaid on sexual difference to provide both style and theme of the books – with an incestuous miscegenation constantly threatening to ruin all identities both linguistic and social. One of the troubling emphases of this work is to suggest that racial oppression is simply the most appalling and evident examples of a process endemic to any form of representation which must always divide in order to identify.

This fundamental philosophical theme is one that runs through the work on Faulkner, pitting Plato against the pre-Socratics and Nietzsche, showing how the Platonic emphasis on identity is unable to solve the paradoxes of representation. It is these paradoxes which Faulkner dramatises again and again – identity is only ever the product of a difference which renders identity constitutionally unstable. Race then becomes both form and content for Faulkner, the necessity to separate black and white becoming sexually, socially and linguistically the neuralgic and impossible centres of his work.

The authority with which Snead deploys his grasp of both the western philosophical tradition and the historic reality of modernism is astonishing but the political force of the book is often pessimistic. Snead is absolutely clear, and makes the point repeatedly, that the liberation of the blacks in the South is inseparable from the liberation of the whites. Faulkner's work makes all too separately clear that liberation cannot simply limit itself to allowing the black man to accede to the position of the white man – that position must be transformed. However, that transformation is never addressed directly by Faulkner and, partly as a result of this, Snead's argument comes close to a pessimism that would see some form of discrimination (not necessarily based on race) as inevitable, the ineluctable accompaniment of the will to power as knowledge.

This pessimism is completely set aside in the current book. Produced under the impact of a black history and a current black struggle, *White Screens/Black Images* is shot through with anger and with hope. The book demonstrates how central the representation and exclusion of blacks has been to the most powerful of twentieth-century art forms. But it also celebrates the growing power of a black cinema which is determined to challenge those representations and exclusions. At the same time, and this might have been the missing conclusion of the book which would have engaged with Lee's films, there is no consideration of the paradoxes of representation which were sketched so forcefully in the Faulkner book. The current struggle over representation in the cinema is not linked to the struggle of representation itself, the Utopian question as to whether the representations necessary to make a world exist can be decoupled from central repressions which would anchor this world in sexual and racial difference.

It might be tempting, if one did not know James, to read the move from European modernism to Faulkner to black cinema as a growing acceptance of blackness of the kind that Stuart Hall has recorded so forcefully in his accounts of his own intellectual development. But James Snead was of a younger generation to Stuart Hall and had been reared on the slogan of 'I'm black and I'm proud'. I myself would therefore read this movement in a slightly different manner. James was, and was conscious of being, the first generation of his race to be raised in the purple of the white educational establishment. He was determined to conduct his intellectual life at the most strenuous level, engaging with the most difficult and central arguments about representation. His development follows his growing belief that those central arguments inevitably involved questions of race. Unhappily he was prevented from following this development to their full conclusion. Whether he would have been able to link the political positions of *White Screens/Black Images* to the profound philosophical pessimism of the Faulkner analysis and to have engaged both across the full range of his experience is a question that is impossible to answer.

What is certain is that this book is in and of itself a major contribution to film theory. In the last decade much of the serious work in film theory and history has been concerned with very local analysis. The overweening ambitions of the early 70s when the semiotic analysis of Metz was linked to Althusserian Marxism and a Lacanian psychoanalysis to produce a general theory of film has given ground to much more precise formal analyses and much more specific film history. There are many positive elements to these developments – it is no exaggeration to say that much of the early theoretical work made assumptions which were entirely based upon ignorance and that our understanding of the multiple determinants of any particular film is now vastly improved. At the same time there is a risk that this correction has in its turn gone too far and that we risk losing sight of the crucial role that film has played in the forming of twentieth-century attitudes and values.

White Screens/Black Images redresses this balance. The analysis of particular films and histories is at the service of a general attempt to understand how film dramatises and enacts fundamental social divisions.

Snead understands

film as (in the words of Jean-Luc Comolli and Jean Norboni) 'ideology presenting itself to itself, talking to itself, learning about itself'. My work on Hollywood film analyzes stereotypes in terms of codes they form, and makes these codes legible, inspecting their inner workings, as well as the external historical subjects they would conceal. (p. 2)

By stressing how codes mobilise a whole series of expectations Snead is able to break out of an analysis which simply analyses representation of blacks in terms of positive or negative images. It is through the deployment of the notion of code together with the associated concepts of 'marking' (the fact that blackness is always over-emphasised) and 'omission' that Snead is able to demonstrate how central the representation of blacks is to Hollywood's overall vision of the world.

One of the great merits of Snead's book is that it reminds us how historical analysis must be informed by contemporary film-making and, at the same time, how our understanding of contemporary film is immeasurably improved if we understand its historical context. Snead's reading of the classic Hollywood tradition enables him to stress the importance of the work of contemporary black film-makers in Britain and America. At the same time his understanding of that tradition grows out of his real engagement with that contemporary work. What James Snead discovered in film was a field in which historical analysis could feed into contemporary practice. I have no doubt that Snead's work will have important consequences for film theory but those consequences will feed back into both black and white film-making as Snead's analyses sharpen our perception of what is at stake in the representation of race.

There could be no more fitting memorial.

10   Gayatri Spivak

One of the great intellectual pleasures of the late 80s at Pittsburgh was to have Gayatri Spivak as a colleague in the English department. There can be few examples of anyone who has so rigorously held together the philological and critical claims of the literary tradition with the epistemological critique of Derrida's deconstructive project and the political force of Marx's analysis of exploitation. If this intellectual trilogy was not sufficiently complex, Spivak has constantly inflected it in terms both of gender and of post-coloniality. The force of her work comes from her continuous refusal to privilege any one of the elements that make up her fields of inquiry. I was delighted when Bill Germano at Routledge asked me to introduce her first collection of essays *In Other Worlds* (New York and London: Routledge, 1987), not least because it forced me to engage fully with the range of Spivak's arguments and references.

Gayatri Spivak is often called a feminist Marxist deconstructivist. This might seem a rebarbative mouthful designed to fit an all-purpose radical identity. To any reader of her remarkable book it will come to seem a necessarily complex description, limning not an identity, but a network of multiple contradictions, traces, inscriptions. The book does not merely state that we are formed in constitutive contradictions and that our identities are the effects of heterogeneous signifying practices: its analyses start from and work towards contradiction and heterogeneity. Illumination is a necessarily transitory and conjunctural moment. Any foreword to this work is, of necessity, asked to address the three fields of feminism, Marxism and deconstruction. However, much of the force of Spivak's work comes from its reiterated demonstration that these fields can only be understood and used in a constant attention to their interpenetration and re-articulation. Any simplifying foreword thus runs the risk of reducing the potential of this productive work. The task is, however, worth undertaking exactly because these texts are of importance to anyone concerned with our understanding of culture. Better: with the relation both of culture and its interpretation to the other practices that shape our lives.

   What aid to the reader, then, is proposed by a foreword? Lurking somewhere, no doubt, is the fear that these essays are 'difficult'. Difficulty is, as we know, an ideological notion. What is manually difficult is just a simple job, what it easy for women is difficult for men, what is difficult for children is easy for adults. Within our ascriptions of difficulty lie subterranean and complex evaluations. So if Spivak's work is judged to be difficult, where is that difficulty held to reside? Although these texts have been published in learned journals, their effectivity to date has largely issued from their delivery as spoken addresses. Judgments of difficulty have thus tended to remain at the level of speech, of rumour. It may be of use to dispel some of these rumours, to enable the reader to engage more quickly with the pleasures and challenges of Spivak's inquiries.

Let us quickly enumerate the ways in which these texts are not difficult. They are not difficult stylistically: this is periodic English at its most pleasurable, interpolated with the occasional sharp American idiom, elegant and concise. Nor is the difficulty that all too typical obscure, omniscient and irritating academic manner, which classes epochs and cultures with a whimsical aside and no reference to sources. Not for Spivak an analysis of Chinese culture based on a few second-hand sources, nor the empty rhetoric of 'since Plato'. Every analysis is carefully annotated, by someone who is, at least in this, a model product of an Indian undergraduate and an American graduate education – probably the most scholarly combination on this planet. Indeed, one of the minor uses of this text is the way the footnotes offer an annotated bibliography to several of the most interesting Marxist and feminist debates of the past two decades.

There is another, more subtle way in which the whispered rumour of difficulty is often intended. What we are talking of is a 'difficult woman', a 'difficult native'. Spivak herself describes so well what is at stake here in 'Explanation and Culture: Marginalia' that I would find it impossible to improve on her acute account of the structures of an academic conference, and the corridors of knowledge and tables of learning where the marginal aside is made with central purpose. All that is worth stressing here is that one doesn't need the substantive, carefully erased from the academic conscious, to grasp the meaning of the adjective. What is at stake here is tone, gesture, style – a whole opera and ballet of sexist racism which continues to dominate the academic theatre and which should be challenged every moment it appears; especially given the difficulty that, when challenged, it vociferously denies its own existence.

There remain, however, two real levels of difficulty in these texts, and although these two levels cannot finally be theoretically separated they can be differentiated at a practical level. The first is unavoidable – it is the difficulty which is inevitably involved in any serious attempt to reflect and analyse the world within publically available discourses. No matter how great the commitment to clarity, no matter how intense the desire to communicate, when we are trying ourselves to delineate and differentiate the practices and objects which are crucial to understanding our own functioning and for which we as yet lack an adequate vocabulary, there will be difficulty. Only those supremely confident of their own understanding – those who would deny all reality to history or the unconscious or matter – can bask in the self-satisfied certainty of an adequate language for an adequate world. This should never be taken as a *carte blanche* or a willed esotericism which figures an equally complacent certainty in the inadequacy of language: the literary countersign of technocratic stupidity. However, there will be a certain difficulty in reading *any* work which is genuinely trying to grapple with some of our most urgent problems which do not yet – and this constitutes their most problematic intellectual aspect – have the clarity of the already understood. To deny this real level of difficulty in Spivak's work could be misleading.

With much of such difficult work there are, however, immediate reference points within existing disciplines and arguments, which easily serve as an initial orientation. But this does not prove to be the case with Spivak's essays. However measurable the style and however detailed the references, Spivak's texts radically transgress against the disciplines, both the official divisions of anthropology, history, philosophy, literary criticism, sociology; and then unofficial divisions between Marxism, feminism, deconstruction. There are few ready-made categories or reading lists into which her arguments fall. This is no accident: one of the major arguments of her book is that the academy is constituted so as to be unable to address the most serious of global questions, and that, in fact, many of the most radical critiques remain completely within terms set out by the constituted academy. Spivak's theme here is large: the micro-politics of the academy and its relation to the macro-narrative of imperialism. But this is a theme without subject: one that lacks reading lists, introductory guides, and employment opportunities. It is not easily located in relation to the established subject divisions (what is a literary critic doing discussing economic theory?) nor vis-à-vis what are becoming the relatively well-mapped fields of Marxist, feminist and deconstructionist criticism.

There is, therefore, some point in providing crude categorisations of these three 'oppositional' positions and locating Spivak's work in terms of them. The problem is also to stress the provisionality of this categorisation; to remember/encode the fact that this homogeneity is, in each case, wrested from a heterogeneity which is forever irreducible to it but which cannot be grasped except as a limit, an excess beyond which, for a particular discourse, intelligibility fades. Such a thought is indebted to the work of Jacques Derrida, and Gayatri Spivak is still probably best known as the translator of his most famous work *Of Grammatology*. She is, therefore, obviously a deconstructionist. She says so herself. And yet this extraordinary collection of essays, gathering together some of her most important work of this decade, lacks the defining features of deconstruction in America.

This paradox is merely an index of the poverty with which Derrida's thought has been received in the US. Norman Mailer, in one of his characteristically acute asides, remarked that Kerouac was an 'Eisenhower kind of gypsy', and deconstruction 'US' style has been a 'Reagan kind of radical theory'. Its significance and importance in the United States is entirely in terms of the development of the academic discipline of literary criticism; indeed, it has become a dominant method of contemporary literary education. It subjects texts to the rigorous forms of analysis developed by Jacques Derrida, analyses which tease out the fundamental oppositions which underpin and make possible any particular discourse and which show how those oppositions are always themselves caught up in their own operations – how they become the vanishing point of a discourse's own intelligibility.

Derrida elaborated this work in the context of Heidegger's meditation on Being and in an attempt to recapture the revolutionary potential of a series of the key texts of literary modernism – Mallarmé, Artaud, Joyce, a project which found its rationale in the situation in France in the 1960s. An adequate account of that period does not exist – we even lack the most banal elements of a positivist cultural history. What can be said with some certainty, however, is that it was in large part a reaction both to the sudden advent of consumer capitalism under de Gaulle and the widely perceived exhaustion within the French Communist Party. In the decade after 1956, France went through one of those periods of accelerated and overdetermined change which were, in retrospect, to be phenomenally rich in social contradiction and cultural production. If one wanted to emblematically grasp this commitment both to radical politics and the analysis of the new and complex text of consumer capitalism, the pre-eminent theoretical text would be Roland Barthes's *Mythologies* (1957). Culturally one could gesture towards Jean-Luc Godard and his films of the mid-60s such as *Deux ou trois choses que je sais d'elle* (1966). Politically one could think of the Situationists and texts such as Guy Debord's *Society of the Spectacle* (1967) and Raoul Van Eigen's *The Revolution of Everyday Life* (1967).

These are, admittedly, very disparate figures but all, at different levels, attempted to grapple with the elaborate signifying systems of advanced capitalist society: the immense network of significations, from advertising hoarding, to magazine, to television – the circulation of signs in which the subject is constantly figured and refigured. The concept of text developed in that period – and associated concepts such as deconstruction – found a specific intellectual and political purpose in the attempt to both articulate the reality of the dominant culture and to escape its stereotyped identifications.

It is easy, particularly for one who lived through its boundless excitement and energy to recall this time as a simple golden age. To do so is to ignore its manifold problems. It too simply assumed the intellectual arrogance of both vanguard politics and vanguard art; and although I would argue that much of its initial emphases came from the explosion of consumer culture in France, it never actively engaged with that culture but instead postulated another radical cultural space constituted largely by a neo-surrealist canon. Its contemporary texts were theoretical rather than literary. Most importantly, it never really articulated a new politics or that thoroughgoing revision of the Marxist heritage that it promised.

By the time this intellectual project was transported to America in the 1970s, following a dubious success in France, it was transported as an individual – Derrida – and its terms were altered. The project was divorced from its attempt to refind the revolutionary force of modernism, in which the institutions of art were always in question, and relocated within a much safer and domesticated Romanism, where art retained a clearly delineated institutional space. 'Text', far from being a concept-metaphor with which to deconstruct both individual and society in order to grasp their complex of contradictory determinations, became metonym for literature, conceived in all its exclusive and elitist forms; textuality became little more than a fig-leaf behind which one could hide all difficult questions of education and class. Deconstruction came simply to name the last privileged defence of the canon in a way brilliantly described in the second essay in this collection. It was reduced to a powerful method which would reveal the sameness and the greatness of the major literary texts.

In her long third essay on Wordsworth, Spivak dots the i's and crosses the t's on this particular development within the literary academy, reintroducing to one of the privileged texts of American deconstruction the sex and politics that Wordsworth is at such pains to erase in his attempt to construct an art which will be troubled by neither. But if Spivak is critical of the domestication of deconstruction, she is not concerned with returning to its radical origins. Independently of any deconstructionist doubt about the originality of origins, Spivak shows no enthusiasm for the project of modernism or the attempt in the 60s to revive its radical potential (she would probably want to criticise the original project and its renewal in feminist terms). The enormous contemporary interest of these essays is that they develop some of the concepts and approaches of the 60s in the context of two concrete but very different dimensions: the development of the university in the advanced world and the developing forms of exploitation in the Third World. Spivak's determination to hold both of these situations, both of her situations, in constant tension, in a perpetual deconstructive displacement, is what provides many of the astonishing insights and measures in *Other Worlds*. Deconstruction, for Spivak, is neither a conservative aesthetic nor a radical politics but an intellectual ethic which enjoins a constant attention to the multiplicity of determination. At the same time, Spivak is absolutely committed to pinpointing and arresting that multiplicity at the moment which an enabling analysis becomes possible. The difference between Spivak and Derrida is best captured in their respective attitudes towards the pathos of deconstruction: 'the enterprise of deconstruction always in a certain way falls prey to its own work', writes Derrida in a comment which surfaces frequently in these essays. But what has become for Derrida, *the* abiding question, is, for Spivak, a limit which cannot obscure the value, however provisional, of the rigorous analyses that deconstruction enables.

To grasp the interest of Spivak's work necessitates going beyond the binary opposition between First World intellectual production and Third World physical exploitation. Running across both in further contradiction/production is her situation as a female academic and as one who has played a significant part in that explosion of feminist theory and practice which has marked the last twenty years.

Spivak's feminism may well seem as initially unreadable as her deconstruction. This stems from her conjunction of a rejection of any essentialism with an emphasis on the crucial importance of examining and reappropriating the experience of the female body. While Spivak avoids the sterile debates of deconstruction, or comments on them only obliquely, she is a willing participant in feminist debates, but a participant who problematically combines positions which are often held to be antithetical. Many feminists have wished to stress an essential feminine, an area repressed by male domination but within which it is possible to find the methods and values to build a different and better society. The most notable opponents of such a view have been those influenced by psychoanalysis, and specifically its Lacanian version, who stress sexuality as a construction produced through familial interaction. Neither male nor female sexuality can be understood *as such*, but only in their interdefinability as the child seeks to locate itself in the complicated exchanges within the nuclear family.

The psychoanalytic thesis thus proposes both a fundamental bisexuality, a bisexuality which finds its primary articulation in the dialectic between being and having the phallus. All questions of direct access to the body are bracketed for psychoanalysis by the need for the body to be represented or symbolised – indeed, failure of such a representation entails psychosis. Thus for Lacan the real is that to which we do not have access and whose disappearance from the field of consciousness is the condition of intersubjectivity. Feminists who accept this account do not question political struggle and the need to supersede male domination, but they argue that it must find its forms and aims in specific situations and cannot be elaborated in relation to an essential feminine nature. Spivak's opposition to essentialism is, in the first instance, deconstructive rather than psychoanalytical.

'Woman', like any other term, can only find its meaning in a complex series of differentiations, of which the most important, or at least the most immediate, is man. It is as ludicrous, in deconstructive terms, to talk of an essential feminine as it is to talk of any other essence. It is not ludicrous, however, on this account to talk of the specificity of the female body. If deconstruction is critically sensitive to any account which bases itself on a privileged moment of experience, it is exactly to allow full force to the heterogeneity of experience. It follows that, for a woman, that heterogeneity must importantly include the experience of her body, an experience which has been subject to the most rigorous male censorship down the ages and finds a particularly shocking, but for Spivak, exemplary, form in the practice of clitoridectomy.

Spivak develops the experience of the female body in two radically different directions. On the one hand she wishes to stress the clitoris as the site of a radical excess to the cycle of reproduction and production, and on the other, to emphasise that the reproductive power of the womb is crucially absent from any account of production in the classical Marxist texts. Further, she argues that it is only when the excess of the clitoris has been taken into account that it will be possible to situate and assess uterine social organisation. It would be difficult to overestimate the skill with which Spivak weaves these themes together in relation to the classic Marxist theme of production.

Before moving on to Marxism, what of psychoanalysis? Only the briefest and most provisional of answers is possible. This is partially because Spivak is never interested in psychoanalytical theory as such but rather in its use by literary theory as a radical fabulation with which to explicate the functioning of texts. Spivak would seem to accept an account of the child's acquisition of a sexual identity which would place that acquisition in the social interplay of desire. She would, however, explicitly, object to the phallus being made the crucial term in this equation and, implicitly, to the description of the family as the only site of significant desire. While it is clear that, for Spivak, the womb must be considered in this exchange, she does not indicate how the relation to the clitoris would differ, nor how she would displace the primacy of vision, which awards the penis pride of visible place in any psychoanalytical account. But, as I have said, psychoanalysis is not one of Spivak's most urgent concerns, and it may remain for others to develop further her extraordinarily suggestive comments in psychoanalytic terms.

Marxism is, however, an urgent concern, one that insists throughout these essays. But it is a Marxism which will be alien to at least a few Marxist critics. For this is a Marxism crucially grounded in Third World experience and is therefore a Marxism which concentrates on imperialism and exploitation, one that is both critical of, and finds no use for, the normative narrative of the modes of production. While most recent Marxist cultural criticism in the developed world has been occupying itself with revising the crude economistic models of base and superstructure, it has always been prone to a repression of economics; it has conveniently forgotten the necessity of locating those cultural analyses within the organisation of production and its appropriation of surplus. Often 'Marxist' now means nothing more than a commitment to a radical or socialist politics and the adoption of the classic mode of production narrative – the transitions from slave, to feudal, to capitalist orders. This, it must be stressed, is not meant simply as a condemnation but as a description of the difficulty of analysing contemporary developed countries in the terms elaborated in *Capital*: the problems posed by the analysis of the enormous middle class; the decline in factory production; and, above all, the growth of computerised production in the last ten years. In this context the claim that labour power is no longer the major productive element within the developed economies becomes plausible.

From a Third World perspective, however, such a plausibility is itself seen as the management of a crisis and the classic Marxist analysis of exploitation, as expanded to account for imperialism, makes more sense – as Spivak indicates in many telling asides. In the essay 'Scattered Speculations on the Theory of Value' these asides are located within a thoroughgoing argument which fully retains Marx's account of exploitation grounded in the theory of surplus value. The argument is both extraordinarily complex and interesting, and all I can hope to do here is indicate its major vectors.

Spivak clearly realises that to retain the theory of surplus value it is necessary to retain its basis, which Marx had adopted from classical economics: the now much questioned labour theory of value. She accomplishes this by a thorough re-reading of the first section of *Capital* volume I, supplemented by the *Grundrisse*. Her most audacious move is to deny that Marx ever adopted the labour theory of value in that 'continuist' reading which proceeds in relations of representation and transformation from labour to value to money to capital. Instead, Spivak argues, we have to understand Marx's account of value not as indicating the possibility of labour representing itself in value but as an analysis of the ability of capital to consume the use value of labour power. By concentrating on use-value as the indeterminate moment within the chain of value-determinations, Spivak breaks open that chain, redefining labour within a general account of value, which makes labour endlessly variable both in relation to technological change and to political struggles, particularly those around feminism. Even if I have understood it correctly, the argument is too complex to do full justice to it here. Suffice to indicate one reservation and one consequence. The reservation is that in order to explain the continuing exploitation of the Third World, Spivak stresses the contradiction whereby capital has to produce more absolute and less relative surplus value. But it is not clear to me that this distinction survives her critique of the 'continuist' account of value. What is clear, however, is that while Marx has perfectly grasped the constitutive crisis of capitalism, he has not provided an account of any other mode of production; for if there is no fixed relation between value and labour, it is impossible to understand the appropriation of surplus outside a full understanding of the organisation of value within a particular community. This consequence may be seen as endorsed by Spivak because, for her, normative accounts of mode of production have impeded Third World struggles.

If she wishes to retain Marx as a theoretician of crisis, she is happy to bracket him as a philosopher of history. This is not simply because the Asiatic mode of production offers a classically inadequate account of historical Asian societies but because the notion of a 'transition' to capitalism has crippled liberation movements, forcing them to construe their struggles in relation to the development of a national bourgeois class. For Spivak, the attempt to understand subaltern classes only in terms of their adequation to European models has been deeply destructive. The political project becomes one of letting the subaltern speak – allowing his or her consciousness to find an expression which will then inflect and produce the forms of political liberation which might bypass completely the European form of the nation. It is this momentous project that produces context for Spivak's final essays.

This work takes place in, and in relation to, the historical collective called *Subaltern Studies*. While Spivak endorses the group's abandonment of the modes of production narrative, she argues that such renunciation is not enough. As long as notions of discipline and subjectivity are left unexamined, the subaltern will be narrativised in theoretically alternative but politically similar ways. To avoid this dominating disablement, historians must face the contemporary critique of subjectivity both in relation to the subaltern (it cannot be a question of restoring the subaltern's consciousness but of tracing the subject effects of subalternity) and in relation to themselves (as they recognise the subject effects of their own practice). It is only when the full force of contemporary antihumanism has met the radical interrogation of method that a politically consequent historical method can be envisaged.

It is such a method that Spivak employs in the final reading of Mahasweta Devi's magnificent and terrible story 'Breast Giver'. Here Spivak demonstrates the importance of undoing the distinction between literary criticism and history or, which is the same undoing at another level, the distinction between imaginary and real events. This is not the aesthetic stupidity of 'all history is literature'. Put crudely, the thesis is no more than Marx's dictum that ideas become a material force when they grip the masses. But what Spivak argues is that to understand this process the analyst of culture must be able to sketch the real effects of the imaginary in her object of study while never forgetting the imaginary effect of the real (the impossibility of fully grasping her situation) in her own investigation. But where Lacan understands that real entirely in relation to a castration which sets the imaginary in place, Spivak understands that real as the excess of the female body which has to be placed in its cultural and economic specificity and only thus can an imaginary be figured.

The force of Mahasweta's text resides in its grounding in the gendered subaltern's body, in that female body which is never questioned and only exploited. The bodies of Jashoda and Dopdi figure forth the unutterable ugliness and cruelty which cooks in the Third World kitchen to produce the First World feasts that we daily enjoy. But these women's bodies are not yet another blank signifier for masculine signifieds. These women articulate (better, construct) truths which speak of our as well as their situation. The force of Spivak's reading resides in its attention to the dialectic between real and imaginary which must be read in these texts and in its attention to how that dialectic reflects back on the imaginary and real of contemporary theory. Spivak's courage lies in confronting both sides of this dilemma: reading Mahasweta's text with the full apparatus of contemporary western critical discourses while also, at the same time, using that text to read the presuppositions of that critical apparatus. Any other position but this would involve that simple acceptance of a subject-position which is, for Spivak, the inevitable sign of bad faith. The force of Spivak's work lies in her absolute refusal to discount any of the multiplicity of subject-positions which she has been assigned, or to fully accept any of them. In that sense Spivak is always in 'another world' – always allowing herself to be pulled out of the true. This is the ever movable ground of these texts, and as one reads one is both illuminated by the thought and moved by the exhilarating and painful adventure that subtends it. But this text is not simply a personal odyssey, it is also the trace of a series of struggles: of leftist politics in Bengal, of the 60s within the American university system, of feminism worldwide. It is only insofar as these texts can be useful to such struggles that they will be effective. No guarantees for such effectivity can be given in advance. These essays on cultural politics cannot be understood simply as a set of analyses; it is only insofar as they serve as an aid to action that they could possibly complete their own undoing. That action is multiple and heterogeneous. I have not the competence to speak of India or the Third World nor the scope to speak of the variety of political struggles in the advanced world. Suffice to say the full significance of this work will rest on events outside its control, and whether it will come to mean something for what comes after is not in any individual's power of choice.

It seems necessary for me, however, to end this foreword by going beyond the limits of Spivak's text, with some specific comments on the micro-politics of the university in the developed world. It immensely diminishes the potential of this book to limit to the one world of the western academy. But of course it is not one world – any one world is always, also, a radical heterogeneity which radiates out in a tissue of differences that undoes the initial identity. One could perhaps talk of here of the dialectic between theory and politics where theory (like travel) pulls you out of the true and politics (like homecoming) is what pulls you back. One could perhaps turn to Wittgenstein here and, misquoting, argue that 'differences come to an end' – in other words that particular identities, whatever their provisionality, impose themselves in specific practices.

There is one formal identity and specific practice that I share with Spivak: it is not simply that we are both university teachers, but that from this year we are teachers in the same department of English in the same university of Pittsburgh. If one limits oneself to the simple and most obvious point, one might begin by reflecting on the limitations imposed by the very notions of a discipline of 'English'. The construction of English as an object of study is a complex history, but it relates to the academic division of the social world enacted by capitalist imperialism in the nineteenth century and neo-colonialism in the twentieth. You can study literature, primitive societies, advanced societies, past societies, foreign societies, economic forces, political structures; you can even, if you move outside the Ivy League, study television and film. You are, however, disciplinarily constrained not to presuppose a common subject-matter. The world automatically divides into these categories.

Of course, it is true that much vanguard research crosses disciplines, but this is written out of the undergraduate and graduate curricula. If, however, the humanities and social sciences are to get any serious grip on the world, if they are to enable their students to use their studies, then it is imperative that there is a general recasting of the humanities and social sciences. On the one hand, students must confront the enormous problems facing the world; on the other, they must understand the relation of their own situation to those problems. The degree of micro-political resistance to any such educational reform will be considerable. The individual fiefs that will fall, the networks of power and patronage that will dissolve are not negligible. But daily, such fiefs disappear; daily, networks dissolve.

Underlying this resistance will be a genuine problem: has not knowledge advanced to the point where the data is so vast and the specialties so complex that any possible programme, which is not technically and specifically limited, will simply produce graduates who know a little about everything but have mastered nothing? This problem, however, carries with it the seeds of its own solution. It is true that knowledge is expanding exponentially, but the problem then becomes one of training students in the use and analysis of data. Within the social field it would become the task of confronting the organisation of data that the child/citizen is offered in the most unified way by television, and beginning to consider the specific form of that organisation. From that analysis it would then be possible to chart a way through the various disciplines in relation to the problems encountered and the questions produced. I am not proposing a media studies for all in which pitifully thin analyses of pitifully thin programmes become the privileged object of knowledge. I am, however, proposing a pedagogy which would take as its starting point the public organisation of social data as the way to provide a possibility of judging and checking both the data and the organisation. Such a pedagogy would be genuinely deconstructive in that the position of the analyst would never be a given but the constantly transformed ground of the inquiry. This would clearly break with many of the educational developments of the past few years in that the role of the individual teacher would become much more important, as the specific starting point of inquiry would be negotiated between teacher and student. At the same time there would have to be generally agreed and assessed levels of common competence attained within these specific programmes. Obviously this suggestion involves a detailed elaboration of curricula and methods. It is a project to be counted in decades rather than years, and it would be unwise to underestimate the time-scale. One point must be stressed again and again. If this critique is seriously to address education, then it will be crucial, as Spivak herself writes in this volume, that one qualifies students to enter society at the same time as one empowers them to criticise it.

The most important problem is, however, neither the micro-political conservatism of any institution nor the genuine problem of elaborating an educational programme which emphasised both individual specificity and public competence. It is that such a project will encounter powerful macro-political resistance. The accusation of 'politicisation' and of 'bias' will be made again and again. It is a powerful accusation and one which when it refers to the inculcation of dogma, or the specific promotion of party position, finds a justifiably large public response. What will be objected to, however, is the school and the university carrying out their historically approved and socially sanctioned function of enabling students to think and empowering them to act. There are vast interests who do not want a people educated about race or ecology or the media, about the various forms of exploitation and domination. And these interests, as Spivak constantly points out, are not forces to be located simply *outside* the university; and First World university teachers must acknowledge a certain identification with those interests.

One of the great virtues of these essays is the commitment to teaching and edu-

142

cation that runs through them. Spivak is rare in combining an understanding of many of the most crucial problems facing the globe and the species with an interest in considering the detailed question of specific educational situations. From the lofty heights of the development of imperialism, the study of sexuality, and the impossibility of representing Being, to discussing the mundane merits of differing composition courses may seem like a fall from the sublime to the ridiculous. It is one of the delights of this book that it shrinks from neither: 'I think less easily of "changing the world" than in the past. I teach a small number of the holders of the can(n)on male or female, feminist or masculist, how to read their own texts, as best I can.' Any reader of these texts of Spivak will be better able to construe and construct the contradictory texts that constitute their own lives.

PART FOUR

Institutional Initiatives

11   On the Eloquence of the Vulgar

The lecture that follows was given in October 1992 as a public event which would launch the BFI's new MA. The lecture was designed to address an audience drawn both from the industry and the academy and to explain the purposes of the degree to both. Above all it was designed to place the development of film and television studies within a very long history of the democratisation of communication. Raymond Williams is not mentioned by name within the lecture but *The Long Revolution* is the book that informs the whole thrust of the argument.

> *The word you want is Dante*
> *He said he loved Beatrice. Whatever he did*
> *He didn't love Beatrice.*
>   VERONICA FORREST-THOMSON
>   'Cordelia or "A Poem
>   Should Not Mean, But Be" '

> *de Latin wasn't hip*
>   JEAN BINTA BREEZE
>   'Riding de riddym'

'And I found myself in mid-life and lost in a dark wood with no direction home.' These are, of course, the opening words of Dante's *Inferno*, or rather they are my rather free translation of Dante's Italian:

> Nel mezzo del cammin di nostra vita
> Mi ritrova per una selva oscura,
> Che la diritta via era smarrita

It is close to impossible for us to project ourselves back into Italy at the beginning of the fourteenth century and to realise how extraordinary was Dante's decision to write the *Divine Comedy* in Italian. One of the first surviving responses to the poem is the shock registered by Giovanni Del Virgilio when he complains that it is quite improper to deal with such weighty topics in a vernacular language and that Dante should really be writing in Latin. '[S]uch weighty themes why wilt thou still cast to the vulgar, while we pale students read nought from thee as bard', he writes in his first epistle.[1] For us, of course, the thing seems clear. Latin – the language of Europe from the Empire through the Dark Ages – was inevitably giving way to the vernaculars of Europe. But that was not how Dante and his contemporaries saw it. Indeed, Dante wrote an unfinished discourse in Latin, *De vulgari eloquentia*, in which he defended the use of the vernacular and from which I have, in punning misconstruction, taken my title. Dante's purpose, however, was not to produce a language which would be available to the common people. He makes absolutely clear that what he is

147

looking for will be noble and courtly. Until Dante, vernacular poetry had been confined to the love songs of the Provençal poets, those knights who wished to make impossible love to their fair ladies. It was in the *langue d'oc* because it was intended for a small and intimate audience which included women. The songs, the *canzoni*, inhabited a different universe from the official language of Europe, that Latin which had been the very language of civilisation since Augustus and the constitution of the Roman Empire.

As Erich Auerbach put it, in what still remains the best single book on Dante:

> It was not from a great, universal moment that Dante drew his first inspiration but from the formal culture of a small circle which consciously adopted the Provençal tradition, all the more enthusiastically in view of its esoteric, foreign character. The social foundations of Provençal poetry were lacking in Italy, but that did not prevent Guinizelli, the founder of the Italian movement, from taking over the Provençal heritage of a highly stylised poetry expressing a select, aristocratic form of life, hostile to vulgar expression.[2]

Dante and his Florentine friends who imitated the poems of Arnault and his circle were not lords at the bitter end of a system which was collapsing as a money economy replaced the complex networks of loyalty which constituted feudalism. Indeed, they were the very representatives of that new money economy, the Florentine traders and burghers who wanted to run their city independently of the heavy hand of Pope or Emperor. We probably owe the *Divine Comedy* (as we almost certainly and very similarly owe *Paradise Lost*) to political failure. If the citizens of Florence had not banished him from '*suo dolce seno*', as Dante puts it in an intensely moving passage of the *Convivio*,[3] it is doubtful whether the poet would have found the time or mental energy (of which his long exile was to furnish him with an overabundance) to compose the first epic of modern Europe.

But when he did compose it, he knew that he wished his audience to be his fellow citizens, the people from whom he felt himself exiled, rather than simply the scholars. If he had written in Latin, he would, he tells us in the *Convivio,* have been advancing his own career, but he would have been prostituting literature. Instead, he wants to write for those who are *volgari e non litterati,*[4] those who are increasingly able to read Italian though unlettered. But if in clear, political terms Dante wants to widen the audience for his work, this does not mean that he is looking for a universal audience. It is the audience of his own class and their social superiors whom he wishes to seduce from the sordid pork-barrelling of papal politics in favour of an impossible imperial ideal in which the political order would fuse with the moral in a society which encouraged instead of frustrated the development of the individual.

So radical is Dante's move that it is actively contentious for more than a century. Petrarch laments that his predecessor was so unwise as to use Italian for such weighty matter; and Boccaccio, Dante's first biographer, was prevented from giving the lectures which would have made the great poet more widely available to readers in his too-much-loved city.[5] Indeed, Dante's political relevance may not even be quite exhausted yet. In a decade which has seen the rebirth, in conscious appeal to medieval times, of the Lombard League, it is possible that Dante's political vision was not exhausted in the Risorgimento, which to many in Italy looks an increasingly false dawn, and that he will yet prove relevant to that dialectic between the local, the national and the European which so dominates current political debate.

If he does, however, it will be very clear that Dante, if he writes in the vulgar tongue, does not write for the vulgar. Probably the most important chapter of the *De vulgari*, Chapter 6 of Book 2, comes just before he leaves the work unfinished and where, having already identified the illustrious vernacular, he turns to the question of style and tries desperately to pinpoint what it is that constitutes the real elegance of language. I will not go into detail of his argument – for that the topic of the lecture would have to be Dante and the lecturer one, like the great Auerbach, totally immersed in the culture of the Renaissance and the late Middle Ages.[6] I will content myself with Dante's final words on the subject where he admits that he is at least sure that he wishes to exclude all vocabulary and constructions which are plebeian in character.[7]

With his exclusion of the plebs, Dante makes clear that while he is concerned to construct a culture which will bypass the dominance of church and priests, he has no interest in – indeed, is unable to conceive – a democratic culture. It is no part of my purpose today to suggest that the pleasures of the *Inferno* are simply those of a certain class. But the briefest reflection on Dante's language indicates how the figuring of an audience excludes as well as includes. What the major European cultures all share with Dante is a crucial moment of exclusion, if that moment is to be read very differently in the works of an English Shakespeare or a French Racine.

I have started my lecture with a consideration of Dante at the beginning of the fourteenth century in order to suggest how difficult it is to consider art without addressing social questions. Text and society are not separate categories but ones which mutually illuminate each other as we think in terms of audiences and their educational and commercial formation. It is no accident that probably the most exciting area of the traditional humanities is now literacy studies as scholars try to determine how and why particular audiences are constructed.[8]

Questions of audience and communication allow me to cast my net wide enough to embrace both subjects of my lecture, for I am not here only to speak to you about the art of film and television, but also of its study, its place within education. The argument of this lecture is that these two questions are inter-linked and that both are complicated methods of communication. But this does not mean that we should confuse the processes that lead to the birth of mediums and genres with those that lead to schools and curricula. In both cases, however, we are dealing with crucial determinants in the definition of our political and social beings. Indeed, it is part of the argument of this lecture that our communal existence is defined as importantly by them as by either our legal and constitutional status as citizens or our private status as daughters and sons, brothers and sisters, wives and husbands, fathers and mothers.

The British Film Institute was founded with the aim of encouraging the appreciation and understanding of the art of film, and in the early 60s the word 'television' was added to that remit. This makes the BFI a very particular kind of institution. Nobody could, in that brutal way, imagine a British Literature Institute because, although there are many societies with this or that particular literary objective, there can be no doubt that the understanding and appreciation of literature is a valued good. Our traditional centres of learning, the universities, have always been concerned with producing what Dante calls the *litterati*, the lettered, though for him that meant a knowledge of the classics; while in an epochal change, focused in the nineteenth century, it comes to mean the knowledge of those national literatures which trace their origins to that moment when the feudal world of the Holy Roman Empire dissolved into the nation states of Europe.

Thus the British Film Institute was set up outside that cultural authority which linked the classics to the national tradition. If the establishment of the Institute's MA in conjunction with Birkbeck College has importance – and I am here to argue that today – it is because it marks the moment at which the Institute's project engages with that authority and because that moment should mark the beginning of a process of real cultural democratisation. If that moment also creates an elite graduate course, it should confuse only those who under the pressure of a facile egalitarianism have confused elite with elitist – a distinction that I shall return to at the close of this lecture.

If the beginning of the twentieth century saw the creation of art forms, through cinema, recorded music, the popular press and radio (later joined by television), which reached audiences on a scale which even the most popular of national literatures could never dream of, it was a long time before these forms (because they addressed themselves to the unlearned) received the kind of cultural and historical analysis which is the unearned right of their contemporary traditional arts – literature, music, painting.

If there is a single individual who by his own efforts altered this state of affairs, it was the French thinker and activist André Bazin. It is astonishing that even today there is no place where one can consult the complete works of this most vital of twentieth-century intellectuals, and it is an omission which I hope the Institute will put right, even if it results in the paradox that his complete works become available in English before they become available in French. And yet it is not so astonishing, nor is it so paradoxical.

Bazin is a child of the Third Republic; the third attempt after the Revolution of 1789 to produce a state based on a secular notion of citizenship.[9] It is a commonplace that the ideological foundation of this state was lay education; and Bazin was institutionally formed within that ideology, moving from his small provincial town to the Ecole Normale Supérieure at Saint-Cloud just before the outbreak of war. But Bazin, whose crucial definition of the role of the teacher is one who both confirms and disrupts tradition and community, was soon in revolt against his own dominant tradition.

His first publications, written in disgust with the institutions of Vichy, reveal an impatience with the narrowness of French education, which he feels lacks the dimension of value or religion. I would like to note in passing that Bazin's religious belief is one fully committed to the development of scientific knowledge. For, it is in the attitude to science that we can identify one of the key elements which distinguishes between those faiths which genuinely try to re-pose the unavoidable questions of religion and those which simply want to respond to all questions with a fundamentalist belief.

It was in the dissident Roman Catholic journal *Esprit* that Bazin was to publish many of his most significant essays. And it was partly through *Esprit* that Bazin was drawn to the cinema; for film criticism was important to the journal, not least because it published the thinking of Roger Leenhardt, one of the few individuals who welcomed the advent of sound, arguing that it displaced attention from the image to the subject filmed.

The end of the silent film and the ever growing dominance of the star system and Hollywood meant that by the end of the 30s there was an ever growing contempt for cinema on the part of intellectuals. The intellectual and political context of the Occupation form the background of Bazin's first ciné-club: its success confirmed his decision to abandon teaching and devote himself to that medium which, as Dudley Andrew puts it in his classic biography, he held to be 'the important advance in the popular and visual arts since the decline of the miracle play and the invention of the printing press'.[10]

It is crucial to understand how vital distribution and exhibition was to Bazin at this time; for him, the role of the critic was simply part of a complex feedback between audience and producer in which the moment of criticism was intimately linked to that of exhibition and distribution. It is also important to realise to what extent Bazin in the immediate post-war years was a phenomenal one-man BFI, animating ciné-clubs as far apart as Germany and Morocco and pouring out article after article at every level of the daily, weekly and quarterly press.

If the extraordinary openness of the Liberation allowed Bazin an extraordinary range of activities and audiences, the bitter struggles of the Cold War were to limit both. He was the first director of cultural studies at IDHEC, the Institut des Hautes Etudes Cinématographiques, but he soon resigned from this state institution (as he had earlier left the education system) to concentrate on cultural animation groups such as Travail et Culture and Peuple et Culture. This was the context for his promotion (both critical and material) of neo-realism, the high point of which came in late 1946 with the attendance of Rossellini at the Paris première of *Paisà*.

The open and international world of cinema was soon to become increasingly offensive to a Left which, under Soviet influence, was to identify America simply as the enemy. It was soon as unacceptable on the popular Left to admire Hollywood cinema as it had always been on the bourgeois Right. But it was above all the Hollywood cinema which fascinated the young men who gathered at Henri Langlois' *cinémathèque* and for whom Bazin was the father-figure to whom all their aesthetic and theoretical efforts were addressed. It was in the course of this dialogue at the end of the 40s that Bazin came under increasing attack from the Communist Left, and the break finally came in 1950 when he refused to praise the contemporary Soviet cinema. The tones in which he was denounced in *L'Ecran français*, by then effectively a journal of the PCF, are revealing:

> These are the same people who are ready to abandon all national independence on the political plane, who are ready to abandon everything which makes us proud in the past and the present for a future triumphant for 'basic French', American films and US atomic bases on our soil.[11]

I recall this post-war history because it is important to remember that when *Cahiers du cinéma* was founded in 1951, it was founded as a magazine which defined itself not only against the university professoriat, but also against political engagement. But there was a third element which defined the young critics; their classicism – the references are to Chateaubriand and Aragon, Valéry and Malraux, not to Leiris or Bataille.[12] For the young critics of the 50s, cinema provided a respite from the modernism which is such a powerful response to the crisis of the national audience, as fully literate populations chose to ignore traditional literature.

Modernism can be read as attempts to make up for the inadequacies of audiences in the present by postulating ideal audiences in the future. The *Cahiers* critics, however, enjoyed having found the classical art of the twentieth century which was secure in its contemporary universal audience. If Bazin had presented them with Welles and Rossellini, then the young critics would present their master with Hitchcock, Wyler and Hawks. But in this presentation there were a host of contradictions which would become much more evident in the early 60s.

From one point of view, *Cahiers du cinéma* was absolutely, securely, the inheritor of the Bazinian project to liberate through education. The magazine was concerned to deepen an understanding of film through an attention to its specific elements: lighting, camera, set design, editing, music, direction. But from another point of view, the project of the magazine's critics was very different. On the one hand, they were concerned, because of their particular battle with contemporary French cinema, to denigrate the role of the script and to promote the role of the director. At the same time, the audience they were in the process of creating, that of the omniscient *cinéphile*, was very distant from the universal audience that they postulated in their classical theory.

In what is a desperately moving and inspiring life, there is something almost mystic in Bazin's final hours. As, in the company of his family, he finally succumbs to leukaemia, François Truffaut, the delinquent child whom he had adopted and nurtured through many difficulties, rushes to his bedside having just completed the first day's filming on his first feature. It is to Bazin that *Les Quatre Cents Coups* is dedicated, and in the euphoria of the next two years as Godard's *A bout de souffle* joins Chabrol's successes, one might have been forgiven for thinking that Bazin's project had been achieved. It is important to realise, however, that by 1951 when *Cahiers* is founded, it is founded because of the impossibility of working with the cultural institutions of either the state or its opposition, and it is difficult to believe that Bazin himself must not have been aware of the impossibility of constituting a whole society out of a simple commitment to cinema.

What happens in the early 60s – and I am going to take Jean-Luc Godard as my exemplary figure, for it was he, above all, who believed that life and cinema were coextensive – is that developments both national and international produce for these young, classical film-makers a belated but none the less deeply felt modernism. In Hollywood the collapse of the studio system and the catastrophic fall in the number of films produced endangers the careers of directors like Nicholas Ray and Robert Aldrich, who were, for *Cahiers*, the very justification of American cinema. In France the growth of the supermarket society threatens to make of film just one more America consumer item, lacking completely the religious aura which had illuminated Langlois' screenings. The crisis of the audience, which for literature stretches from Baudelaire to Eliot, is condensed for the *Cahiers* directors into a few short years.

For me, the film of this period is *Le Mépris* (1963), in which the doubts and anxieties about the relations between culture and commerce, Europe and America, are articulated most clearly. The American producer Prokosch erupts into the world of European cinema and culture. He represents that generation which has already buried the Hollywood *Cahiers* loved and which now, through international co-productions, threatens European cinema in its own studios.[13]

It is important to realise how serious Godard was when he continuously claimed that he was waiting for '68 because he could no longer work with the available structures of cinema. What happened in '68 is that, increasingly disappointed in the available audiences and structures, Godard and *Cahiers* both attempted in a moment of revolutionary enthusiasm to create the perfect audience. This required two apparently complementary strategies. On one hand, one would short-circuit all existing structures to produce films which would find their audiences through political networks; and on the other, one would use the full panoply of semiotics, psychoanalysis and Marxism to transform the classic films of the Hollywood past into texts that bore witness to the contradictions of both cinema and society. *Vent d'est* (Wind from the East) and the reading of *Young Mr Lincoln* are two sides of the same coin, a coin which wishes to withdraw itself from circulation.

It is easy now to mock the messianic utopianism of those times, but if I will yield to no one in my scorn for the stupidities of that period, I also refuse simply to dismiss the desire for a better society which animated them. It is one of the obvious idiocies of the present age that everybody talks blithely of the end of both Communism and Marxism. That the societies formed in the wake of the Russian Revolution, for whom utopia was a planned industrial society providing for the already understood needs of its population, were, for their populations, dismal failures is apparent to all except that quarter of the world's population which lives in the People's Republic of China. That, however, the Communist ethic which manifests itself every time friends gather or when a family sits down to a meal – to claim that this ethic, which is fundamental to our very survival and existence as a species, is exhausted can only be read as ludicrous or terrifying.

As for Marxism, it must be said that the current global crisis of overproduction would seem to confirm the analyses of *Capital*. Whether, in a narrow sense, there is any life in Marxism depends, I believe, on whether it is possible to produce from Marx's writing a theory of money adequate to its function as both representation and sign. (Marx's explicit account of money at the beginning of *Capital* is woefully inadequate.) But, independently of that narrow question, anybody who struggles to understand the relationship between cultural and economic forms in the belief that a better understanding will lead to real possibilities of social emancipation – in that sense Marxism continues to provide one of the essential contexts to the vast majority of serious attempts at cultural understanding, although I have deliberately chosen formulations which could as easily embrace the Annales School as the Birmingham Centre for Contemporary Cultural Studies.[14]

If, however, Communism and Marxism continue to abide our question, what is certain is that the dead end reached in the late 60s in France was terminal. Godard himself only just survived. It is perhaps no surprise (for the whole history that I have been relating is, with one or two significant but minor exceptions, entirely a boys' story) that his survival in every sense of the term was due to a woman – Anne-Marie Miéville.

153

It is equally significant that, unlike Godard's previous partners, Miéville's role was behind rather than in front of the camera. The first fruits of their collaboration is the singular (if little seen) *Ici et ailleurs* (Here and Elsewhere), in which Miéville makes clear how, in the search for a perfect film and a perfect revolution, the male film-makers had gone further and further *elsewhere*, while never managing to confront or interrogate a *here* which was composed of television, consumer products and the domestic home.

Godard's work since then has eschewed both the universal audience of classicism and the perfect audience of modernism in favour of local and plural audiences. His work of the last twenty years constitutes one of the most astonishing investigations and celebrations of the image that history records. It must be said, however, that it has taken place outside any contexts in which feedback from the audience, which Bazin saw as so crucial, has been possible.

In many ways, *Cahiers* never recovered from its terminal moment. The magazine's original strength has been to read film from the point of view of the audience: the fan was turned into an expert viewer equipped with all the technical and material knowledge of the film-maker. However, there was always an ambiguity in which the *Cahiers* viewer became the privileged fan who distinguished himself from the rest of the audience in his ability to recognise not just art but the guarantee of art – the artist. It was this privileged position which the positions of '68 tried to break from. But, deprived of any institutional engagement with education or distribution, *Cahiers* could only finally, when it rejoined the land of the living, reproduce in various etiolated forms the earlier aesthetic and political discourses.

There was, however, one institution which was shaken by the Wind from the East. That institution, the BFI, was, to my knowledge, the only British institution which was really affected in its innermost workings by what in shorthand we call '68 – not simply in the high farce of the 1970 Annual General Meeting, when the members' action group voted off all the Governors, but in the following years when, particularly through its grant-in-aid client SEFT, the Society for Education in Film and Television, it tried to explore the intellectual and political consequences of some of the positions advanced in France in the late 60s.

There is one figure who, like Bazin, demands to be identified in this context: Paddy Whannel. If France was bitterly divided by the war and its Vichy collaboration, Britain was famously unified as the last great national war was articulated with the international struggle against fascism. While some of the possibilities of the BFI had been laid in the 30s, when it was established, there can be no doubt that it was one of those institutions which had life breathed into it by those returning from the war and bringing with them very changed experience and attitudes: Leslie Hardcastle and Denis Foreman are the most obvious names in this context.

But, from the perspective of this lecture, the real force of the social transformation of the war arrived in 1957 when Paddy Whannel took up the post of Education Officer. After working as a projectionist for six years, he joined the Royal Navy in 1942, aged twenty; later, after qualifying as a teacher, he spent nearly ten years in secondary-modern schools.[15]

It was this experience which led in 1963 to the publication of *The Popular Arts* by Paddy Whannel and Stuart Hall. It is in my opinion a much more fertile book than Richard Hoggart's almost contemporary *The Uses of Literacy* (1957). While

Hoggart's eyes are firmly fixed on the past, sketching the ethnography of a previous, and in my opinion largely illusory stage of working-class culture, Hall and Whannel focus on the working class of the 50s and on the possibilities of developing contemporary working-class taste in radio, film, television and recorded music. While the book places evaluation clearly at the centre of its project, and it is the argument of this lecture that such a process is critical to any study of film and television, it does so within a Leavisite discourse.

> In the end we are driven back to a qualitative definition based on critical judgements of individual pieces of work. Such judgements are often dismissed by sociologists as 'subjective' or 'impressionistic'; but there is a difference, surely, between vague opinion and the considered view based on close analysis which presents itself for debate and discussion controlled by 'evidence' from the work in question.[16]

These terms and considerations were about to become more than unfashionable as considerations of value disappeared before the desire for scientific knowledge either in its classic semiotic form or its more engaged Althusserian variant. This work found its British introduction through the efforts of Paddy Whannel, and one of his most influential decisions was to recruit Peter Wollen to the Institute. The result of that recruitment was both *Signs and Meaning in the Cinema* (1969) and the elaboration of a policy to aid universities to set up posts in film.

It is a truth which I have garnered from experience that one is rarely if ever punished for professional failures, but that it is very difficult indeed to survive professional success. If, in retrospect, it is clear how important and fruitful was Paddy Whannel's work, the then Governors of the Institute saw it very differently. A Governors' committee on Educational Services, chaired by Asa Briggs, declared that too much time was spent on 'sophisticated research' and that the Educational Department, to be renamed the Educational Advisory Service, should content itself with a purely reactive role in responding to teachers' requests. Paddy and five other members of the department resigned. But what looked like defeat was from another perspective victory and so strong was the case they had made that the then Chairman accepted in a policy report (whose very existence was another testament to an argument won) that there was indeed need for research, even if it should now take place outside the Institute.

> So far as educational interest in film goes, the Governors believe that in the long run film study should and will become a recognised part of formal education, from secondary-modern level right up to postgraduate studies. Meanwhile they believe it is our job to serve teachers with the advice and tools they need. Grants-in-aid can help research into political, social or aesthetic critical theories. The Governors want to encourage research of this sort in universities and other bodies of higher education, but not within the Institute. We will do our best to help finance such projects.[17]

It was this commitment which was to sustain the funding of SEFT and its magazine *Screen* over the next two decades. And it was in the pages of *Screen* that the theoretical and political projects of '68 were explored.[18] I am the last to undervalue the enormous understanding of film which that period marks – I think particularly of Stephen Heath's astonishing analysis of *Touch of Evil* and Laura Mulvey's essay on visual pleasure – but I want here to dwell on its failures.[19]

155

Bazin had dreamed of an active and participatory criticism, a crucial element in the circulation between producer and audience. *Cahiers du cinéma* substituted for that a more limited circulation between director and aesthete and when that failed had imagined a utopian dialectic between text and reader. What Bazin needed was a theory of institutions which would have enabled the feedback between audience and producer to have been enacted on many levels. The situation in France after the war provided no such institutions and *Cahiers*, a direct result of this failure, was unable, two decades later, to produce them. For *Screen* to have engaged with these possibilities, it would have had to take both education and television more seriously than it did (and it seems to me no accident that *Screen Education*, which did take these issues seriously, was by the end of the 70s the more vital and important journal). There are no doubt many reasons for this failure, but I want to concentrate on two: the auteur theory, and value.

For someone who has had the privilege to work with a genius like Terence Davies, there can be no doubting that films can have authors, that is to say films the founding possibilities of which are articulated in one person's particular existence. But, and this is a crucial point, I doubt whether one can in that sense talk of an author except when the director has also written the script. Most film-making, and almost all television, involves a much more collective production. It might be possible to argue that this inevitably means that film and television are going to be without enduring value, since once we move from the individual to the group, it is impossible to find the necessary complexity, social and psychic, essential for the production of great art.

The simple answer to this is that it is wrong. *Casablanca* is a great film despite the fact that it had no original origin, and indeed it is even difficult to produce a coherent account of the group which made it. But it is in terms of group, both of producers and audiences, that we need to think, if we are to understand questions of value in relation to film and television.[20] Most contemporary theorising about value emphasises its situational nature. The radical subjectivism which characterised Anglo-Saxon moral philosophy for much of this century has given way to analyses which stress that the expressions of preference will always take place within a specific forum.[21]

These forums are what now reorganise our sense of the public and private and there is no more important example of such a forum as television. One thing I now want to suggest is that a significant way in which we currently explore our communality is through our evaluation of the media. At its simplest, this is stating the obvious. One only has to look at the time devoted to soap-opera stories in the tabloids to reckon their importance in our understanding of what constitutes the acceptable range of the private. The tabloids, however, are basically reactive.

If I had given this lecture in another place, I might have devoted it to one of my favourite forms – the *Sun* headline. Prolonged study of this most pithy of tropes has forced me to the conclusion that while it embodies the great plebeian virtue of derision, there are few other virtues, of any kind, to which it can lay claim. Television, however, is deeply concerned with the construction of values, and I say 'construction' because it is a complicated process of circulation and dialogue.

I want to take my example from the current autumn season of BBC1. This season is – and a glance at the last thirty-five years of public-sector television would

156

establish this as standard procedure – a response to a period of ITV success in drama, with such titles as *Prime Suspect, The Darling Buds of May* and *London's Burning.* The BBC has spent some more money and come up with a season which includes *Eldorado, Between the Lines* and *Civvies.* Verity Lambert and Tony Garnett are the two television producers who have given me the most pleasure over the years and if I had longer I would like to try and address their programmes.

I want, however, to concentrate on *Civvies,* because when I first saw it, and this is why it is crucial to my argument, I could not make up my mind whether I thought it good or not. My problem was that the use of the Dire Straits' 'Brothers in Arms' track over the presentation of extreme emotional situations was almost guaranteed to provoke sympathy for the discharged paratroopers independently of any resources of narrative or truth. As I have become increasingly impressed by its authenticity (and authenticity is the key term, I feel, with which to develop Bazin's concept of realism), it has seemed to me to be an extraordinary investigation of community.

The world of the paras is demonstrated as limited and cripplingly masculine, and yet this world offers more genuine solidarity and human sympathy than the civilian society into which they have returned and which has no interest in their dominant experience. In a country where it is impossible to represent the situation in Northern Ireland on television screens, *Civvies* offers a meditation on what is involved in this repression. It shows through the effects on the paras what happens when a society is involved in a conflict to which it has not given its assent. Perhaps the weakest parts of the programme are the flashbacks to Northern Ireland, because, on the old horror principle that you should never show the monster, they make the mistake of attempting to represent what the programme itself argues is unrepresentable.

In its determination to engage every part of the population in the dialogue as to what makes us a community, the BBC seems genuinely to be a national institution and it is, I suspect, for that reason that it is so hated by political parties which no longer seem quite so confident in their ability to fulfil that function. The worst future for our television would be one that absolutely divided us by taste and class, which perpetuated indefinitely our most disabling differences. The next worst thing would be to limit the possibility of investigating and deepening our enabling differences, the mission that both Channel 4 and BBC2 are primarily charged with.

If I may use this occasion to make a polemical point: What is disturbing about the current attitude of the BBC Governors and their Chairman is that they seem to be offering no public support for Jonathan Powell's ambition to try to produce 'passionate popular television' (to use his own memorable phrase), to rearticulate popular forms that engage with Britain in the 90s. They would seem by their very public silence to be abandoning the BBC's most valued heritage.

Before ending, I want to consider the argument, close to one that I have myself advanced, that it is impossible for television any more to fulfil this national function, because the audience is irretrievably fragmented, technologically and socially, and because television itself in the 60s accelerated the fragmentation in cultural terms.[22]

The conservative response to this generally acknowledged explosion of differences has been focused on education and a national curriculum which will ensure a communality of knowledge. I must confess myself broadly in sympathy with this endeavour, provided that the curriculum so constructed relates to the realities in Britain today and not to the vain desires of politicians. And I want to suggest that if a national curriculum is really concerned with improving the common stock of knowledge, then television will be at the heart of it.

If one studies the Cox Report on English, one is struck by the acumen and intelligence of its remarks on language, which balance the plurality of voices that make up this island, with an insistence on a common tongue that we must all read and write. It represents an extremely sophisticated and democratic form of cultural nationalism. This cultural nationalism is clear at the level of language, but totally absent from the section on literature. It is brief and anodyne. One cannot object to assertions about the centrality of narrative to human experience or the importance of linguistic play, but the lack of examples, except for a ritualistic bow to the universality of Shakespeare, makes it difficult to engage with this section of the report. Most importantly, and perhaps surprisingly, given its chairman's Leavisite formation, there is no reference to a national culture either in minority or majority forms.

It is perhaps a deep historical irony that, at the moment we elaborate a national curriculum, it becomes quite clear that it is close to impossible to teach our central literary tradition, even at undergraduate level, because the book has now been joined by so many other sources of information and entertainment that many of the fundamental categories required to inhabit this tradition are simply no longer present.

The comparable debate in history is instructive. The conservative position wishes to stress the importance of English history and the political and constitutional development of democracy; the crude progressive alternative is to sample a whole variety of experience from a wide range of the past. My own solution is simple: one teaches the history of the British Empire which not only has the virtue of giving an account of the world which explains to most of the children in the classroom why they are there, but also allows the telling of the story of British liberty so that it inevitably has to confront some of its less appealing subplots. The contribution that Cromwell made to the development of political and religious liberty was very real: real, too, were the Irish massacred in their thousands at Drogheda and Waterford. In literature, the argument opposes progressives defending relevant literature (which would seem to allow pupils to run the whole gamut of English literature from William Golding to Ted Hughes) and conservatives who want set texts which many teachers (and not, it should be noticed, educational experts) feel are beyond their pupils' range. The first step towards making this literary tradition available to the majority of contemporary pupils is a conceptual scheme which would render this tradition intelligible. The only subject which can provide this is media studies.

My colleague Cary Bazalgette has worked with a host of pupils and teachers to produce a primary curriculum statement which expects all children aged eleven to be able to understand the following concepts: media agencies (who is communicating and why), media categories (what type of text it is), media technologies (how we know what it means), media audiences (who receives it and what sense they make of it) and media representation (what the relation is between text and reality).[23]

It is only with these concepts that children can make sense of what is now a very distant culture. It is a paradox only for those who could not care less what happens to our literary tradition, that if we are going to teach it to our children, it will have to be in the context of media studies. Let there be no mistake about the radical proposition I am advancing here. My argument is that there can be no sense to a teaching of literature which is not a branch of media studies.

It is my own belief that, in the development of the subject in schools, a greater stress needs to be put on production, so that the ability to record and edit sound and image will be as necessary a part of being a citizen as reading and writing is already. But now I take off into a utopian future in which we will have become a nation of independent producers, all with sweetheart deals with the BBC. The immediate present does, however, give some grounds for optimism.

The new MA which we are here to celebrate today is designed to accomplish two objectives. The research placements which lie at the heart of the course will enable the BFI to develop another layer of reflection on its activities so that it can continuously orient itself towards new developments in the moving image and its audiences. It will also enable the accumulated wisdom which the Institute embodies in such venerable figures as John Gillett and David Meeker to be reproduced and passed on to future generations. What I have hoped to demonstrate is that by encouraging the art of film and television, the Institute will also be of necessity be arguing for a more democratic Britain.

When I was trying to raise money for this course, I had a standard pitch in which I would try to encourage sponsors by offering them the chance to participate in the foundation of the first elite educational institution in England since Oxford and Cambridge. Of course, like all pitches it followed *The Player's* explicit injunction and was twenty-five words or less; it also imitated that film in being remarkably inaccurate. If there is an institutional equivalent, it is probably the founding of the London School of Economics, and even that is probably not a very good analogy, particularly for a project which has not yet proved itself and may fail absolutely in its own terms or contingently in terms of available funds and resources.

There is, however, a determination to construct an elite course, in the etymological sense of choosing out the best, but one which will avoid elitism both in its recruitment and in its functioning. The aim is not to turn out cohorts of students who have mastered a discipline and feel that it is equivalent to mastering the world, but to turn out students who have learnt a variety of intellectual skills through research placements that will teach them the multitude of talents involved in the production, distribution and exchange of images. Film and television studies are now well established in the universities; what this course adds to the existing provision is a determination to inform theoretical development through practical knowledge. At its best, the British Film Institute has always represented a dual commitment to the rigours of intellectual inquiry and the demands of practice across the range of film and television. I hope that this MA course will deepen that commitment within and without the BFI.

If it does, it will be in large measure due to the backing of those who have sponsored studentships, and I would like to thank publicly Frank McGettigan and Channel 4, Melvyn Bragg and LWT, Michael Kuhn and Polygram, Alan Yentob and the BBC. I am particularly grateful to Sir Richard Attenborough whose support extended beyond words to the personal endowment of a studentship. I must also acknowledge Anthony Smith, who first made me realise the possibilities of the BFI as a new kind of research institute, and Wilf Stevenson, who determined to make these possibilities actual and who convinced me that any serious research institution can only function if it has at its heart the formation of graduate students.

It is usual that events of this kind at the National Film Theatre are followed by a question-and-answer period. However, the realities of exhibition make this difficult, as the first screening of the evening follows shortly. I am, however, very happy to answer any questions in the congenial atmosphere of the party to which you are all now invited in the television studio of the Museum of the Moving Image. However, making, as is my wont, a virtue of necessity. I am not sure what purpose a brief question-and-answer session would serve.

What I have produced is not the pleasing and intimate form of the *Guardian* Lecture, the purpose of which is to elicit questions from the floor. What I have pronounced here today is the slightly chilling and distant form of the *cours magistral*, an inaugural lecture, if one prefers an English term. The theses I have produced will be available for public consumption in the near future and will then provoke comment or apathy as they deserve.

They will, however, be subjected to searching scrutiny in a seminar with the MA students whose new existence is the very occasion for this lecture. And I must confess that there is a very personal pleasure for me in the fear with which I anticipate that seminar. After leaving Cambridge, I had many good and challenging students at Strathclyde. I have not, however, had to face such a collective number of very able students since I conducted my last seminar at Cambridge. If I have enjoyed this experience at Pittsburgh, and I must particularly mention the cultural studies programme at that university, it has always been in a national context which is not my own.

The failure at Cambridge to build an English Tripos, which would have encompassed television and film and which antedated my own Warholian fifteen minutes, meant that I was bound to leave in any case. My one professional regret was that I was unlikely to know again that curious mixture of pain and pleasure as a group of perfectly informed students tear one's argument to pieces and make it into something better.

Notes

1 Michael Cesar (ed.), *Dante: The Critical Heritage 1314(?)–1870* (London: Routledge, 1989), p. 106.
2 Erich Auerbach; Theodore Silverstein (ed.), Ralph Manheim (trs.), *Dante, Poet of the Secular World* (Chicago: Chicago University Press, 1961), p. 26.
3 Dante Alighieri; G. Busnelli, G. Vandelli and Antonio Enzo Quaglio, 2nd ed., *Il Convivio.* (Florence: Felice Le Monnier, 1968), p. 20.
4 Ibid., p. 158. Dante did not understand Italian as a historical development of Latin (this realisation came much later in the Renaissance), but thought of Latin as an artificial construct, a *grammatica*, underpinned throughout its history by a vulgar tongue. To

write in the vulgar was thus a significant political decision – one much clearer to his contemporaries than to us.

5 Cesar, *Dante*, pp. 167–8.

6 The question of how to use that philological tradition without producing institutions which would act in the tradition of the spineless German universities which kowtowed to Hitler is still alive. The starting point for my answer remains Erich Auerbach's great work of political allegory *Mimesis* (Berns: A. Francke, 1946).

7 'Subsistant igitur ignorantie sectatores Guictonem Arentinum et quosdam alios extollentes, nunquam in vocabulis atque constructione plebescere desuetos.' (So let the disciples of ignorance stop praising Guittone of Arezzo and some others, who never lost their habit of aping the vocabulary and construction of the people.) Warman Welliver, *Dante in Hell: The De Vulgari Eloquentia: Introduction, Text, Translation, Commentary* (Ravenna: Longo Editor, 1981), p. 109.

8 See Margaret Ferguson, *Limited Access: Female Literacy and Literary Production* (New York: Routledge, forthcoming).

9 My knowledge of Bazin's life is drawn from Dudley Andrew, *André Bazin* (New York: OUP, 1978) and Antoine de Baecque, *Les Cahiers du cinéma: Histoire d'une revue*, vol. 1, *A l'assaut du cinéma, 1951–1959* (Paris: Cahiers du cinéma, 1991).

10 Andrew, *Bazin*, p. 61.

11 Oliver Barrot, *L'Ecran français, 1943–1953* (Paris: Editeurs français réunis, 1979), p. 214.

12 For a demonstration of the attachment of the young *Cahiers* critics to the classical traditions of French literature, see the elliptical manifesto by the 22-year-old Jean-Luc Godard, 'Défense et illustration du découpage classique', *Cahiers du cinéma*, vol. 2 no. 15, pp. 28–32. Both the title and style are a reference to du Bellay's sixteenth-century defence of the French language as a worthy vehicle for literary expression. Not only does Godard produce, in his effort to break a lance with '*l'inoubliable Bazin*', an alternative history of the cinema in which German Expressionism and Alfred Hitchcock occupy a central position, but he links this twentieth-century history to a revisionist account of French literature which dismisses fiction (particularly Sartre) and even insists that the first of the moderns, Baudelaire, must be understood in terms of the classical Diderot.

13 Godard's purpose is particularly clear if one considers his transformations of the Moravia novel on which the film is based. In the novel, all the characters are Italian and it is the producer who is wedded to the classical interpretation of the myth. There is an excellent account of Godard's relation to his source in Michel Marie, *Le Mépris* (Paris: Nathan, 1990), pp. 26–30.

14 See Patrizia Lombardo, 'Cultural Studies and Interdisciplinarity', *Critical Quarterly*, vol. 34 no. 3, Autumn, 1992, pp. 3–10.

15 Geoffrey Nowell-Smith, Obituary, *Screen* vol. 21 no. 2, Summer 1980, pp. 10–12.

16 Stuart Hall, Paddy Whannel, *The Popular Arts* (London: Heinemann, 1963), pp. 35–6.

17 BFI Policy Document, November 1971, p. 8.

18 For a brief history of *Screen* in the 70s, see Colin MacCabe, 'Class of '68: Elements of an intellectual autobiography', *Theoretical Essays: Film, Linguistics, Literature* (Manchester: Manchester University Press, 1985), pp. 1–32. On a more personal note it is difficult for me to express adequately the personal debt I owe to Sam Rhodie and Ben Brewster.

19 Stephen Heath, 'Film & System: Terms of Analysis', *Screen* vol. 16 no. 1, pp. 7–77, no. 2, pp. 91–113; Laura Mulvey, 'Visual Pleasure and Narrative Cinema', *Screen*, vol. 16 no. 3, pp. 6–18.

20 Although I have improved the text of the lecture that was actually delivered on 13 October 1992, and I must particularly thank Simon Frith and Tony Rayns for their comments, I have not substantially altered this argument. However, I should note that after the lecture John McGrath convinced me that the group simply reproduced the problems of the category of the author and needs to be replaced with a much more difficult and complex concept of social experience. A real investigation of that might well start with case histories of *Z Cars* and the Garnett-Loach productions of the 60s and 70s.

21 See Barbara Hernstein Smith, *Contingencies of Value: Alternative Perspectives for Critical Theory* (Boston: Harvard University Press, 1988).

22 Colin MacCabe, 'Death of a Nation: British Television in the 60s', *Critical Quarterly* vol. 30 no. 2, Summer 1988, pp. 34–46.

23 Cary Bazalgette (ed.), *Primary Media Education – A Curriculum Statement* (London: British Film Institute, 1989), pp. 8, 20.

12 Cultural Studies and English

The one administrative task that I undertook at the University of Pittsburgh is to participate in the establishment and administration of a postgraduate programme in cultural
studies. Much of the discussion of cultural studies within the programme has divided those
who understand it as a continuation of the Birmingham Centre's original political project
from those who understand that project as exhausted and in need of replacement. This
paper was a contribution to that discussion.

It is one of the ironies of history, one of Hegel's ruses of reason, that at the
moment in the early 80s when the project of the Birmingham Centre expired in
the face of working-class support for Thatcher, it was reborn in the United States.
Despite the fact that its original class project is equally difficult in an American
polity dominated by Reagan, Bush and Perot, cultural studies, in the early 90s, is
the most active and vigorous element within American humanities and social science programmes. Its current fashionable status masks of course a curiously
overdetermined present. On the one hand it can function as a convenient administrative and intellectual excuse into which one can pretend to shovel any topics
not covered by the current curriculum; on the other it provides a site of political
consolation in a world which offers few such pleasures.

It would none the less be completely wrong to think that it is a purely fashionable phenomenon. If one may be forgiven for the rational calculation that in a
decade's time it will be the most barren administrative and political logics which
will dominate cultural studies, it is nevertheless the case that cultural studies is the
crucial site for the interrelation between the disciplines, and, which may be
another way of saying the same thing, the crucial point of the intersection
between the academic and the non-academic, between the university and the
world.

I want to start with a quotation:

> It must be a study in concrete terms of the relations between the economic, the politi-
> cal, the moral, the spiritual, religion, art and literature, and would involve a critical pon-
> dering of standards and key-concepts – order, community, culture, civilisation and so
> on.[1]

Apart from the reference to 'the spiritual and religion', almost any casual reader
would take this as a contemporary definition of cultural studies. In fact it dates
back more than fifty years and is taken from Leavis's manifesto for an English
school. What it does demonstrate and demonstrate quite clearly is firstly that the
subject Leavis is proposing is both interdisciplinary and constitutionally focused
on questions of methodology (the elaboration of key-concepts). More import-

antly it makes evident that there is a crucial link between English and cultural studies – that their relation one to another is not simply that which obtains between cultural studies and other disciplines but that there is a privileged genealogy in which English *is* cultural studies. Certainly Leavisite definitions of English are directly related to cultural studies – and not merely in their imperial attitude to the rest of the university nor in their breeding of rancorous and ill-natured debate. What differentiates cultural studies clearly from Leavisite definitions of English is that Leavis still presupposed a clearly defined object of study: literature.

If the current definitions of cultural studies are most importantly fought out in America, it is to nineteenth-century England and the familiar figure of Matthew Arnold that we must turn if we want to understand the pre-history. It is important to realise that Arnold's project starts not from literature but from a bleak judgement about the current social reality of England in the mid-nineteenth century and a crisis of value. Neither the decaying aristocracy nor the emerging proletariat offer any hope for a future which will preserve and enlarge civilisation. If, however, we look to the middle classes, we find them trapped between a religion which has lost all power to console or inspire and a newly emergent capitalist culture which provides a flood of newspapers and books which are certain in their ease to provide no locus whatsoever for value. It is to this problem that literature arrives as a solution – we must study literature in order to find a secure locus of value – to find a way of educating taste so that it can ignore the operations of the market. What is important to recognise about these formulations is that the Arnoldian view of the subject focuses value and taste as the crucial elements of this new form of study. Literature as object is curiously secondary within this rationale. It is, to caricature, merely the misfortune that we have lost our belief in God and have entered an era of economic development that encourages the production of valueless reading matter that places literature at the centre of the agenda. It is exactly because the justification for the study of literature is so baldly ideological that the academy is throughout the late nineteenth and early twentieth century so troubled by it. If it is to be made an object of study then it must be presented as the acquisition of objective knowledge. It is this fact which from the start confuses the ideological investigation of value and taste with the grounding in a philology which has been elaborated throughout the nineteenth century. It is this struggle between evaluation and philology, between criticism and scholarship, which is to dominate the early history of the discipline. What gives Cambridge its peculiar place within this history is that it was founded very late and at a particularly auspicious moment for the complete dominance of criticism within the curriculum. London had its first chairs of English in the 1830s and 40s, even Oxford began a serious English degree in the late nineteenth century, but the price for setting the pace was that these degrees were encumbered with a great deal of philological baggage. It was Cambridge at the end of the First World War that established a degree which was centrally about the criticism of modern English literature. Three very different kinds of reason underpinned this decision. The first was that even institutions like Cambridge were affected by the First World War. The periodic debates in the Cambridge senate before the war about the wisdom of introducing an English degree are couched in predictable scholastic tones. 1914 changed all that and the need for a 'modern subject for modern times' found a very easy audience. Second, and in a much less optimistic tone, philology carried with it all the rhetorical weight of the 'German science' and thus one could be both right-thinkingly progressive and unthinkingly chauvinist at one and the same moment. Finally, the then Professor of Anglo-Saxon – in a gesture which is probably unthinkable in any present-day university – declined to approve any compulsory inclusion of Anglo-Saxon on the grounds that he wanted no students who had not elected to grapple with the language and literature of Old English. The stage was thus set for a self-consciously modern study and it was this stage that I. A. Richards occupied throughout the 20s as he developed a theory and practice of literary criticism.

It must be stressed that, like Arnold, Richards's interest was not in literature as such. The problem once again was one of value, this time understood above all in terms of communication. Richards, who had studied moral sciences with G. E. Moore, was concerned to elaborate a theory which would at one and the same time ensure optimum forms of communication (and thus avoid a repeat of the carnage of the First World War) and at the same time produce optimum psychological states. Richards's immediate interest in returning to Cambridge in 1918 was to begin a course in the natural sciences so that he could go on to engage with psychoanalysis, but that interest was quickly replaced by an appointment for the new Tripos and for the next ten years Richards was concerned to produce a psychology and an ethnography that would be adequate to account for the effects of both good and bad literature. It is crucial to realise that, as for Arnold, the development of taste in literature is above all a response to the forms of writing that are the major form of contemporary anarchy. Arnold's worst fears had now been triumphantly realised with the completion of compulsory schooling and the development of the yellow press in the 1890s – one now had a totally literate population which none the less chose to ignore literature.

Richards's efforts are admirable both for their rigour and their democracy. The aim is to develop an account of the literary text so that its exemplary effects are an objective quality of its linguistic organisation. The role of the critic, and the major purpose of an English course, is to rectify the bad habits developed by the commercial products of capitalism and thus produce minds that are objectively better and which can in turn pass on the benefits of this superior organisation to others. At the same time what Richards finds is a method – that of practical criticism; the patient examination of critical texts. Leavis continues the method and the concern with value but ditches the democratic psychological theory in favour of an elitist social practice. English is transformed from a disciplinary adjunct of psychology – to become the formative influence on those who are to be the bearers of value within the society. The value of a text is not given by linguistic fact and psychological effect but is to be found in the agreed elaboration of meaning amongst those who have proved themselves sensitive to the values that literature proposes.

While this conception of English, even in Britain, is never totally dominant – a struggle within an older philology continues to occupy a certain amount of time – in the fifteen years after the Second World War it is massively successful. This success presupposes that English is an interdisciplinary enterprise. Further, it is an enterprise to which the rest of the humanities and social sciences are subservient – they only find their full justification in their utility to an English discipline which is less a discipline than a sacred mission and which is guaranteed by the values that repose in the canon.

Canon-formation is the major function of the discipline. Whether to include Milton or Shelley (both, amongst other things, unacceptably political and unacceptably androgynous) in the past and who, other than Eliot and Lawrence, to admit from the present make up the doctrinal struggles of this powerful sect. From within its ranks it is challenged on two fronts, fronts which are never clearly distinguished but which are, none the less, of radically different import. The first is provided by those students and teachers who, while accepting the Leavisite analysis, are troubled by the way in which it automatically devalues their own working-class experience and who want, within that experience, to value previously unvalued literary forms. The bible of this tendency is Richard Hoggart's *The Uses of Literacy* and it is he who founds the Birmingham Centre for Contemporary Cultural Studies using money donated by Penguin in gratitude for his crucially important evidence at the trial of Lady Chatterley. This tendency – which in disciplinary terms was concerned with an ethnography of working-class life (and, predominantly, Northern working-class life) – is an important but not dominant part of the Centre's concerns.

The radical edge comes from a very different experience than that of the Northern working-class; it comes from teachers at secondary-modern schools in post-war England. Two such teachers, Stuart Hall and Paddy Whannel, write in 1964 a book called *The Popular Arts* which attempts to reorganise the canon completely to include new forms of communication – radio, cinema, recorded music. Given how little attention is paid to this truly vital work (compared, for example, to Hoggart's), it is worth stressing that the whole institutional framework in which cultural studies developed in the 60s and early 70s is dominated by these two men: Hall through his direction of the Centre at Birmingham and Whannel through his work as Head of the British Film Institute's Department of Education.

For a long time the commitment to an ethnography of the working class and the commitment to the analysis of contemporary cultural forms are difficult to distinguish. It is not clear that those associated with the Centre would have made such a distinction and the most important work, crucially that of Raymond Williams, fully subscribed to both tendencies. In fact their confusion was crucial for what binds them integrally together is the appeal to the working class as an alternative locus of value. It should be noted that this appeal is not an appeal to Marxism – it is only in the 70s that the Centre's leading figures choose to reaffiliate with what by then is a much more complex intellectual movement – but an appeal to a source of moral authority.

Cultural studies in the early 60s inherits from Leavis the emphasis on interdisciplinarity and a belief in its key position for the articulation of the humanities and social sciences. Literature, however, has gone. It remains as an object, amongst others, but it is no longer the key locus of value. Indeed, Leavis's socially disenfranchising move – you are without value if you cannot recognise the value of literature – is analysed within a class history. The repository of value now becomes the working class; a working class whose specific national formation is chronicled in Thompson's *The Making of the English Working Class*. Indeed, the whole project of the communist history group of the late 40s who go on to become the founding fathers of British social history is crucially linked to cultural studies. It is no accident that both Hill and Thompson start their research with literary topics and late in their life deliver themselves of major studies of Milton and Blake. In the appeal to the working class cultural studies is not professedly or orthodoxly Marxist – it is, however, political. The enabling definition which Leavis finds in literary value, cultural studies finds in an emancipatory social project.

If we consider cultural studies at the beginning of the 60s, it is perfectly adequate to describe it within a specific national history. The late 60s, and 1968 is the orthodox dating for a much longer period, marks an internationalisation of academic culture which brings it into line with the newer cultural forms of the twentieth century. Immediately these developments eclipsed cultural studies. The emergence of theory challenged cultural studies on two separate fronts. From within a Marxist perspective, theory dismissed both sociology and the appeal to interdisciplinarity in favour of the elaboration of a science in which the class struggle was the key concept and all attempts to construct the social as an object were doomed to failure. As importantly, the cultural theory that emerged from these Marxist perspectives completely ignored the new media and found their critical edge in a series of revolutionary claims for certain texts of high modernism. If, in a British context, these positions were elaborated in the context of a film journal, *Screen*, the perspective on culture was largely derived from the literary and political avant-gardes of the 20s and 30s.

In America, the emergence of theory was even more inimical to cultural studies. If the full cultural history of the complex transformation of French theory as it made the Atlantic crossing is impossible until much more time has elapsed and a full inventory can be made, it is now possible to see clearly what was at stake in the de Manian appropriation of Derrida. De Man transformed Derrida's use of literature to interrogate the philosophical tradition into a celebration of literature as the timeless bearer of sceptical truth. The endless paradoxes of de Man's essays circle around literature's privileged ability to stage the paradox of language continually claiming to name a reality that escapes it. It is no accident that these paradoxes are crucial to Romanticism, for one of de Man's major aims (and this sharply differentiates him from the Derridean work which he took as his stimulus) is to read Modernism back into Romanticism. The necessity for this is above all to avoid that interrogation of the category of literature which modernism offers. Romanticism remains secure in the privileged position of literature (indeed it invents both word and concept); modernism (be it in the progressive tones of a Joyce or the more conservative accents of Pound or Eliot) questions the very distinctions which separate literature from the explosion of written language which accompanies the development of capitalist forms of production. Modernism replies, in a variety of complicated ways, to the problems posed by the new literate populations of Europe, literate populations the vast majority of which simply ignore literature. The Romantic privileging of literature runs up against the rocks of majority taste unless the audience is retheorised. One famous reaction is Leavis's definition of a 'minority culture', but an equally important reaction in the first half of the twentieth century is to theorise, either aesthetically or politically, a future space in which whole populations will come to enjoy what is henceforth unavoidably a minority culture. Nietzsche, indeed, can be read as exemplary in his writing for an audience 'which is far off', a Utopian vanishing point which can repair the damage of contemporary incomprehension.

In fact the most radical edge of modernism (Joyce and Nietzsche spring immediately to mind), combines a Utopian modernism with a contradictory post-modern conception of audience. The post-modernist revels in the multiplication of audiences and accepts the local position thus allocated to the intellectual, while the conservative, whether of the Left or the Right, will continue to hold out the promise both of a unified audience for literature and a central position for the intellectual, albeit in the imaginary future. De Man participates in neither of these moments, effectively trying to avoid all the complications of the twentieth century be they modern or post-modern.[2]

If the historical project is to arrest literary development with the Romantics, then the corresponding critical project, which is why the demystifying of literature is seen as the most important critical position to undermine, is to retain the canonical study of literature. At this point the radicalism of deconstruction becomes moot. The anti-humanist ethic of literature as the perpetual staging of linguistic crisis remains absolutely wedded to the traditional curriculum, that curriculum constructed to salvage the substantial moral truths from the best that has been written and thought.

What is absolutely striking about theory in America of the 70s and early 80s is how it is used to exclude from cultural study all contemporary cultural forms. At the same time this serves as a useful reminder that one of the crucial features of the great wave of French theory in the 60s was its missed encounter with mass culture. Of all the great names – Lévi-Strauss, Lacan, Derrida, Althusser, Foucault, Barthes, Deleuze – only Barthes ever engaged in any way with popular culture, and that interest was a feature of the early *Mythologies* (1957) and the semiotic analyses of the early 60s. In the late 60s even Barthes abandoned any central interest in popular culture when he aligned himself with the late 60s politicisation of the magazine *Tel Quel*. *Tel Quel* simply ignored popular culture as mere consumerist repetition in favour of the revolutionary potential of the great texts of literary modernism. In that sense de Man was pushing at an open door. Once he disengaged this primacy of literature both from its political context and its crucial engagement with science, he was able to fashion a practice of reading which could ignore politics (along with all contemporary culture) in favour of a powerful scepticism which would re-read the canon but leave it completely intact. It is then no accident that all criticism can do, at its best, is to reproduce the paradoxes of literature because to suggest anything else would allow an extra-literary set of concerns to intrude.

If in the mid-70s the Birmingham Centre might have seemed to have been displaced by these two new international contenders, by the late 80s its version of cultural studies looked set to become dominant. The rapprochement with what one might crudely call Althusserian Marxism was the less surprising. Political positions had always been shared and the differences (crudely put, the difference between the appeal to the party and to the class) became less than crucial as both appeals failed. The European failure of Euro-Communism and the British success of Thatcher spelt the end of conventional Marxist politics of both kinds. The strength of the Birmingham Centre at this point was its commitment both to the contemporary and the local. It was this long-term tradition which underpinned Stuart Hall's magnificent analyses in both *Policing the Crisis* (1978) and *The Politics of Thatcherism* (1983). At the same time Hall's analyses underlined the extent to which the imaginary working class in which the Centre had invested its ethical project was no longer a tenable source of value. It is this paradox which continues to haunt cultural studies.

In the mean time, however, cultural studies began to win a much more surprising battle. The dominance of theory in America gave way to an increasing interest in cultural studies. The reasons for this are complex and, as often in writing about a contemporary situation, it is very difficult to weigh definitively the competing causes. I want to advance two explanations. The first, which is both less important and more speculative than the second, is that theory's fate was always linked to Marxism. If there was no real engagement, Marxism always functioned as a kind of limiting alibi for theory. The evidence for this is less textual and discursive than anecdotal and institutional. One might think of de Man's recruiting of Jameson for Yale and further back ponder the juxtaposition of Derrida and Althusser at the Ecole Normale Supérieure in Paris. Theory never really embraced its nihilistic genealogy, preferring to comfort itself with a mere gesture to a politics. As this politics had very little concrete engagement, the events in western Europe which so clearly marked both cultural studies and the fate of Althusserianism had almost no impact whatever on American developments. The events of 1989 were, however, of such staggering import that they did remove the last vestiges of any supposed link between theory and Marxism.[3]

These political events, which in retrospect may have been the final knell for the dominance of theory, were preceded by a much more serious contestation of the traditional canon. If there were many competing forces demanding that literary study pay attention to contemporary forms, the most unanswerable challenge came from those concerned with the differences between black and white, North and South. Whereas those who questioned the canon from working-class or feminist positions could often find alternative written traditions, black students who wanted to value their own traditions had to oppose both the equation of culture with writing and the identification of tradition with nation as they sought new values in black music and a variety of diasporic literatures.[4]

Cultural studies with its commitment to an ethnography of popular cultures and its refusal to privilege literature was an obvious framework for this new work. At the same time the problem of value which I have argued is crucial to understanding the development of both English and cultural studies is now more difficult than ever. The belief in the working class as a privileged source of cultural value, either as author or audience, is no longer tenable after decades which have thrown up the claims of women, gays, blacks. At the same time the simple annexation of cultural studies as the academic equivalent of identity politics constantly presupposes that those marginalised identities can themselves produce criteria of value in the same way as the working class within the original model.

If the dominance of identity politics provides the most obvious reason for the success of cultural studies, there are two unrealised potentials within cultural studies which may well determine what its long-term effects will be. The first is that, contrary to almost all of the theory that emerged from the late 60s, cultural

169

studies' appeal to the working class was based in a traditional humanism. If that traditional humanism remains subject to all the anti-essentialist arguments, it is clear that a revision both of that tradition and of the separate but aligned liberal tradition is going to be crucial to any new elaboration of value.

It may well be, however, that the anti-essentialist arguments will prevail; that it will prove impossible to articulate any serious criteria for evaluation which are not hopelessly mired within the specific situation of their articulation. At that point cultural studies promises another and very different solution. The whole academic tradition stresses the importance of the recognition of value independently of the conditions of that recognition. It may be that the point is to focus on the production of value. This emphasis will inevitably stress an engagement with local conditions and with collaborative methods of working (both features of the Birmingham Centre) and may well conceive intellectual projects finding their dissemination in contemporary audio-visual media as well as more traditional written forms.

The challenge facing cultural studies is nothing less than to become the discipline that English, in its ideological form, always claimed to be, but to undertake this task at the intersection of different disciplinary concerns in their engagement with the contemporary world. It may be thought that such a future is over-optimistic but it does raise the intriguing question of what then is to happen to English. Does English simply merge with cultural studies or has it an autonomous future? The answer is much more evident in the United States than in England. The university discipline in America has retained a much closer link to the primary concerns of English as a training in literacy, and in both composition and creative writing programmes there is the potential for a discipline which places much more emphasis on production rather than criticism. English would indeed find its constitutive definition in the written word, but that definition would have as much to do with writing as reading.

Notes

1 F. R. Leavis, *Education and the University: A Sketch for an 'English School'* (London: Chatto and Windus, 1943), p. 49.
2 It is only in this context that one can provide a serious analysis of the controversy over de Man's politics.
3 This should not be read either as endorsing the 'end of Marxism' or as suggesting that there is not a continuous need for theoretical reflection. The unorthodox suggestion is that deconstructionist theory often implicitly assumed a congruent Marxism.
4 In the faculty seminar at Pittsburgh at which the first version of this paper was delivered, Patrizia Lombardo made a most telling criticism when she complained that my account of the genesis of cultural studies was a traditional literary historical one, tracing ideas through individuals rather than producing an account which fully analysed the social and institutional matrix in which they develop. This criticism could only be fully answered with a much more detailed study. A more temporary reply would simply propose much of the argument as a hypothesis which needed further empirical work. Nowhere would such work be more crucial than in analysing the role of black and Third World students in graduate programmes of the 80s.

13   Decisions

In February 1995, the Architectural Association, Birkbeck College, the British Film Institute and the Tate Gallery, launched a new PhD programme with a conference entitled Decisions. Those reflecting on decisions they had taken included Paula Rego, artist; A. S. Byatt, writer; the Lord Browne-Wilkinson, judge; Jeff Kipnis, architect; Steve Woolley, film producer; and Bernard Williams, philosopher. The four participating institutions had created the London Consortium to administer this new degree and it was as chairman of this new venture that I introduced the day.

In the month that marks the anniversary of his death, it would be fitting to mark the founding of the London Consortium with a simple tribute to Derek Jarman. Were he alive, he would undoubtedly be an enthusiastic member of the visiting faculty; in death, he is undoubtedly our patron saint. But it is not just personal or institutional piety that prompted us to commence today with two extracts from Derek's films. The parting scene from *Edward II* which is followed by Annie Lennox's extraordinary rendering of the Cole Porter classic 'Every Time You Say Goodbye' and early scenes from *Wittgenstein* which end with white dots appearing on a black screen, demand for their analysis an incredible range of knowledges. My task today is both to introduce you to the London Consortium and to the day itself. The quickest way of suggesting to you why we need a multidisciplinary doctoral programme of the kind that the Consortium will provide is very rapidly to reflect on that range of knowledges. As an initial check-list let me suggest the following. Literary history both in terms of Marlowe's place in that Renaissance drama which was so crucial in providing the image of England and the language of English that is still dominant today and in terms of the rediscovery of the complexity of that drama in the 20s with which one could associate the names both of T. S. Eliot and Dadie Rylands. Art history and that particular moment in the 60s in which Derek began his career as a painter. Popular music and particularly the moment of punk which Annie Lennox evokes. Philosophy and that extraordinary cultural conjuncture which makes the greatest English philosopher of the twentieth century an Austro-Hungarian Jew. And that before we get on to film itself where one at a minimum would have to conjugate Ken Russell who pulled Derek out of the world of painting because he wanted to get away from the dominant traditions of realism in British cinema and Stan Brakhage without whose experiments in avant-garde cinema it is difficult to imagine that extraordinary moment when we watch for several seconds white spots against a black background as Wittgenstein turns off his hose.

Even such a long list omits any mention of British television which provided the money for both projects, but I shall return to the question of culture and commerce, art and money later in this argument. But if I have already convinced you of the need for a multidisciplinary training to understand contemporary art why have we decided to launch this project with a day devoted to decisions, and decisions which are not simply the artistic ones that Paula Rego, Antonia Byatt and Jeff Kipnis will describe but the legal, political and commercial considerations which will inform the contributions of Lord Browne Wilkinson, Bernard Williams and Steve Woolley? We have chosen to focus on decisions because we feel that that is the easiest way to bring out in a single day the founding emphases of the Consortium. The first of these is the absolute requirement to train postgraduate students in more than one discipline if they are going to be able to analyse and engage with the contemporary world. Again and again today I hope we will be forced to recognise in the heterogeneity of the accounts that we will be offered that knowledge of a single discipline is simply an inadequate preparation for analysis of culture and society; although I will stress later in this talk that it is absolutely crucial that students are grounded in disciplines and not encouraged to believe that the need to move between disciplines is confused with a belief that one can ignore them.

More than this, however, we hope that in concentrating on decisions we will be able to contest an epistemological, ethical and aesthetic relativism which is ever more dominant in contemporary thought. Unlike almost all other study of contemporary culture, evaluation will be at the centre of the Consortium's teaching. In talking of value I and the Consortium are setting our faces against much of the orthodoxy of the past twenty-five years in which evaluation has increasingly vanished from the academic study of art and culture. Those of you who attended the conference here eighteen months ago on Art and Value may not be surprised at such sentiments but as they are a fundamental part of the rationale of the London Consortium and as our conference today is, in a real sense, the second part of that previous conference, I want to start by rehearsing the arguments as to why value is central to this new academic endeavour.

If there is one phrase that lies behind the flight from evaluation in the traditional humanities it is Walter Benjamin's chilling aphorism that 'Every monument to civilisation is also a monument to barbarism'. That phrase must be one of the most quoted phrases of the last twenty years and the historical record increasingly proves it all too accurate. The imaginary country of *The Faerie Queene* is a transcription of Ireland whose real inhabitants Spenser was keen to starve to death so that the English colonisers would enjoy an unencumbered view of their new possessions. Prospero's isle was full of many voices but we now know that we must include among them the screams of the murdered inhabitants of the brave new world and the moans of those transported to provide the labour to exploit it. The art historians have directed our gaze to the dark side of the landscape to glimpse the figures whose labour provided the surplus which allowed the aristocracy to patronise the arts. The feminists have taught us to be suspicious of all these masculine representations of women, to read in their very idealisations the lineaments of repression and exclusion.

One very common reaction to the recognition of these facts is to take refuge in relativism. Art is simply what one group of people have chosen to like: we can find no values which are not expressions of interest and we must be careful to make no claims for our own taste which would impose it on others or to condemn other's choices because we do not share them. This position, which I think is probably now dominant in the educational system at every level from primary school to university, has two disadvantages. In the first place it is incoherent at the level of what one might call the grammar of value – we do not speak as if our expressions of value could be reduced to expressions of interest. Indeed, if someone says to me 'you just like opera because the whole experience confirms a certain social superiority' and I accept that judgement, then my evaluation of opera is likely to change. We don't adopt or change our valuations in relation to interests but in relation to a whole variety of arguments which touch both on the work itself and its relation to the world and ourselves. Any real debate takes place as though our standards of evaluation are objective.

This philosophical point is given real edge when one considers value from the national perspective. In the past few years we have gained both a national curriculum and a department of national heritage. Both effectively are making major aesthetic choices which determine what literature will be read in schools and what arts will be supported and preserved. How are those decisions going to be made? This political setting transforms an arcane aesthetic problem into a fundamental question about whether the nation has any reality or substance over and above a set of legal and constitutional relations. The reason that so many are unwilling to carry over the objective standards of value that they use in their local conversations and situations is that they are uncomfortably aware of how objective standards have been used historically to denigrate, exclude and marginalise both popular forms within western culture and art both high and low from outside the western tradition.

But in thus stating the problem we can also begin to glimpse a solution. For it has been possible to widen the terms of the debate to allow claims both for popular and non-western forms to be made. The way to the traditional arts as well as our understanding of them are enormously enhanced when we consider them from the viewpoint of media which were developed to address the whole population. It may seem that the question then is whether these claims are to be made at the expense of the traditional canon or as an enlargement of it. But this is a false dichotomy. The very process of argumentation is one of enlargement even if that will always leave very hard questions about what will be included in this specific curriculum here or that particular museum there. The traditional canon will continue to abide our question even if we must now weigh its barbarism as well as its civilisation but that weighing is simply the deepening of the process of civilisation itself. It is here worth emphasising, which almost all those who use the Benjamin quote forget, that Benjamin was not attempting to ignore or reject the claims of civilisation but simply to emphasise how far that civilisation had not yet begun to meet its own proclaimed standards.

The argument is not one of absolute against relative but of a debate about absolutes which requires the widest participation. We do not want a relativist culture but we do want a pluralist one. The process of debate must not be one of simply hearing those who have already spoken but of keeping our ears attuned to voices that have not yet been heard. This indeed was my own experience as a state funder when Head of Production at the British Film Institute. When we were choosing what films to fund we used a discourse which was resolutely objectivist: this script was better than that but when we were deciding how to allocate time and energy to development, we deliberately chose elements of the national experience who had not yet been able to express themselves in sound and image. In some ways apparatuses of funding that have grown up present a more sophisticated grasp of the relations between margin and mainstream than the education system which opts for a relativism which is intellectually weak and which, if seriously followed through at every level of national life, would leave us a series of non-communicating enclaves and ghettoes. When Toni Morrison and Derek Walcott offer from the perspective of global culture a renegotiation of margin and mainstream, we should not lightly give up the task of defining and constructing a national culture which will deepen and enrich the value of our lives. There may always be a risk of domination and exclusion but there are also possibilities of emancipation and empowerment. One of the great weaknesses of contemporary Britain is the sheer difficulty it has in imagining itself. Mrs Thatcher called for a return to Victorian values – but these are narrow values and an image of Britain which is unacceptable at every level from child prostitution to imperial exploitation. To build a powerful image we will need much more generous and long-lived values than those of Victorian England.

If the London Consortium and the teaching that it offers has the elaboration of those values as its explicit aim, it is not simply the failure of the traditional humanities that is at stake but, more importantly, the failure of cultural studies. To talk of the failure of cultural studies is, at one level, so paradoxical as to border on the perverse. How can we talk of failure when over the last ten years cultural studies has entrenched its dominant position in the new universities in Britain and swept all before it in the United States where new programmes have been set up in university after university?

There are two major problems with cultural studies as it is currently constituted in most of the academy. The first is that it is by and large entirely the study of contemporary culture. When the Birmingham Centre was set up (with money donated by Penguin following the Lady Chatterley trial), the classics faculty objected to it being called a centre for cultural studies on the grounds that cultural studies already existed – it was called 'classics'. This objection was met by renaming the centre's concerns as 'contemporary cultural studies'. The anecdote is telling. The analysis of contemporary capitalist forms of culture is almost always divorced from the analysis of traditional forms with a remarkable impoverishment of both. In particular, questions of comparative value are impossible to pose except in the terminally stupid forms of 'we want Shakespeare not soap opera' or 'Keats is better than Dylan'. The London Consortium is absolutely committed to studying contemporary forms of cultural production within the most long-term historical perspective. And this perspective inevitably involves a very serious engagement with the established disciplines. The call for interdisciplinarity is a very old one: it can be heard in Leavis's formulations for an English school in the 40s, in the establishment of the Committee for Social Thought at Chicago, in the birth of area studies after the Second World War, in the foundation of the post-Robbins new universities in Britain. The impulse is sound – the world, by and large, does not present itself to us, as this day is designed to demonstrate, in forms that correspond to the disciplines. However, there is little doubt that by and large interdisciplinarity has failed to deliver – that it often deserves the obloquy heaped on it by academic conservatives as a recipe for ignorance. The Consortium is committed to taking the disciplines with total seriousness but as practices rather than representations. What is fundamental to a discipline is not this or that picture of the world but practices that sustain it: textual criticism in English, participant observation in anthropology, the exploration of an archive in history. The very ambitious aim of the Consortium is to fashion students who are seriously trained in more than one discipline and who, in that training, understand what it is to apprentice oneself in a new discipline. We want to produce students who are neither terrified nor complacent when they realise that the problem which they wish to understand requires them reading in a wholly unfamiliar bibliography.

All this is ambitious but it is an ambition which it is possible, at least, to entertain in any properly staffed and resourced research university, Birkbeck could undertake such a project here, my own university in Pittsburgh is committed to such a project in the United States. There are undoubtedly other institutions pursuing similar paths. The real excitement and possibilities of the London Consortium are much greater than that.

I hope the audience will excuse the hyperbolic tone but to indicate what is at stake here I want to take us briefly back to Prussia in the early years of the nineteenth century when the crushing defeats imposed on it by Napoleon had rendered it all but a vassal state. It was as part of a desperate desire for national regeneration that Humboldt was summoned back from diplomatic service to undertake the founding of a new university at Berlin. If the charming legend that would have Berlin immediately producing Blücher's general staff which, with Fichte riding along as tutor in arms, would finish Napoleon's and France's dream of European domination on the fields of Waterloo, rescuing a Wellington whose staff had no training but the playing fields of Eton – if that charming legend has unfortunately not survived the detailed work of intellectual historians over the past twenty-five years – it is the case that what Humboldt did in the short year between 1809 and 1810 was to establish the research university as we know it. It is to the dominance of Berlin in the succeeding years that we owe the international ubiquity of the PhD adopted in America through Johns Hopkins in the 1870s and later in Britain against considerable opposition at the beginning of the twentieth century. The revolution and the Committee for Public Safety had had no time for universities. Medieval anachronisms, hangovers from a feudal past, the universities had been totally abolished in favour of new schools in which teaching and technology had total priority over the abstract pursuit of knowledge. Humboldt's university, which built on developments in the German universities of the late eighteenth century, took a very different path. The abstract pursuit of knowledge was at the centre of the university but the definition and evaluation of that pursuit was not the business of a single university but of disciplines defined by specialist publications and by a recognisable research community.

We are so used to the dual nature of the contemporary university in which the individual teacher is constantly negotiating two competing collectivities – that composed by the teachers and students within her own institution and that composed by the international research discipline which defines the subject in which she works – that it comes as a shock to realise how comparatively recent that structure is.

Every graduate student works with this same dual address: on the one hand concerned with the undergraduates and teaching in his own university and on the other preparing his work for the research community to which the PhD certifies his admission. What the London Consortium offers is a third element – the audiences which flock through the Tate gallery and the BFI on the South Bank and the regional Tates and film theatres. The work of the graduate students will be intimately bound up with the contemporary organisation of knowledge in terms of its presentation to audiences well outside either of the academic communities as currently defined. It is this which constitutes the real excitement and risk of the new venture which we are here to launch today.

There are many ways in which this new relation between knowledge and audience may inflect the concerns of the students of the London Consortium but there are two that I wish to emphasise today. The first is that the students concerned with pursuing topics in cultural theory and analysis will be constantly confronted and engaged with cultural practices with the artists, architects and film-makers who are currently engaged in creating new cultural forms. It is here that the model of the Architectural Association is so vital to the new venture, an institution created in the nineteenth century precisely to establish new relations between theory and practice and, above all, to ensure that knowledge was to be developed in relation to current problems.

In this relation to practice there will perhaps be no single theme more dominant than the relations between commerce and culture. It is impossible for the traditional university not to constitute these two areas as antithetical both in disciplinary and ethical terms. But for those engaged in the practice of culture, there are no such easy oppositions. It is close to impossible to conceive of any art as being produced without a potential audience. But to talk of audiences is immediately to talk of money and it is in the very complicated set of relations between artist and audience, between product and market, that the new degree will find much of its edge. If I may return to the example of Derek Jarman with which I started, a full analysis would necessarily require an analysis of the way in which the BBC chose to fund a feature film through the same production company, Working Title, which three years later would use a writer reared in the best tradition of British comedy to produce the most successful British film to date – *Four Weddings and a Funeral*. In the case of *Wittgenstein* we would have to consider an initial commission from Channel 4 from their Education department for a one-hour television programme. It was supplementary funding from the British Film Institute which allowed the film to exist at a longer length. It also allowed it to exist as a 35mm film which was the condition of it reaching an international audience. In thinking of audiences it is impossible not to think of money and in thinking of money one is led ineluctably to the law. When I first became Head of Production at the British Film Institute my first three months were engaged in securing the copyright on the script of Derek Jarman's *Caravaggio* which the Board had already decided they wished to finance. Derek had signed an initial development contract which had no limit to the option thus acquired. The contract produced to secure the copyright ran to some 200 pages and gave me a crash course in copyright law and the realisation that the relation between copyright and audience is one of the most pressing cultural and political problems of the twenty-first century.

If the relation to audiences will be crucial to the new degree, it must finally be stressed that the relation to the international research community will also be maintained. If this new project is unthinkable without the new perspectives provided by the BFI, the Tate and the AA, it is also unthinkable without the massive research expertise provided by Birkbeck College. Nor should it be surprising that it is the college established to allow adult education which is a partner in this new venture in the organisation of knowledge.

We have chosen to launch our new programme with a day discussing decisions. We have chosen decisions because as we examine them through the day we hope that the two main themes of our new programme will recur again and again. First, that when we look at the complexity of the modern world, it is impossible to understand it from within one disciplinary perspective. We hope that the heterogeneity of the factors going into a particular decision will make evident how crucial a multi-disciplinary training is. Second, we trust that the claims of relativism will evaporate as they do as we approach a decision. Many perspectives may be brought to bear on a decision but at the moment of making there is no relativity whatsoever – in the moment choosing that relativity disappears. It may seem strange that in a day devoted to decisions, we have found no space for a discussion of decision theory. Decision theory, after all, is the hottest of current academic subjects. It is to the 90s what structuralism was to the 60s. But its failure to percolate through to humanities faculties is not simply due to the traditional insularity and mathematical incompetence of most of those who profess the humanities – it is due to the fact that the formalisations which so fascinate logicians and economists are so obviously inadequate to the kind of decisions that we are discussing today. If marketing analysts are fascinated by that paradox by which a person in a restaurant on being told that there is only chicken and steak on the menu chooses chicken, but when the waiter returns and says that the chef has told him that he also has fish and the customer then changes his order to steak, it seems clear to me that the kind of decisions we are discussing today escape any axioms which do not include infinity. When we were discussing how I should organise this talk my assistant Paulene Turner said to me that I should obviously discuss the decision to set up the PhD. I hope that I have given some of the very complicated historical factors at work. There was, however, for the British Film Institute a moment of decision and it came in the summer of 1988 when Wilf Stevenson, the then newly appointed director of the BFI, asked me to create a Research and Education division which would include the direct teaching of graduate students. I confess that my first reaction was to think that the director had taken leave of his senses. Why on earth should the Institute form graduate students directly? Wilf persuaded me that there were two overwhelming reasons. The first was that the practices of the Institute were an untapped educational resource which would allow us to produce students who had genuine familiarity through exhibiting, distributing, producing, curating, archiving – who had direct experience of the complicated negotiations which establish images and their meanings. The second was that there was a desperate need for film and television to occupy the centre of intellectual and academic life.

It is impossible to write a history of twentieth-century literature or twentieth-century painting without reference to the cinema. I say it is impossible but it is done time and time again just as histories of the cinema are produced which ignore the literature or painting which are crucial to understanding them. Students on the London Consortium will, in their first year, encounter *Birth of a Nation* but they will do so in relation to Man Ray and Mallarmé. When they look at Indian cinema they will be thinking of narrative and how the cinema has profoundly affected the possibilities of the novel. Joyce and Rushdie are literally unthinkable in the forms we know them without understanding their deep engagement with the cinema. It is these courses which will enable them in their second year to approach British cinema in the 80s, knowing that to analyse Peter Greenaway or Ridley Scott it is crucial to understand the history of post-war British art, just as it is impossible to understand Stephen Frears or Lindsay Anderson without understanding the development of drama in the 50s and 60s. But it is not only the arts to which film and television are central. Any serious thinking on contemporary society in many of its aspects from politics to the family has to pass through an understanding of the moving image. As Newt Gingrich starts a seminar on the care of uncared-for children with a screening of Spencer Tracy's *Boys' Town*, the need for the analysis of the moving image to be at the very centre of our most systematic attempts to understand society and culture could not be given more obvious proof. I referred earlier to Humboldt's founding of the University of Berlin. This was proceeded by a substantial grant of land direct from the monarchical treasury. Needless to say in our present straightened age, this new endeavour must be a nil-cost activity. It is the students of the Consortium that will pay for this new degree – it is to those students that this day is addressed.

Index

306.44
Mac

MacCabe, Colin.

The eloquence of the
vulgar.